RICHARD SCHLATTER, GENERAL EDITOR

Humanistic Scholarship in America

◄§ THE PRINCETON STUDIES §►

THE COUNCIL OF THE HUMANITIES
WHITNEY J. OATES, CHAIRMAN
PRINCETON UNIVERSITY

ANTHROPOLOGY

Eric R. Wolf

ART AND ARCHAEOLOGY

James S. Ackerman   Rhys Carpenter

CHINESE PAINTING

Wen Fong

CLASSICS

Eric A. Havelock

HISTORY

Felix Gilbert   John Higham
Leonard Krieger

LINGUISTICS

William Haas   Karl D. Uitti
Rulon Wells

LITERATURE

David Daiches   Howard E. Hugo

Their Authors

MODERN AMERICAN CRITICISM
Walter Sutton

MUSICOLOGY
Frank Ll. Harrison Mantle Hood
Claude V. Palisca

THE ORIGINS OF AMERICAN
HUMANISTIC SCHOLARS
Robert H. Knapp

PHILOSOPHY
Roderick M. Chisholm Herbert Feigl
William K. Frankena John Passmore
Manley Thompson

RELIGION
Paul Ramsey, ed.
James Luther Adams Philip H. Ashby
Robert M. Grant J. H. Nichols
Harry M. Orlinsky John E. Smith
Claude Welch

RELIGION, A HUMANISTIC FIELD
Clyde A. Holbrook

The aim of these volumes is to present a critical account of American humanistic scholarship in recent decades. They have been commissioned by the Council of the Humanities, Whitney J. Oates, Chairman, of Princeton University and were made possible by a grant from the Ford Foundation.

—Richard Schlatter, General Editor.

RELIGION,
A HUMANISTIC FIELD

ॐ ॐ

CLYDE A. HOLBROOK

WILLIAM H. DANFORTH
PROFESSOR OF RELIGION
OBERLIN COLLEGE

94026

PRENTICE-HALL, INC.   ENGLEWOOD CLIFFS   NEW JERSEY

PRENTICE-HALL INTERNATIONAL, INC., LONDON
PRENTICE-HALL OF AUSTRALIA, PTY., LTD., SYDNEY
PRENTICE-HALL OF CANADA, LTD., TORONTO
PRENTICE-HALL FRANCE, S.A.R.L., PARIS
PRENTICE-HALL OF JAPAN, INC., TOKYO
PRENTICE-HALL DE MEXICO, S.A., MEXICO CITY

FOREWORD

What is the purpose of humanistic scholarship? What, in fact, does the humanist scholar do?

The job of the humanist scholar is to organize our huge inheritance of culture, to make the past available to the present, to make the whole of civilization available to men who necessarily live in one small corner for one little stretch of time, and finally to judge, as a critic, the actions of the present by the experience of the past.

The humanist's task is to clear away the obstacles to our understanding of the past, to make our whole cultural heritage—primitive, pre-Columbian, African, Asian, aboriginal, Near Eastern, classical, medieval, European, American, contemporary, and all the rest—accessible to us. He must sift the whole of man's culture again and again, reassessing, reinterpreting, rediscovering, translating into a modern idiom, making available the materials and the blueprints with which his contemporaries can build their own culture, bringing to the center of the stage that which a past generation has judged irrelevant but which is now again usable, sending into storage that which has become, for the moment, too familiar and too habitual to stir our imagination, preserving it for a posterity to which it will once more seem fresh.

The humanist does all this by the exercise of exact scholarship. He must have the erudition of the historian, the critical abilities of the philosopher, the objectivity of the scientist, and the imagination of all three. The scholar who studies the history of science, for example, must combine a knowledge of languages, history, and philosophy with the knowledge of a scientist. And so on with the scholars who study music, art, religion, literature, and all the rest.

The job is, obviously, impossible for any man; and the humanist scholar, knowing he can never attain his true goal, is always tempted to run after wooden idols whose cults are less exacting and which proffer an easy bliss.

Sometimes the humanist is tempted to bypass the rigorous training of the scholar and to wrap himself in the cloak of the sophist. Then he lapses into a painful wooliness and becomes the "literary" sort of humanist whose only accomplishment is a style which achieves the appearance of sublimity at the cost of an actual inanity. His opposite number is the hardheaded humanist who reacts against empty loftiness by becoming a pedant: he devotes himself to antiquarian detail no less trivial than the banalities of some social science or the mere collecting spirit which is sometimes found in the natural sciences. "Physical science can be at least as trivial as any other form of inquiry: but this is less obvious to the outsider because the triviality is concealed in the decent obscurity of a learned language."

Given the magnitude of his task and the impossibility of total perfection, the humanist scholar must, of course, specialize and his works will often be esoteric. But the belief persists that somehow specialization must be converted to generalization if the humanist scholar is to complete his job. Humanist scholars have not solved the problems of excessive specialization and must share the blame for that catastrophe of communication which besets modern learning.

Humanist scholars have been accused of being overly genteel, contemptuous of popular culture, snobbish and anti-democratic after the fashion of their aristocratic Renaissance progenitors, backward looking, hostile to the present, fearful of the future, ignorantly petulant about science, technology, and the Industrial Revolution—"natural Luddites." "It is a sad thought indeed that our civilization has not produced a *New Vision*," a modern technologist complains, "which could guide us into the new 'Golden Age' which has now become physically possible, but only physically. . . . Who is responsible for this tragi-comedy of Man frustrated by success? . . . Who has left Mankind without a vision? The predictable part of the future may be a job for electronic predictors but the part of it which is not predictable, which is largely a matter of free human choice, is not the business of the machines, nor of scientists . . . but it ought to be, as it was in the great epochs of the past, the prerogative of the inspired humanists." (Dennis Gabor, "Inventing the Future," *Encounter,* May 1960, p. 15.)

Scholars in the humanities may modestly reject the suggestion that they can ever be the inspired prophets of a new age. But their scholarship is essential to enable us to distinguish the inspired prophets from the fanatical Pied Pipers.

The Ford Humanities Project under the direction of the Council of the Humanities of Princeton University is looking at American humanistic scholarship of recent decades, describing it, and attempting to sift the imaginative, the original, and the admirable from the pedantic, the conventional, and the superficial.

We have commissioned about a dozen volumes by recognized scholars in each field. These volumes will give us an account of American humanistic scholarship enabling us to see just what that scholarship has contributed to the culture of America and the world.

In the course of our discussions at Princeton about the volume having to do with scholarly work in the field of religion, we came upon a peculiar difficulty—peculiar that is to the field of religious scholarship. A considerable body of American scholars are of the opinion that religious studies are no part of the humanities, no part of the liberal arts, not an objective scholarly discipline. These scholars think of traditional religious scholarship as a professional study preparatory to the tasks of indoctrination and conversion and want it relegated to the seminaries of the various denominations. On the other hand, undergraduate and graduate departments of religion have recently begun to flourish in both private and public universities in this country and many members of the academic community feel that religion has been wrongly excluded from a formal place in the curriculum.

We asked Professor Holbrook to review the arguments and state the case. This he has done with grace and impartiality. The issue is an explosive one and is, consequently, often obscured with the flames and smoke of passion and prejudice. Clyde Holbrook brings to the discussion calm rationality, urbanity, objectivity, and the wisdom of a very successful teacher and scholar. Whether the reader agrees with the conclusions or not, he will certainly talk about the issues and problems more sensibly from now on.

RICHARD SCHLATTER
General Editor

PREFACE

In keeping with the general purpose of the Ford Humanities Project, this book interprets a particular field primarily for the benefit of those outside the field in question. In this case religion is treated as a humanistic area with the nonspecialist in mind. I have assumed that religion understood as a liberal arts subject is less commonly considered in this manner than are other subjects of a humanistic nature. Accordingly the aim of providing a technical discussion which would be of interest only to professors of religion has been subordinated to that of acquainting a larger public with religion's role in the ensemble of the humanities. Of course, I hope that my colleagues within the field will recognize the value of this approach while, at the same time, they find I have considered issues of some consequence to them.

Some professors of religion or members of the clergy may bridle at omission of matters they count to be of paramount significance. If, for instance, they are of an evangelical Christian stripe, they will perhaps be disappointed to see that I have not represented the study of religion in "religious" terms or as a challenge by the Christian faith to what is sometimes referred to as "the godless campus." The religious task, in distinction from the educational task, I hold to be the special responsibility of religious groups and chaplains on campuses. Therefore I have largely bypassed this issue. Those who seek a theological analysis or rationale for the study of religion may look askance at my slighting of this area. Since analyses of this type are usually the in-group activities of theologians and since I believe them to be of limited interest in the present context, I have drastically reduced their treatment. For good or ill, higher education, even in many church-related colleges, is imbued with a mentality to which theological considerations are not only foreign but also more confusing than illuminative. Although many, including myself, hold theological considerations to be of importance in understanding trends in higher education, they cannot be depended upon today to bear the weight of arguments for the entry and support of religion as a humanistic subject. It has therefore seemed unrealistic to pitch religion's case on a theological rationale. There also may be those who feel I have given short shrift to the role of religious bodies in the establishment and support of colleges and universities. Since this study is intended to deal only with developments during the past some thirty years, extensive treatment of historical origins appeared to be diversionary. I would remind the secular-minded reader of the immense debt owed to religious groups for the establishment of institutions and for many of his academic rights, but I have declined the opportunity of arguing the case from historical precedent.

On the other hand, some people outside the field may well ask why major attention has been paid to theological seminaries since these institutions are not usually regarded as being dedicated to humanistic studies. The answer lies in the fact that theological faculties stand at a most influential juncture in respect to higher education in religion. They still provide the largest source of training for professors of religion; they influence the content of the field itself and they are responsible for much of the scholarship produced. Unfortunately in some respects theological schools have had a deleterious effect upon graduate education and upon religion in the undergraduate program. It has been virtually impossible, therefore, to sidestep consideration of the impact of these institutions on the field.

However, I have not entered into the problems which face theological education as such.

A further preliminary word can be offered on the frequent references made to the ethos of the free university. I am not ignorant of the many pressures and distorting ideologies which turn higher education away from its loftiest goals. No university lives in an atmosphere free of all bias and human frailties. The crosscurrents of too many divergent values, prejudices, and opinions mingle in its halls to allow successful claims for its absolute freedom. I am sufficiently convinced, however, of the values for which the university at its best strives and which it fitfully exhibits to rest the case for study and scholarship in religion on that ground. Furthermore, I see the chances for the successful implementation of these values enhanced rather than endangered by the integral inclusion of religion by the university.

This book, in short, endeavors to show the generally accepted conformation of the field of religion, its place among the humanities, its peculiar problems and opportunities, and its contributions to humane learning. I have conceived the nature of religion along as broad lines as possible without accepting a doctrinaire nontheistic interpretation of the humanistic spirit which would arbitrarily read out of court those forms of thought and belief which take account of the superhuman. My mandate was one which called for interpretation rather than a catalog of activities within the field and I have accordingly rejected the role of a polltaker or a compiler of statistics. My critical interpretations, for which I am alone responsible, I hope have evaded the trap of sheer idiosyncrasy.

I owe especial gratitude to members of the Religion Department of Princeton University for their cordial reception and enlightening conversations which helped me to formulate and reassess my ideas. I also thank the Council of the Humanities at that institution for accepting me as a Senior Fellow. I am debtor to both Princeton University and Oberlin College for their several courtesies. Appreciation is due Dr. Richard Schlatter of Rutgers University, Director of the Ford Humanities Project, for his helpful services and friendly interest in my work. And I surely cannot repay Mrs. Jone Tobin, secretary for the Project, for her typing and retyping of what was too often an incomprehensible manuscript.

CLYDE A. HOLBROOK

Oberlin College

CONTENTS

xv

CONTENTS

xvi

◄§ I §►

INTRODUCTION

HISTORICAL ANTECEDENTS

The intellectual life of man has never been far removed from the manifold concerns of religion. The instruction which a Plato, Aristotle, or Plotinus gave his students and followers repeatedly touched upon the perennial issues of religious consequence. Speculation on nature's way and upon mathematics was intermeshed with thoughts on man's nature, his possibilities for good and evil, his conduct, his eventual destiny, and the nature of a supreme or ultimate being. Knowledge of such matters was not deemed tangential to the main efforts of the philosophical enterprise. Indeed, at least for Plato and Plotinus, knowledge in its fullest sense moved toward a climax of spiritual illumination which could be called nothing less than a form of personal salvation. The education provided by these thinkers assumed a continuity of experience whereby knowledge of worldly matters and of oneself passed over eventually into a transformation of the self. Deciding whether the masters of Greek philosophy would have called their systems religious in purpose is less important than recognizing the intimate association between knowledge normally known as secular and the attainment of a life whose fulfillment was to be discovered in realms which transcended the immediacies of sense experience or even speculation itself. Philosophy not only sought knowledge; it yearned for a wisdom which would grasp and alter the deepest well-springs of the human spirit. Thus learning and the spiritual quest for man's destiny walked together.

Both Christianity and Judaism took to themselves the resources of this tradition, weaving much of it into the structures

3

of their beliefs, and maintaining for the most part the mutual attachments of learning and religious faith. The early apologists and teachers in the Christian catechetical schools took up the simultaneous tasks of developing a reasonable defense of the faith and the instruction of converts in the faith. In the performance of these tasks the insights of the pagan Plato were put to good use in the service of a developing Christian theology and Judaism. Studies of the Bible texts in several languages and their translation into others, exemplified by Jerome's great Latin translation of the Bible, gave evidence also of the possibility of Christianity's laying under tribute the secular learning of the time. No less active, though commonly less widely known outside its learned circles, was the work of Jewish scholars and rabbis who preserved and translated ancient texts, wrote extensive commentaries upon them, and instructed their own people and willing gentile auditors in the lore of their scriptures and their religious and ethical conceptions.

If the purpose of the education offered by Plato and Aristotle was to prepare men for participation in the Greek city-state, and in Plato's case, for a life beyond, the early Christian teacher prepared men for induction into a visible institution whose purposes extended far beyond this world, but which as yet had not produced a dominant culture of its own within the world. The Jewish teacher taught to strengthen his people's sense of their spiritual history and destiny, their uniqueness as a people, and to maintain a culture which, although seldom possessed of political or military authority, provided a habitat hopefully immune to the attacks of Christians and pagans.

Soon the central question emerged as to whether the incorporation of pagan learning into these religions could be carried out without dangerous disruption and dilution of concepts held to be of crucial significance within the religion itself. That Augustine of Hippo's intellectual and religious wanderings cul-

4

minated in his conversion to Christianity reveals his answer to this problem. Tertullian might ask "What has Athens to do with Jerusalem, the Academy with the Church?" or "What is there in common between the philosopher and the Christian, the pupil of Hellas and the pupil of Heaven?" and return a negative answer. Not so Augustine. Although he was convinced that his learning from secular sources had not brought him to that calmness of mind and resoluteness of soul which he observed among simple and untutored Christians, he did discover that a believer could relish pagan learning and convert it to the purposes of the faith. This he proceeded to do with neo-Platonism. The point established by Augustine and from which he worked as one of the most influential theologians of the Christian movement was this: to know the truth one must believe; one must give more than intellectual recognition to the area of knowledge in question. Or as E. H. Harbison puts it: "To Augustine there could be no such thing as a purely secular search for the truth." [Harbison, *The Christian Scholar in the Age of the Reformation* (Scribner, 1956), p. 18.] Christian faith and knowledge of the truth must join hands.

Augustine's thought reveals another facet of the problem. Could there ever actually be a separation not only of religious conviction but of religious knowledge from knowledge which sprang from sources quite independent of avowedly religious purposes? The language and images which colored Christian faith could not be set aside as irrelevant by the most intransigent defender of the uniqueness of Christian revelation. Views of the cosmos, the heavens, and the earth; conceptions of the soul, the physical body, and their relation; as well as moral ideals had flourished independently of and antecedently to Moses and Jesus. The deep yearnings of the human spirit and their assuagement had not begun with Christianity's arrival. These facets of human experience had received telling repre-

5

sentations in the dramas, myths, and "sciences" of Greece, Babylonia, and Egypt. The religious concerns of man and his thought about them could not be confined within the structures of an independently conceived Christian theology and its cultic practices. How, in the face of these considerations, could it be seriously maintained that religion develops with such originality as to be impervious to prevailing cultural forces?

The answer of Augustine and those who came after him was that even a religion insistent upon its peculiar doctrines and practices could lay hold upon secular knowledge and insist that its insights better illuminated, criticized, and employed that knowledge than did its originators and earlier developers. Thus a religion, through its interpreters, found a way to incorporate secular knowledge safely into its very structure. Both Augustine and Aquinas accomplished this for Christianity by erecting imposing intellectual syntheses. Secular philosophy was employed not only as a preparatory step to the "higher" truths of Christianity but served to structure the insights of faith itself.

When possessed of sufficient authority and power, the Western church was not satisfied with this accommodation and at times dictated the legitimate bounds to which the search and development of knowledge could be pressed. Thus it proclaimed a sovereignty over all fields of knowledge, even those remote from doctrinal matters. By doing so, it brought to focus in the Western world the latent tension between the truths of faith backed by ecclesiastical authority and the truths which arise independent of religious sanction and purposes. It need scarcely be remarked that this tension remains to our day. It is reflected not only in the problem of Christianity's relation to culture generally but in the suspicion which has surrounded efforts to place the study of religion among academic disciplines at all educational levels. It is more easily forgotten sometimes that religious institutions have not been alone in their attempts to control and dominate learning. In more recent days other structures of thought possessed of far more influence and power than the church possesses have repeatedly made forays into the provinces of man's spiritual and intellectual life while the churches have sometimes stood as the champions of a freedom without which the life of the mind in any field is impossible.[1]

In the Middle Ages, as the great universities grew, there could be little doubt of the relation between religion and secular truth as represented in educational practices. Generally it was assumed that the study of the Trivium and Quadrivium provided what might be called a liberal arts basis for the students' advanced work in one of the superior faculties of the university, law, medicine, or theology. Although the first universities and their predecessors, the monastic and cathedral schools, were primarily in the service of the church,[2] the relation of these universities to the church was seldom a completely peaceful or passive one. The papacy promulgated bulls which authorized the existence of universities; it often protected the university from molestation by state or local officials; it decided what books could be used and what ideas could be taught, employing cardinal legates to enforce its decisions. It also expected assistance from its theological faculties, especially that at Paris, in the forms of aid in detecting heresy and of judgments on moot points of doctrine. On the other hand, neither the arts faculties nor the theological faculties were completely pliant

[1] The ambivalent relation between religion and intellectual freedom has been sketched by R. L. Calhoun in his essay, "The Historical Relation between Religion and Intellectual Freedom," in *Religion and Freedom of Thought* by Perry Miller, R. L. Calhoun, N. M. Pusey, and Reinhold Niebuhr (Doubleday, 1954).

[2] Although education for various age levels was sponsored by secular authorities, the scholars, teachers, and the location of schools were connected with the church. [See R. F. Butts, *A Cultural History of Western Education,* 2nd ed. (McGraw, 1955), pp. 125-32.]

7

before the orders of the church. The disputations held by the Paris theological faculty were often watched with suspicion and apprehension by both state and church, because of their freely speculative nature, and the same faculty repeatedly embroiled itself in the internal politics of the church, even setting afoot plans to end the Avignon schism and from time to time aligning itself with French interests against those of the Italian-dominated papacy. The model or ideal relation for the high Middle Ages might be that of a harmonious cooperation of church, state, and university, but the facts seem to point to a far different picture. The church, in its strongest popes, might claim hegemony over state and university, but neither of these bodies proved tractable. Education was largely but not entirely in the service of the church and was carried out under its auspices, but as Rashdall pointed out, in theology "again and again Paris led the way and Rome followed." [*Rashdall's Medieval Universities,* vol. I, ed. F. M. Powicke and A. B. Emden (Oxford, 1936), p. 549.] The truth of the matter would seem to be that although religious truth was the customarily acknowledged goal of the highest learning—this, every theological faculty would have maintained—the church at any given time was not the sole arbiter of that truth, a distinction which probably would not have been publicly advertised although it was assumed in practice.

Whatever else may be said of the domination of learning by the church in the Middle Ages or of the sterility of its learning after the initial enthusiasm for Aristotle had waned, it should not be overlooked that the church assisted in the introduction of humanistic studies in the opening phases of the Renaissance. Chairs of languages were encouraged by several of the popes. Innocent IV encouraged the study of Oriental languages, and Clement V ordered teachers of Hebrew, Greek, Arabic, and Chaldean to be appointed in the universities of Rome, Paris,

8

Oxford, Bologna, and Salamanca. [Powicke and Emden, *op. cit.*, pp. 565-66 n.] Presumably this support for language study was not offered solely for the purpose of encouraging study of humane letters for their own sake.[3] The wider concern of the church lay in the defense of the faith and the strengthening of its theological resources. Thus the pattern held firm. Education, although it served other important needs, at least ideally, was directed to the production of servants of the church, and learning, again ideally, could reach its maximum fulfillment only in that knowledge of supernatural truth of which the church was the jealously possessive guardian.

The Protestant Reformation was in very large part a scholar's revolt, directed not only against moral abuses in the church, but against those modes of thought which scholastic thought had fastened upon Christianity. Luther might rail against "reason" and despise certain works of Aristotle, but he, like the other principal reformers, did not despise education or humanistic studies. He could write "I believe to owe it to the Lord to fight philosophy and to exhort people to read the Scripture," since philosophy for him was "a study of vanity and disaster." But he could also urge the establishment of schools and the study of biblical languages in these words: "We shall not long preserve the Gospel without the languages. The languages are the sheaths in which the sword of the spirit is contained; they are the casket in which we carry the jewel." [*Works*, vol. 14, p. 114; Philadelphia edition.] His translation of the Bible into the German vernacular was a spur to literacy at all levels, as scripture was held to be a norm of doctrine and the vehicle of God's own word to man. Calvin was at home in the learned

---

[3] Even at a relatively early date in the Middle Ages some teachers read and taught classical literature for its own sake. John of Salisbury is one who did so at Chartres. [See Robert Ulich, *The Education of Nations* (Harvard, 1961), p. 5.]

world, having been trained both in the humanities and in law. His keen dialectical mind was honed not only by the subtleties of scriptural translation, but also on the practices of scholastic dispute. Even the so-called radicals of the Reformation, of whom Luther, Calvin, and Zwingli held savagely low opinions, were no strangers to the realms of humane learning. Franck, Grebel, Castellio, Hubmaier, and von Hutten, and many others who soon wandered from the path being beaten out by the giants of the reform movement, were scholars in their own right, but their insistence upon the validity of immediate promptings of the Spirit, or the free ranging of a reason infected by humanistic studies, brought inevitable clashes, both with Protestants and with Roman Catholics. Their contribution to the reform movement was to move Protestantism along its ambiguous course, hovering between the extremes of a radical antinomian enthusiasm and a rationalistic humanism which was to flow into the liberalism of the nineteenth and twentieth centuries.

Protestantism therefore found itself presented with a curious situation in respect to humane learning. It developed with the rise of humanism and helped to free the minds of men from the strictures of medieval thought at the same time that it called for a fresh subordination of learning to its interests. Protestantism helped to produce critical minds at the same time that it preserved elements of the medieval pattern of education in the service of divine truth. It lauded learning, but also feared its outcome when improperly directed.

If for the moment the cultural forces of the Renaissance and the rise to dominance of the nation-state be omitted from consideration, we can see embedded in the theological stance of the reform movement as a whole the elements which have ever since made difficult its development of a coherent viewpoint on the relation of liberal learning to religion. Protestant doctrine called for the use of three norms of true doctrine and faith: right reason, scripture, and the witness of the Holy Spirit. Yet these three each held serious dangers in Protestant eyes. Reason, to which even Luther appealed for his justification against Roman Catholicism, was long associated with the notion of a natural knowledge of God and natural law which, it was feared, could subordinate religious truth as given in scripture to human determination as exemplified in Roman Catholicism. The unique and sole revelation of God in Jesus Christ and the precious doctrine of justification by faith alone would be swallowed up in the vain speculations of man. If appeal were made only to scripture, the question soon arose as to who should interpret it and in what manner. Among stubborn and unsophisticated Protestants the Bible could be turned into a code book of laws and information covering all aspects of human experience. Worse yet, for some it could be employed by sinful men to squelch the impromptu outpourings of the divine spirit. Of course, the plain fact was that reason could not be cast aside when one took the scriptures seriously, and even with the best scholarship of the time, serious differences of opinion concerning the teaching of holy writ soon breached the momentarily united front of the Reformation. Zwingli and Luther at Marburg futilely disputed the meaning of the words "This is my body" and parted, each unconvinced by the other. Those of the radical party elevated the Holy Spirit to pre-eminence, only to find that on this basis also no agreement was possible among convinced Protestants. Those who elevated the openings of the Holy Spirit to a supreme position over scripture and reason were soon wandering in the fogs of antinomianism and antirationalism. In their most extravagant excesses, they promoted disdain for learning of all kinds, and even refused to recognize the most elementary moral restrictions as binding on them. The dangers to the Protestant movement which lay in this direction were so obvious that its leaders were castigated and persecuted without stint. With horror and disgust Luther and Zwingli insisted that they had never intended to countenance as divine wisdom the loose-lipped flighty sentiments of men who mistook their subjective fancies for immediate disclosures of the Holy Spirit. Eventually, the main Protestant streams settled for an uneasy but nevertheless fruitful interplay of the three norms, none of which could be left out of account, but each of which threatened the other. The heavy emphasis which the Reformation leaders and the rationalistic left-wing reformers placed on knowledge of scripture and the uses of reason helped saved humane learning for Protestantism, whereas repeatedly the "enthusiastic" radicals appear in history protesting the debilitating effects on pure faith which learning exercises.

Other theological factors have also affected the development of a Protestant rationale for education and humane learning. For the classical Protestant tradition, salvation came by faith, not by the accumulation of worldly knowledge, significant as that might be in its own right. God's free gift of grace embraced in faith came from beyond man, and was distinctly independent from man's efforts antecedent to its coming. There was a radical disjunction between God's action and those activities which men carried on as natural beings, and over which they held control. This disjunction had profound effects on attempts to relate learning to religious studies. Since worldly studies in themselves did not provide stepping stones to the goal of spiritual knowledge given only in revelation, the relation of these studies to soteriological ends remained in doubt. Those branches of study which dealt with God's revelation, his mode of salvation, the history of Christian and Jewish tradition, and the Bible could be pursued by any scholar, but, by virtue of the area which they covered and the nature of the processes with which they dealt, they could not be smoothly placed in integral relation to humane studies. The deepseated suspicion of the Protestant theologian was directed against any intellectual move which smacked of a return to the concept of a natural knowledge of God—a knowledge which in his view was not a saving knowledge of deity. He feared the religious consequences of building intellectual structures by which the "natural" man might deceive himself by believing that he could move from his spiritually unenlightened position into a domain of which God alone was master. To be sure, a Calvin could see a place for a type of natural knowledge of God, but one recognized this natural knowledge only from the side of faith. It was not a firm bridge erected by man's unaided efforts. The tools for expressing revelational theology were those provided by humane studies (e.g., knowledge of the Bible, texts, and translations), but revelational theology possessed an autonomy of a quite different kind from that found in the Roman Catholic rationale for learning and theology.

One of the most important consequences of this Protestant disjunction has been the freeing of secular learning from control by theological interests, and at the same time the freeing of theology itself from any organic relation to other branches of learning. The logic of the Protestant position ideally led to the emancipation of the arts and sciences from theological supervision, even when in specific cases the practice has been to the contrary. Probably the development of this logic is nowhere better seen than in Luther, who, in the words of H. R. Niebuhr, "affirmed the life in culture as the sphere in which Christ could and ought to be followed; and more than any other . . . discerned that the rules to be followed in the cultural life were independent of Christian or church law." [H. R. Niebuhr, *Christ and Culture* (Harper, 1951), p. 174.] The Christian man, understood in Protestant terms, was free to pursue the aims of humane education among other vocations; the theologian was equally free to go his way. What was not to be assumed was that such learning as the scholar might amass in any way put him in a more favorable position for the advent of divine grace than the most humble stonemason or farmer. The principle of the freedom of the arts and sciences in those countries where the Reformation worked itself out on Lutheran lines opened the way for the beneficial effects of freedom of inquiry, but it also threatened severely the possibility of a meaningful relation between these diverse parts of learning and made difficult the development of a coherent Protestant rationale of education. Perhaps even more decisive for our contemporary scene was the possible implication which denied that the God of which theology spoke had any profound relation to secular knowledge and man's nonreligious pursuits. The full force of this implication was to make itself felt in succeeding centuries.

Insofar as the Reformation took the theological direction laid out by Luther, and insofar as theological ideas have social power and convincement, the divorce of theology and the liberal arts was bound to occur eventually. On the other hand, Calvinism, because of its strong emphasis on divine sovereignty and its activistic attitude toward the social and cultural world, could be expected to retain more of the medieval image of the relation between theology and the liberal arts although it remained suspicious of too close a relationship between the two.

Another factor, however, eventually more decisive than the theological impact, was moulding the future relations between the arts and religious learning. It was, in certain of its forms, to exploit fully the door left ajar in Protestant theology. By the fifteenth century the study of and delight in the literatures and movements of classical antiquity had already made itself decisively felt in the Roman Catholic Church and in its educational programs. Similar interests flourished in the sixteenth century alongside and intermingling with the religious ferment of the

Protestant movement. In both contexts there arose a sense of independence from religious concerns and a delight in man's creativity as exhibited in an antiquity which owed nothing to Christianity's appearance on the stage of history. The humanists' impact on education was to challenge the assumptions of Roman Catholics and some Protestants that true learning should consummate in the edification of Christian men, and that secular learning properly fell into a context provided by Christian truth. Christian humanists such as Erasmus and More could see no reason to give up either Christian truth or the enrichments of classical learning. More defended the latter to Oxford authorities by admitting that it was secular, but pressed the contention that the secular trains the soul in virtue. "There are some who through knowledge of things natural construct a ladder by which to rise to the contemplation of things supernatural; they build a path to theology through Philosophy and the Liberal Arts. . . ." [Quoted in Harbison, *op. cit.,* pp. 88-89.] In these words More bespoke the model of Roman Catholic learning which Protestants, as we have seen, could not wholeheartedly accept. But other winds blowing from ancient Hellas and the Seven Hills were to cool the enthusiasm of learned and witty men for the gentle accommodation of humane learning and Christian verities. Even the moderate Erasmus sat loose to convictions which others counted of life-and-death importance for the victory of either Protestantism or Catholicism. The effect of the gathering impact of the humanistic movement was to put irreplaceable weapons for theological polemics in the hands of both parties, but also steadily to encourage the suspicion that the issues about which they contested were of slight import compared to the values of worldly experience. Perhaps an educated man might better turn his talents from the pursuit of unanswerable conundrums about the supernatural to the enormously exciting and more immediately satisfying pleasures of humane letters and to the creation of forms of art which exhibited the potentialities of man's creativity rather than his degradation.

To be sure, the age-old themes of man's religious yearning and speculation were not thrown out of court in the literature of the humanists, but clearly the question had been raised as to whether secular learning called for acknowledgment of the superiority of theology in any of its forms. Was not secular learning in itself a sufficient terminus of education? Was there need to go further, or for that matter, to respect those who went further toward religious truth? The Reformation in its time sheltered humanism rather than destroyed it, although the humanist aims of education did not agree with those cherished by the leading reformers. With a measure of oversimplification, but also with an amount of validity, Robert Ulich has suggested that the humanists looked to the breeding of young noblemen and scholars, while the reformers emphasized the upbringing of Christian youth. The humanist no longer spoke of self-negation, Christian humility, and the sinfulness of man, but harped on the well-rounded person taken up with his own glory, honor, power, and self-advancement, practicing the arts of elegant writing and living, whose service more likely than not was placed at the disposal of his country, prince, or king. [See Ulich, *The Education of Nations,* pp. 50-51, 202-03.] But insofar as the reformers themselves were humanists, they were humanists with an ulterior motive of contending for their faith, the defeat of Catholicism, and the salvation of men.

The inroads of humanistic culture had set afoot another significant train of thought. The structure of university education, so far as the position of the medieval superior faculties was concerned, remained, but the function of the faculty of theology was being reinterpreted. In one sense the theological faculty had always been a professional faculty, preparing men for the service of the church. It had enjoyed an autonomy in the university structure. But it had also been, at least in the eyes of the church, both Protestant and Catholic, a symbol of the superiority of religious truth over all other truth. It represented, even when it did not actively prosecute, the church's overarching interest in the whole range of learning of the arts and sciences. It had not surrendered its rights to supervise or interfere in the education which went on beneath its own level. With the decisive spread of humanism in the universities, a process of reinterpretation of the role of the theological faculty began, and the image, abetted by the theological posture of Protestantism, has remained contemporary both abroad and in the United States. The theological faculty retained its position as a superior faculty, but it lost its symbolic value. Its professional character increasingly came to the foreground, while it lost its prestige as a center of dedicated learning in the eyes of the university, which went on its way with less and less interest in or knowledge of what theologians were doing. The theological faculty increasingly lost touch or was put out of touch with those branches of learning which, developing in their own right, had less and less to say of relevance to theology, or theology to them. The liberal arts and sciences were on their way to discovering that they could manage very well without an eye cocked to theology, and theology, while retaining its posture of a superior faculty, lacked significant relation to what went on elsewhere in the university. In the slow but sure drifting apart, there emerged a distaste, if not a downright dislike, for the theological enterprise and its practitioners. Theology was paying a heavy price for its years of dominance over learning, a price which unfortunately in Protestant and secular centers of higher education it continues to pay.

The fifteenth and sixteenth centuries saw the rise of the nation-state. With this major transition in the political structure of Europe came the loss of the universal aspects of education and the growth instead of national responsibility for education. The medieval model was conceived as a relation of the empire to the church and university operating in a threefold harmonious fashion in the service of the Christian faith. The assumption that religious uniformity and political uniformity went hand in hand was not yielded by the Reformation or in the development of the nation-state. But now the university was a national institution and its theologians, though not without bitter opposition, served the interests of the state. Protestant, Anglican, and even Roman Catholic universities found themselves expected to provide not merely Christians, but Christians whose loyalties would be firmly bound to the political aims of the state. Rulers expected, in return for their founding and support of universities, the production of secular as well as religious leaders who understood the high stakes for which they played in international affairs. This assumption cut squarely across the universalistic intent of humanistic studies, though they continued to flourish under its auspices. It vastly complicated the duties of theologians whose fields of study and teaching now had to be undertaken on the principle of the nationalization of education. It reduced the autonomy of theological thought, threatened the cultural intercourse of humanistic scholarship, helped to promote national churches, and eventually to lay a nationalistic structure on top of the rapidly emerging denominational diffusion of the seventeenth and eighteenth centuries. Finally it deposited the firm notion in men's minds that religion, as instruction and study, should promote the welfare of those within a limited political domain. The notion of a study of religion conceived in universal terms or as possessing intrinsic merit of its own was to wait a long time for its advocates.

The Puritans who established Harvard and Yale could not

transplant a Cambridge or an Oxford to the new land, but they did bring a model for education as worked out in Britain, now to be transformed by a frontier situation and their own self-consciousness as true representatives of the Reformation. They were Calvinists by way of Ames, Preston, Bradshaw, and other neo-Calvinists, and they retained that respect for a learned ministry which earlier generations of Puritans had fought for against the "dumb" clerics of Anglicanism and the undisciplined outbursts of the sectarians. The kingdoms of this world were to be God's kingdom, and by his aid and covenant faithfulness, by ceaseless study of the Bible, by a fair admixture of humane learning, and by a regard for a strict sense of discipline, they intended to make their colonies lights to the world, and this not least by the establishment of colleges. To Harvard, as S. E. Morison points out, "they brought a new zeal for scriptural religion and the humanist tradition." Although their equipment in scientific and mathematical learning of the day was "meagre and obsolete," they did not in the main oppose what science they knew. For them "no amount of godliness, good will, or inspiration could compensate for want of learning" in the clergy. [Morison, *The Founding of Harvard College* (Harvard, 1935), pp. 57, 77, 160.] They also assumed that so far as possible an educated laity should be provided for by the establishment of lower schools whereby a continuous flow of divines and leaders would be brought up to and through the colleges. Religion naturally suffused the origins and development of early colleges, but as at Harvard and Yale, the purposes of education were not solely those of an ecclesiastical nature. The purposes of these establishments, it was taken for granted, were linked to the welfare of the society as well as of the church. They were not divinity schools; they were liberal arts colleges, and many of those attending had no intention of entering the ranks of the clergy. [Cf. Morison, *op. cit.,* pp. 247-48.] "For all the

19

preoccupation with religion, the colonial colleges were not theological seminaries or given to the education of ministers exclusively." [G. P. Schmidt, *The Liberal Arts College* (Rutgers, 1957), p. 24.] True, President Clap of Yale interpreted the college's character as a religious society of "a Superior Nature to all others" and scouted the idea held by some that colleges were only designed for teaching the arts and sciences. But, after all, Yale, like Harvard, was founded for the production of those who would take positions of secular leadership in the colony.

The principle inherited from the old world was maintained. Education in college and university promoted the welfare of both state and church, and at least for the earlier collegiate foundations, a theological or religious training was of equal importance for clergymen and secular leaders. The practical relation and importance of religion was taken for granted. The ordinance of 1787 for the Northwest Territory enunciated the obvious when it stated: "Religion, morality and knowledge being necessary to good government and the happiness of mankind, schools and the means of education shall forever be encouraged." [*The Teaching of Religion in American Higher Education,* ed. Christian Gauss (Ronald, 1951), p. 5.] A strict Puritan might have bridled at the use of the term *happiness* unqualified by reference to things spiritual, but he would have understood the intent perfectly.

The nineteenth century saw a change in the relation of religious studies to higher education, though some patterns remained firm. Denominational colleges sprang up in profusion, but in the main their aims were not directed to theological education as such, but "rather toward a Christian general education. The colleges founded by the churches were designed to prepare men for the ministry by the study of the Bible and of the humanities." Other factors, however, were reshaping the re-

lations of religious scholarship and higher education. The revivalism of mid-eighteenth century, in spite of its eccentricities,
helped to create colleges such as Dartmouth and Princeton, and
the prestige of learning was upheld by the best minds on both
sides of the conflict between New and Old Lights. The revivals
of the nineteenth century, on the other hand, made explicit the
dangers inherent in those of the eighteenth century. Respect
for learning, including theology, fell before the strenuous ex-
hortations for a practical pietistic and highly individualistic
Christianity. A robust anti-intellectualism, reminiscent of the
attitudes of some of the radical reformers of the sixteenth century, came to the fore and remained a feature of American culture. Theological disciplines increasingly were pointed to practical ends in the seminaries which burgeoned in this era. The
tension between the American spirit of experimental, practical
religion regnant in revivalism and the Reformation and Puritan
ethos of a learned clergy still in touch with sources of classical
and even scientific learning, was felt in the divinity schools of
the period, and has continued to influence the work of these
institutions. [See H. R. Niebuhr, J. M. Gustafson, and
D. D. Williams, *The Advancement of Theological Education*
(Harper, 1957) pp. 1-5.]

While Protestantism was spawning colleges and seminaries,
and was itself expanding numerically, other forces were moving
in a direction which at last would transform the Protestant hue
of American culture. The growing influx of non-Protestant
populations from abroad and the increasing recognition given
to Judaism were forces which made themselves felt. The century swarmed with new and esoteric sects, each clamoring for its
place in the life of an expanding nation. The tardy rays of the
Enlightenment touched the intellectual life of America with
their rationalistic and sometimes skeptical light. Public education on an unprecedented scale was called for; an education

which would undergird democratic procedures, which would prepare for practical and professional forms of employment and, above all, an education which would faithfully respond to the ever growing religious pluralism of American society. Since it was taken for granted that the term *religion* meant "church," and the term *church* in turn implied "sectarianism," the new state universities of the period usually implemented the principle of separation of church and state by formally excluding religious affiliations and the study of religion from their campuses. What remained near the center of academic interest at church colleges was in these new institutions moved to the status of an extracurricular activity. Thus at a time of vigorous religious ferment in American society, religion studies were confined to denominational institutions and private universities. By the early decades of the twentieth century it was widely understood that tax-supported institutions through whose doors more and more students were to pass had no place for the academic pursuit of religion. The changes had been gradual, but their results were clear and decisive.

Religious pluralism gave new emphasis to the principle of separation of church and state and helped to eliminate religion as an academic field from publicly supported institutions of higher education. The pressures for a practically oriented education continually threatened the central position once held by classical and humanistic studies. Secular interests supervened upon the religious life of Americans, tending to shrink its perspectives to those of nationalistic interests.

No society lives long without some core of values which functions as a religious faith. If none of the traditional faiths could provide this center, what was needed was some common denominator about which spiritual and moral force could be rallied. The American experience had established the value of a hardy kind of pragmatism and the relative unimportance of airy metaphysical and theological speculations. Consequently, there developed a form of nationalistic religion which leaned heavily upon moralistic elements. It was an amorphous blend of Christian, Enlightenment, humanistic, and democratic ideals. So far as the traditional forms of religious faith advanced this amalgam, religion, understood as a practical way of life, has flourished as a popular and important aspect of American culture. Education similarly has in general seen its purposes in terms of this secularized, nationalized, but authentically religious form of faith. Thus, for example, R. F. Butts finds the goal of college education today to be the democratic process itself. The purpose of higher education "should be such that after college days the young people of the United States would know how to live democratically in an interdependent world and would strive earnestly for a truly democratic society in that world. . . . To enable them to become liberally educated persons with high professional and vocational competence and an urgent sense of social responsibility for democracy should be the goal of higher education in the United States." [Butts, *A Cultural History of Western Education,* 2nd ed., p. 584.]

If Butts is correct, the purposes of higher education can be subsumed under the heading of "democracy." His reference to "liberally educated persons" is to be seen in that light and he summons such persons, in almost evangelical tones, to convert the world to a "democratic society." But the term *democratic* also has its nationalistic coloring; it is American democracy which proves to be the guiding image of education and the ultimate end of man's striving. Higher education then is to be limited to a practical and social end, conceived in terms of the particular culture in which it is being carried out. Or to put the matter in a different focus, education is now conceived to be in the service of a political and social ideal when once education and the political ideal were conceived to be at the disposal of universal religious goals.

These transitions in American culture and higher education during the nineteenth and early twentieth centuries set the stage for the consideration of religion understood as a field of study and scholarship among the humanities. Some may feel that religion in any form has no place in higher education; others feel that education without the study of religion is a truncated affair. But in any case it is evident that there no longer exists on any major scale that close identification of religion with higher education which we have seen was once taken for granted in Europe and in America. There are few today who would disagree with Princeton's President Goheen when he states: "Most of the realms of culture for which the university takes responsibility . . . have attained a variety and maturity which require that the worldly pursuit of learning in them be free from explicit connection with the enterprise of religion and theology." [Robert F. Goheen, "The Seminary and the University," *Princeton Seminary Bulletin,* LIV, 1 (July 1960), 8.]

The remarkable fact about the modern situation is that in this freedom of secular learning from theological pursuits, studies in religion pursued not only for ecclesiastical ends but for purposes of their intrinsic or humane value have flourished. Ways for fuller interpretations of the relation of religion study to the academic and general cultural life are being explored. Perhaps most important of all is the self-consciousness of those working in the area of religion who conceive their task not as an advancement of sectarian interests, or as an occasion to reestablish the hegemony of distinctively theological viewpoints over higher education, but as an opportunity to use their services for the liberalization of education itself.

≈§ II §≈

RELIGION AND THE HUMANITIES

◄§ 2 §►

CLARIFICATION OF TERMS

Few terms conjure up so many different ideas as does the term *religion.* It is associated with institutions such as churches, synagogues, and temples; with attitudes such as devotion, faith, belief, and prayer; with traditions and systems of thought such as Protestantism, Buddhism, Judaism, Thomism, and Lutheranism; with objects such as a supernatural being, the ultimate one, gods, and natural entities. The vastness and variety of forms religion takes would seem at the outset to preclude success in determining the meaning of the word. So ambiguous is the term that some are willing to call quits to all efforts to bring the phenomenon into manageable intellectual focus.

Attempts to define *religion* are fated to end in the same predicament as do efforts to delineate abstractly such broad human activities as art, philosophy, and politics or such generalized objects of experience as "life" and "nature." People obviously experience these activities in a variety of ways. They are identifiable activities, but the names given to them represent somebody's judgment of what identifies or constitutes them. Art is not first of all defined and then done. Philosophy does not begin by defining *wisdom,* if that even is its goal; it proceeds to think as vigorously as possible about certain problems. The result is called philosophy. Politics does not await the dictum of the political scientist before states are governed. Neither is *life* defined in advance of its study by the life sciences. These sciences determine after study how the term *life* is to be used. Thus when these fields of study are identified, definitions made in advance of investigation are not employed as controls.

27

Certain objects of experience and behavior, in a remarkably rough fashion, are seized upon by the mind for investigation. After prolonged study, those engaged in it describe or define the nature of what they have investigated. But the term by which they summarily identify the results of their work is often the same as that used to identify the activity or object of experience. Thus, for example, *art* refers both to artistic creativity and to the various fields by which this activity is studied. Definitions, as Whitehead once remarked, come at the end of investigation, not at the beginning.

So, also, one does not define *religion* as a precondition either of the religious activity itself or the study thereof. However, as in the case of *art,* one term, *religion,* is used to designate both the activity and the study of it. At this point misunderstanding of its usage easily arises.

In spite of an inevitable awkwardness, the term *religion* will normally be employed in this essay to refer to the study and scholarship which takes as its province certain activities and beliefs commonly known as religious. When it is necessary to use the term to refer to religious attitudes, beliefs, and actions themselves, the context, it is hoped, will make the meaning clear. The nature of what is "religious" is determined by the examination of the phenomena, and this is not, for our purposes, done by any casual observer or self-appointed authority, but by those who have the requisite preparation and ability to carry out such studies. At the outset then, it is necessary to understand clearly that the term *religion* is used to refer to a field of study and not to religious behavior as such. The definition of *religion* called for is not one which describes what people do and believe as a consequence of certain experiences, but a description of the nature of those techniques and approaches by which religion as a human activity is studied and assessed.

It has been argued that the term *religion* should not be used

as a title for the field of study, lest it becloud the distinction between study and activity. *Theology* has been suggested as the
more suitable and exact word, since it appropriately refers to
the discipline which investigates religion as an activity. A number of analogies are offered in support of this usage. Mathematics is not called a number-concept department, philosophy
is not known as the wisdom department, nor is history identified
as the department of past experience. Furthermore, the ambiguity which surrounds the term *religion* is itself sufficient warrant
for the use of another title. [See Edwin M. Good, "The Purpose
of Religious Studies in General Education," *Journal of General
Education,* XIII, 3 (October 1961).]

Some weight may be given to these considerations, but it is
not easy to see that much has been gained in accuracy and
clarity. Few of the terms by which disciplines are identified in
college curriculums are univocal—*history, art,* and *music* are
patent examples of the vagueness of academic shorthand. It is
also obvious that the term *theology* carries with it as troublesome problems of definition as does *religion,* and its relation to
the liberal arts is no less problematical.[1]

More importantly, however, the word *theology* has come to
have a more restricted meaning than that assigned to *religion*
among academic subjects. Certainly theology in a Christian
vein wrestles with the presence and significance of religious
structures other than its own in the world, but it becomes a
misnomer when either as *theology* or *Christian theology* it is
employed to designate the whole range of disciplines which
deal with religious phenomena. It seems singularly inappropriate

---

[1] What is one to make of Alexander Miller's statement in this connection? "It is the nature of theology that it cannot be dealt with as an
intellectual discipline among others, as if the problem of the relation of
theology to other intellectual concerns were merely a problem in the
sphere of ideas." [*Faith and Learning* (Assn. Pr., 1960), p. 120.]

as a title referring to the scholarly examination of the religion of preliterates, world religions, literary and textual studies of sacred literatures, and religious phenomena in general. Neither is it a term congenial to much of Judaism or applicable to those forms of religion for which the idea of theology is connected with notions of deity, e.g., certain forms of Buddhism. [See Robert Michaelson, "Religion as an Academic Discipline," *Liberal Education,* XLVII, 1, 72-83.] It would be preferable to reserve the term *theology* for a specialized discipline involving systematic explication, articulation, and defense of a particular standpoint of faith rather than to substitute its use for the field of religion of which it is but a part.

As such, in spite of a certain illiberalism which remains suspicious of the term itself, theology properly belongs to the field of religion. Without its insights, learning in religion would be immeasurably impoverished and would tend to move off into realms of vague unstructured religiosity. It is a vigorous enterprise which by virtue of its intellectual accomplishments and relevance shapes large segments of human experience. It therefore cannot be regarded as alien to the domain of the humanities, unless they be conceived with such narrowness as to deny entrance to any form of thought which takes seriously the existence of a supernatural realm. To be sure, not all theology is bound to conceptions of the supernatural, but those which are so rooted need not apologize for seeking inclusion among the humanities. H. M. Jones has pointed out: "The fact that the material studied by the humanist often has to do with man's faith in a supernatural order does not mean . . . that the humanist per se has an uncritical faith in this or that order of supernaturalism. However, learning values any expression of a noble faith in life, whether or not that faith rests upon supernatural assumptions or upon more nearly temporal values." [Jones, *One Great Society* (Harcourt, 1959), p. 11 n.]

Regarded from a different standpoint, theology itself stands to profit by sustaining a vital connection with religion broadly conceived as a field of study. Many of the principal currents of thought which oppose theology run through colleges and universities. These theology must confront on their home grounds and in doing so will find itself invigorated and reshaped. Indeed, it has been remarked that already there exists a type of Protestant theology which by virtue of its setting in the university atmosphere has moved into a profounder relation with the secular world of thought than that developed in the theological seminary. Although it does not cast off its associations with the church, neither does this theology appear to be linked inextricably with the church's interests. Whatever may be the fortunes of a theology which moves away from traditional conceptions of its task, it has developed a vigor of its own and has raised the question as to whether theology by definition is a function only of the church. It should not be forgotten, however, that the recent rejuvenation of interest in theology in the colleges and universities owes much to the work of theologians whose principal responsibility lies in the ecclesiastical arena.

The word *religious,* when applied to instruction and scholarship, is another awkward term. Many working in the field of religion consider it desirable to distinguish their functions from those of an avowedly religious character, but the distinction is difficult to maintain. Although seldom does one speak of an art course as artistic, a history course as historical, or a course in Greek as classical, religion courses are often referred to as "religious" courses. The suggestion is thereby planted in the minds of students, church members, college administrators, and faculty colleagues that the intent of such courses is to persuade the student to adopt certain attitudes favorable to those held by the instructor or to a particular religious tradition. The manner, content, and purpose of teaching accordingly are expected to be quite different in character from other courses in the curriculum. Since it is assumed that the purpose of teaching religion is to produce religious persons, it is also easily assumed that there can be no other purpose for offering work in the field. This expectation may be especially prevalent in church-related institutions where the sponsoring denomination regards the college as a source of dedicated laymen for its churches. Similar misunderstandings appear when scholarship is labeled *religious*. The supposition then is that the writing has been undertaken in a spirit of pietism or devotion with a view to persuading the reader to adopt attitudes akin to those of the author. Persons who entertain these expectations are shocked to discover that there are professors who do not conceive their tasks in these terms. They are bewildered to learn that these professors refuse to regard their teaching and scholarship as having an explicitly religious purpose and that they consider themselves educators contributing to the general expansion of human understanding rather than agents of the church or purveyors of religious sentiments.[2]

From the standpoint of the professor, the maintenance of the distinction between *religion* and *religious* becomes a matter of even greater delicacy than that suggested. Among other purposes of his teaching stands his desire to transmit to students an appreciation of the nature and forms of religious experience. But to move along these lines seems immediately to involve him in accepting a religious goal for his instruction. Like his colleagues in other fields, he presumably is vitally interested in his field. He wishes his students to share, at least in some measure, his enthusiasm and his sense of importance of the field. He

---

[2] Morton White, for example, has found it necessary to belabor this point as though it were a novel concept: *Religion, Politics and the Higher Learning,* chap. 8 (Harvard, 1959).

recognizes that without their having some sense of the data within the area his instruction fails of any purpose. Is he not then forced by his materials and his own dynamic as a professor to admit that his purpose as a teacher is "religious"? Can he honestly avoid, at last, the charge of indoctrination?

The problem of indoctrination will be dealt with later; it is sufficient here to draw a distinction and a comparison which may be helpful in understanding the religion professor's position. A distinction not always noted is that between the professor's enthusiasm for the study of his field and the religious commitments which may or may not underlie his interest in the field. In keeping with his function as a teacher he should be expected to have a concern for encouraging others to enter as deeply as possible into the study of the field. His enthusiasm for the importance and value of such study should be communicated to students, but it need not follow that he is thereby encouraging them to adopt for themselves religious attitudes which he believes to be desirable. His purpose then is "religious" only to the extent that he desires to make lively and relevant the nature of the content of the field and to develop in his students that degree of participation in understanding which will set before them the extent of religious phenomena. If the professor in classics, French literature, or even chemistry ultimately desires that his students not only gain knowledge and mastery of the techniques of analysis, but also become personally involved in the issues and insights pertinent to his area, is the religion professor to be debarred from anticipating a similar result from his students? Moreover, does not teaching in the humanities entail developing evaluative attitudes? And if so, should not the religion professor, like his colleagues, assume the responsibility for their development? Unless he can bring before his students the rich variety and concrete detail of religious experience itself and enable them to appreciate and to evaluate critically what he brings, his efforts will simply go by the board.

The problem of the relation between *religion* and *religious* also arises in another context. In recent years the religion scholar and professor has declined to accept as the limits of his study those manifestations of the religious ethos which happen to be theistic, related to churches, or which bear in the popular mind and in conventional usage the title *religious*. He may see the term as one which refers to a quality of experience associated with forms of human conduct and experience more often named as secular. It may seem to him unnecessarily constrictive to limit his studies to those forms of the religious spirit which have become crystallized in credal or institutional structures or which, in some cases, have become moribund. Instead he may reach out to consider those postures which have been assumed in defiance and opposition to conventional religious beliefs, such as agnosticism or atheism, yet which bear qualities of the religious attitude. He finds in these a genuine striving for an ultimate coherence to life or integrity of mind which the principal religious traditions have failed to achieve. The religion scholar therefore knows no proscriptive reason which forbids him to discuss a Nietzsche or a Camus, since they manifest that seriousness about human existence which makes up so large an element in historic religion. Neither is he denied the right to detect in such thinkers an authentic religious spirit which bears the marks of the Christian or Hellenic traditions against which they have rebelled, since there seems no record of an atheist or agnostic who is not at the same time an atheist or agnostic by reference to a Christian, Jewish, or Hindu tradition, i.e., who is not influenced in the definition of his posture by that against which he rebels. In short, the category of the "religious" is not one to be determined by the holding of certain beliefs, but rather by the quality of a concerned response which one makes to the mystery of human existence itself. To the evaluation of these responses the field of religion properly addresses itself. Religion is not a divine creation, but a human development of the religious responses of man. Whether these responses be negative or positive in respect to the existence of a deity or deities, the question of their validity is properly a part of the work of the religion scholar as well as the philosopher.

To some, the discovery of a religious dimension in positions so patently at odds with conventionally accepted notions of religion and the religious seems plainly wrongheaded and downright misleading. Thus W. K. Frankena, a contemporary philosopher, offers the opinion that "these positions are not church-related, and it is only confusing to call them 'religious' on the ground that they embody answers to ultimate issues." ["A Point of View for the Future" in *Religion and the State University,* ed. E. A. Walter (U. of Michigan, 1958), p. 96.] It must be replied that a thoughtful examination of religious phenomenology, such as that carried out by van der Leeuw, in his "Religion in Essence and Manifestation" suggests the enormously varied forms which "religious" responses take, only one phase of which may properly be designated as *theistic* or *church-related* even in the broadest sense. Thus it seems proper to conceive the field of religion in more extensive terms than some outside the field would allow.[3]

[3] A certain irony exists in a philosopher's attempt to define in narrow terms the field of religion, when Western philosophy in the grand metaphysical style prevalent up to the nineteenth century is now under attack by the "analytic" school of philosophers, the most zealous of whom seem ready to define the field of philosophy solely in terms of methodology. They intimate that the great thinkers of the past were quite misguided in their philosophical attempt at securing a comprehensive view of "the good, the true, and the beautiful." If a theologian were to suggest that sheer analytic methodology was no longer philosophy because metaphysical constructions are seldom erected by contemporary philosophers, it would seem proper to direct his attention to the fact

In spite of the genuine difficulties encountered in maintaining a differentiation between the uses of the terms *religious* and *religion,* the distinction must be made. The category of the religious, signifying that quality of human experience which is directed toward a diverse range of objects and which is expressed in varied patterns of responses, such as convictions, insights, revelations, beliefs, and cultic practices, is identified by a concerned sense of the ultimate significance of these objects and the appropriate responses made to them. Religions are the formulations into structures of belief and practice which men create, and in which they participate. But *religion* in this essay will normally be used to signify the systematic study of both the "religious" as a quality of human experience and "religion" as formulated structures. It is hoped that where there is the possibility of doubt as to usage of these terms, the context will provide clarification. Accordingly, to describe adequately the field, a concept of considerable breadth is required.

Stated in comprehensive terms, religion embraces the study of those forms of conviction, belief, and behavior and those systems of thought in which men express their concerned responses to whatever they hold to be worthy of lasting and universal commitment. Religion takes for its province of study not only the normative beliefs, practices, and literatures of the world religions as commonly classified, but also manifestations of religious attitudes which impinge upon cultural contexts— political, economic, or artistic—often considered foreign to religious aims.[4]

Conceived in these terms, religion finds its principal aims of

---

that there is such a thing as the historical development of a field of inquiry in which those who work in it are the appropriate authorities to consult.

[4] See *The Humanities at Oberlin,* C. A. Holbrook, co-author (Oberlin College, 1958), pp. 27-28.

instruction and scholarship consonant with those of liberal edu‚ cation. Emphasis falls upon informative, appreciative, and critical purposes rather than upon the stimulation of devotional attitudes or the inducement to doctrinal conformity. Instruction in religion certainly has affected the personal convictions of students, as does study in other fields, but under circumstances appropriate to liberal arts education these effects must be counted as by-products or secondary consequences of the instructional process rather than its goal. Judged by the tenets of either church or explicitly antireligious groups, these changes in point of view are not always regarded as beneficial, since the validity claims of both groups may be brought under critical surveillance and seldom settled to the full advantage of either party.

Religion is often referred to as a field rather than as a discipline because it has no techniques for investigation or evaluation which are peculiar to it, or which set it apart from other humanistic studies. It is an area to be examined by a diversity of methods which are as appropriate to other fields as they are to religion. To ascertain the most probable construction and understanding of a text, the methodology employed by a religion scholar in translating and analyzing a passage from the Bible or the Rig Veda is no different from that employed by a classics scholar. The investigation of the relation between seventeenth century English sectarianism and the rise of religious toleration calls for no less or more critical appraisal of sources than does a historical study of the military campaigns of General Grant. The comparative appraisal of Buddhist and Christian analyses of the nature and goal of human existence demands no more or less unique devices than does the comparison of Mandeville's and Rousseau's outlooks upon life. The opening of the bronze scroll found among the Dead Sea Scrolls or the presentation of the fragile fragments of papyrus manuscripts calls for the same diligent and patient use of technical and scientific knowledge as that needed in any other archaeological or anthropological operation. In short, the difference between religion and other fields lies first of all not in methodologies, which are many, but in the nature of the material to be studied, which in turn naturally demands as a minimal condition an interest in and abiding sense of the significance of the field itself. As in other fields or disciplines, there should be an appreciable growth in sensitivity for religious data, an advance in subtlety of analytic approach, and a resultant development of knowledge, but these characteristics are less techniques than correlates of the emergent attitudes of the instructor and scholar. Of course, there are specialists who may develop their own ways of going at their materials, and who may have their own presuppositions about the ultimate purposes of their studies, but it seems impossible to distinguish these specialists from those working in other areas solely on the basis of scholarly techniques.

The nature of religion itself, furthermore, is so pervasive an element in human culture that any attempt to conceive its study in terms of methodological norms immediately breaks down of its own weight. Its interplay with philosophy, music, art, and literature, as well as with government and economics, presses the scholar to recognize that no matter how disciplined his own contribution may be, it at last finds its proper focus and setting only in an enormously extensive territory to which in his own limited right he cannot lay claim. He is much like the scholar in history who, recognizing the claim of disciplined insight in his own special period, or limited segment of the human process, nevertheless also realizes that history as a field embraces the telling of the entire story of the human venture, inclusive of science, art, religion, politics, and economics. The term *discipline* then properly refers to the development of methods appropriate to a segment of the whole, but not to the total territory. But this is but another way of expressing what is true of all humanistic disciplines. No matter how technically a scholar may operate in his own limited area, that area, by virtue of its coextension with human experience in general, is never a self-contained entity except for procedural purposes. The dimensions of scholarship are not first of all divisions of human experience. They are the products of man's need to examine wide ranges of experience in a disciplined, piecemeal fashion in order to grasp and to penetrate to the significance of the whole.

The moral to be drawn is that just as other major areas of human culture, such as fine arts, literature, or history, touch many facets of human life, yet are studied and taught by common disciplines and in distinct departments of the college structure, so religion, although it profoundly interacts with many other areas of human experience, when interpreted as a field of study also employs disciplines common to the humanistic enterprise and calls for treatment in a department where research and instruction may make their contributions to both liberalizing and preprofessional ends.

❤§ 3 §❤

RELIGION IN THE HUMANITIES

Humanistic scholars in these latter days of scientific prestige and technological achievement have become sensitive about the importance of their respective disciplines. In times when large grants for research have been forthcoming from the government and from private foundations for scientific work; when issues of national defense have pre-empted the attention of scholarship, university administrations, and the general public; and when the "deterioration" of public taste has been widely lamented, humanists have often turned to the defense of their provinces with vigor if not outright bitter aggressiveness. The impetus to the study of foreign languages given by recent events and governmental grants has proved to be ameliorative, but a rankling sense of deprivation of status and support continues to distress many.

On the other hand, the fulsome assertions made in defense of humanistic studies have embarrassed some humanistic scholars who feel that claims for the pre-emption of the area of value judgments by the humanities are not only evidence of provincial inaccuracy, but also indications of an unnecessarily debilitating uncertainty about the validity of the humanistic enterprise itself. Furthermore, extravagant claims made for the influence which humanistic studies wield over human conduct have an embarrassing way of escaping from the quantitative verification of results which is possible in the natural sciences. Hence, it appears that the proper, if more modest, approach to the defense of the humanities lies in the production of scholarly works and in instruction at a high level. The results must then speak for themselves.

The humanities find their characteristic subject matter in those significant achievements of the human race which illuminate and illustrate the distinctive characteristics of man as a rational and spiritual being. Man's capacity for self-transcendence in the forms of reflection, imagination, volition, self-awareness, and his ability to project his mind into the future enable him to experience a dimension of existence which, however much it depends upon the physical and sensate, has an authenticity of its own which no reductionism can ultimately erode or destroy. In this realm, experiences and reactions range from awe in the presence of the underlying mystery of existence itself to ecstatic participation in the intrinsically enjoyable, from tragedy to comedy, from contemplation of nature to the introspective probing of the psyche, from the creation of art forms which reflect the varying moods and insights of man to the development of rigorously logical structures of thought, from ingenious play with languages and sounds to the celebration of crucial experiences of human life. From this almost inexhaustible source of wealth have emerged those patterns of thought and action which collectively are called the humanities, each of which takes for its domain some segment of man's experience to interpret, to preserve, to evaluate, and in some cases to create.

Humanistic learning as it looks to the past attempts to make available to the present the worthy embodiments of man's creativity. As it faces the present, it insists upon a critical dialogue among diverse evaluations and continued reflection upon the criteria of worth. In moving toward the future, it strives to lure into fresh channels man's creative powers. Its overarching goal is to produce in men an "ordered insight" into life "in which intuition, reason, and imagination fuse into a whole." [Douglas M. Knight, "Religious Implications in the Humanities" in *Liberal Learning and Religion,* ed. A. N. Wilder (Harper, 1951), p. 96.] Or to put the matter differently, humanistic learning aims to enrich human existence by placing before it a vision of the heights and depths of the human spirit. It offers no ready-made philosophy of life; the interplay among alternatives is too vigorous for that. It can deepen and broaden man's self-awareness and sense of values by confronting him with variant forms of the ways in which men past and present discover or deny the human possibility.[1]

Although the purposes of the humanities may be couched in terms of heroic proportions, as above, it must be quickly admitted that humanistic scholarship and teaching are seldom carried on with explicit reference to such lofty sentiments. Much of the work in the humanities is more prosaic and it often is technical and piecemeal—the translation of a text, the development of a better technique for teaching foreign languages, the study of the detail on a Gothic cathedral, the analysis of the concept of "cause," or even the composition of music for a computer. The learned journals are not usually filled with broad studies of values or proposals for the "humanizing" of men. More often they contain specialized articles whose connections with the ultimate purposes of humanistic education are tenuous in the extreme. It is not uncommon to find scholars and instructors in the humanities scoffing at those of their colleagues who offer

---

[1] "The purpose of humane learning is to offer those wise enough to want to accept the lesson of human experience an interpretation of the life of man—its tragedies and aspirations, its brutalities and its comic relief. The lesson of human experience in this sense constitutes whatever wisdom man has learned from the process of history and from those enduring expressions of interpretations of experience we call philosophy, religion in a broad and generous sense, works of literature, and works in the form of arts, including music, architecture, and the dance." [H. M. Jones, *One Great Society* (Harcourt, 1959), p. 9.]

comprehensive statements on the purposes of the humanities.

In spite of the pedantries by which all scholarship is occasionally victimized, humanistic scholarship, learning, and instruction must operate on the principle that however irrelevant and esoteric any piece of scholarship appears at the moment, it may in some way eventually contribute to man's understanding of himself. A particular scholar or instructor may care not a whit about the exalted aims which others profess and yet he may contribute richly to the realization of these aims by his own dedicated labors in one small portion of the field. So also the instructor who seldom refers to the goals of humanistic learning may open the way into the richness of humanistic experience.

The role of religion among the humanities has been questioned in recent years. The first specific issue is not how religion shall be studied or taught, but what grounds exist for its acceptance or rejection as a humanistic field. Books which deal with the nature of the humanities reveal a certain uneasiness about its presence. Some simply omit religion from their review of the disciplines and fields within the humanities, presumably on the grounds that the term *religion* signifies sectarianism, or the inculcation of religious attitudes at odds with the purposes of liberal education. Others reveal an uncertainty about the use of the term *religion*. While accepting religion as systems of thought, belief, and action as part of the human scene which no fair-minded projection of humanistic studies can omit, a certain diffidence appears about its role as an identifiable field of scholarship and instruction. Thus David H. Stevens in *The Changing Humanities* speaks of one source of "humanistic strength and sensitivity" as coming through experience in religion. So emphatic is he in asserting the relevance of religious experience that he asserts flatly that "an atheist is not a humanist." Religion cannot be for him simply a matter of objective study; it must be "a personal influence in the life of a man if he is to appreciate humane values." Stevens also sees religion as a strong cultural force, to which humanistic studies must pay heed. The term *religion* is used to refer to the processes of personal appropriation of some beliefs about the ultimate and as an influential factor in human culture. On the other hand, Stevens apparently subsumes consideration of religion in these two senses under the rubric of philosophy, and offers no indication that religion in either sense should be treated as a field of study in its own right. [See Stevens, *The Changing Humanities* (Harper, 1953), p. 23.]

A different position is taken by H. M. Jones in *One Great Society*. He does not discount religion as an aspect of culture, and he goes so far as to suggest that the "Christian ethic" provides "a general religious sanction" for value judgments in the humanities. He notes that religion courses are taught in the division of humanities, sometimes distributed among literature, philosophy, or history; however, he explicitly rules theology out of the humanistic area on the grounds of its historical development and the common practice of confining its study as a technical subject to divinity schools. He does allow that in a broader sense, theology "as a group of religious ideas concerning the nature of man" does markedly influence contemporary "humanism." [P. 3 n, pp. 12-15, 167-70.] Again, it is questionable whether Jones is willing to admit religion to the precincts of the humanities as an identifiable field of study and instruction. His reference to theology as a technical or professional subject taught in divinity school recalls the medieval pattern in which theology is one of the "superior" faculties, but also implies the university structure to which Protestant theory and practice has led, in which theology is separated from other subjects.

Thus there are those of diverse religious persuasions who recognize the historical and contemporaneous significance of theology, but who are manifestly relieved to find it securely set outside the university and collegiate structure, at several removes from the humanities. In this way, it seems, the tensions between humanistic pursuits and religious doctrine are believed to be reduced.

The place of theology among the humanities is not the only issue involved in the tension between religion and the humanities, since it is but part of the field of religion. However, the memory of the clashes between certain forms of theology and other branches of learning still mischievously distorts the relation between religion and the humanities. Jones may be over-optimistic in his opinion that "modern humanism . . . has shed its original hostility to theology" [p. 84], but his comment suggests the possibility that this memory need not be decisive in the evaluation of the place of religion. There also have been increasing indications of the possible compatibility between religion and the humanistic mind. Although the Harvard report on "General Education in a Free Society" was widely regarded as doing much less than justice to the role that religion instruction and scholarship could play in higher education, it should be recalled that its authors were careful to interpret their use of the term *humanism* in such a way as not "to exclude the religious idea" [p. 76]. President Goheen of Princeton has suggested that the search must go on for freer and fuller ways in which theological and liberal studies may interpenetrate with scientific and humanistic disciplines. Speaking for his own university, he added that its Religion Department was mainly "a department within the humanities which young men going into various professions may choose as the focus of their liberal education." [*Princeton Seminary Bulletin,* LIV, 1 (1960), 8, 10.] Gustave Weigel, S. J., in commenting upon the relation of "contemplative theology" to humanistic education has also underlined the possibilities of a rapprochement between the two. The liberal arts college, he observes, has as its "whole function"

45

that of making "the young man or woman pass through a program of humanistic education" not in order to become experts but to see the ways in which "the human being can function on a level other than the pragmatic." The aim of the college is humanistic, for it "essays to show to youth the spiritual (not religious) good in human life. . . . The student is being taught to know and esteem the good. That is the whole essence of humanism." ["The Meaning of Sacred Doctrine in the College" in *The Shaping of the Christian Message,* ed. G. S. Sloyan (Macmillan, 1958), p. 175.]

The sharpening of the issue, however, comes sometimes from personnel in the field of religion itself. There are those in seminaries and churches who fear that scholarship and instruction carried out in the college or university will lose the particularly sympathetic handling which church institutions provide. They are apprehensive lest their own reading of religious convictions be construed simply as one option among others, thereby destroying the uniqueness of their reading by identifying it with religion as such. A contemporary interpreter regards religion as "in essence man's upward reach for secure relation to some eternal or absolute reality" and concludes that religion so conceived is what Christianity opposes, since Christian faith finds man's sinful nature reflected in religion. [C. C. West, "Christ the Light of the World," *Theology Today,* XVIII, 3, 288.] This position, influenced by Dietrich Bonhoeffer and Karl Barth, has won increasing support among certain theologians. But if religion be construed in this derogatory fashion by Christian theologians, the possibilities of a fair understanding of other religions seem drastically reduced. One theological position, presumably exempt from the charge of "sinfulness," would then not only determine the nature and validity of alternative religious faiths but would also limit the scope of intellectual inquiry within the field of religion itself.

Whereas the position represented by Dr. West could be explored and evaluated within the field of religion broadly conceived, it is impossible to employ his view of the nature of religion as the context for scholarship and instruction in the university. It would only exacerbate the tensions between humanistic and religion scholars, and in fact, give a highly distorted picture of what the latter were doing. The point of interest, however, lies in the fact that the question of the possibility of including the study of religion among humanistic disciplines has been raised by theologians rather than by humanistic scholars.

From another standpoint, Father J. Courtney Murray has sharply expressed the sensitivity of those concerned for the fate of religious faith on the campus. Referring to the presence of committed Protestant, Jewish, and Roman Catholic students in the university, he states: "The university as such has no right to judge the validity of any of these commitments." [*Religion and the State University,* ed. E. A. Walter (U. of Michigan, 1958), p. 22.] His comment appears to strike at one of the basic principles upon which the free university operates, for it places the religious commitments of these three faiths in a privileged category where they would be immune from the same critical analysis to which other religious commitments and value systems are subjected. Construed in broader terms, Father Murray's statement could mean that religious commitments of any kind were to be exempted from evaluation. Yet clearly one of the crucial dimensions of humanistic learning, inclusive of the study of religion, is the critical investigation of those loyalties and beliefs by which men interpret and direct their lives. It is neither likely nor desirable that the university should surrender its intellectual freedom to claims of privilege and certainly no scholarly study of religion could be carried through under such limitations.

47

One other ground of possible tension between religion and the humanities moves from a quite different stance. There are those who find not that the university's conception of its task is too sweeping or broad, but that it is too confining and limiting in respect to the study of religion. They consider the opponents of religion to be moved by uninformed impressions of what scholarship and instruction in this field means, and they discover in the university, in spite of the professed liberality and breadth of humanistic studies, a tendency to lay restrictions on the thought and modes of instruction which competent scholars and professors in religion seek to achieve. If, for example, an instructor in religion asks searching questions about the competence of reason to serve as the very foundation of the humanistic enterprise, he may be regarded less as an ally in the attempt to penetrate to the understanding of man's nature than as a traitor to the Enlightenment spirit of much humanistic learning. If he seeks the same freedom which his colleagues enjoy to interpret beliefs or literatures from the "inside," striving to enable his readers or students to appreciate why some have felt these beliefs or viewpoints to be viable options, he may be charged with indoctrination rather than given credit for his efforts to make the past and present intelligible. The scholar in religion, therefore, is sometimes moved to a cynicism about the freedom and liberality of the university, and he may feel that a more genuine freedom for teaching and scholarship lies outside the university setting, perhaps, albeit doubtful, in the divinity school or seminary.[2]

[2] Charles L. Taylor notes the rise of the Kirchliche Hochschule in Germany as a protest against the domination by the state over theological studies. The parallel, of course, is not in exact correspondence to the position sketched above, but it does suggest that the grounds of tension between religion scholarship and other groups and viewpoints are based on other than purely sectarian grounds. ["Seminaries and Universities in Partnership," *Princeton Seminary Bulletin,* LIV, 1 (1960), 14.]

Strange though it may seem to interpreters of the humanities, some scholars and teachers in religion feel that it is they who are threatened by illiberality rather than that they threaten the free flow of ideas and conflict of convictions dear to the heart of the humanities. In this case the tension is not due to sectarian interests on the part of the religion professor, but to the failure of the humanistic proponents to live up to their avowed liberality at some points.

We have here touched upon what appears to be the "nerve" of the problem. Insofar as the humanities in some acknowledged or unacknowledged way maintain the assumption that their work is carried on solely in the spirit of the Enlightenment ethos, in which man is seen as capable by reason and inspired insight to save himself from the downward drag of base passions and animal instincts, there will be a tension with those forms of scholarship in religion which view man as a "sinful creature" whose most fervid efforts at salvation from aimlessness and ignoble satisfactions cannot succeed without divine grace in some form. If humanistic studies even at their best proceed on the basis of a humanist philosophy which by definition rules out all consideration of the possible relevance of the existence and nature of a suprahuman being to the fulfillment of a truly humane possibility, then inevitably some religion professors will sense that the humanities have arbitrarily limited their scope without pausing to argue the case with the counterclaims of other alternatives. If the grounds of acceptance of religion as a humanistic field depend upon a premature limitation of the scope of investigation and instruction, there are those in the ranks of religion scholarship who would decline the option, less for sectarian reasons than in obedience to the claims of a free university and a truly humane educational process.

On the other hand, it seems crystal clear that the religion scholar must accept the ground rules of university education at its best, and not seek special privilege among the humanities for his field of competence. He enters the university scene and takes his place among the humanities in the name not of an esoteric faith, but as one as dedicated as his colleagues to the elimination of ignorance and superstition, arrant dogmatism and provincialism. These ideals he must be willing to accept. His is the task of portraying in his segment of the totality of learning and instruction as informed and sensitive a picture of the human scene as his competence permits and of making that picture live as a representation of and an enlightening contribution to man's knowledge and wisdom. He enters the humanities with the aim common to them of making the past intelligible to the present and of showing wherein the hope of man may lie. He enters with the implicit understanding that he will give and take in the conflict of ideas which any truly lively academic atmosphere engenders. He will not allow himself to be disarmed in advance for the prosecution of his work, either by the prescriptions of church, state, or the ethos of a particular campus. His work is education in the best sense of that term, though he may come to it, as may his colleagues, with some undergirding personal faith concerning the validity of the enterprise and his vocation within that enterprise. Without this acceptance of and devotion to the ideal of the free university and the humanistic aims it affirms, whether in private, state, or church-related university, the scholar and instructor of religion has forfeited claim to his presence within the university.[3]

The tensions which have played a part in defining the relation of religion to higher education and specifically to the hu-

---

[3] Some institutions supported by religious denominations are presumably exempt from this judgment since, although they are not to be counted out entirely on grounds of scholarship, they interpret *religion* primarily in their own doctrinal terms, rather than in the broader context of the free university model.

manities may not be easily eliminated. But the direction of their dissolution lies in a closer attention to the use of terms which apply to the field of religion and in an understanding by all parties of the expectations appropriate to the study of religion in a liberal arts program. Even more it depends upon the actual practice of the arts of instruction and scholarship in religion within that setting.

The issue which now calls for attention is that of the grounds upon which religion can properly take its place among the humanities. Is it, when construed in the broad terms of this essay, a liberalizing or humanizing area of instruction and scholarship? A convincing answer to the question cannot be given by a simple recital of the courses customarily offered in religion departments. No more can the humanistic character of religion be defended solely by the assertion that the content of these courses is intrinsically "humanizing" than can the humanistic intent of an English department be affirmed by citing courses in Milton and Shakespeare. There are certainly some who teach in the humanities who make no special virtue of humanistic goals regardless of the announced titles of their courses. The apocryphal story of the professor who in the teaching of Plato announced to his class "Gentlemen, we now embark upon Book III, a veritable morass of philological peculiarities!" suggests a conception of instruction which falls far short of humanistic ends. Courses in literature or philosophy do not become humanistic simply by being placed among the humanities. So also with subjects within a religion curriculum. On the other hand, it is quickly realized that the vaguer but no less genuinely influential factor of a humanistic approach to material does not alone determine the fitness of a particular subject matter to fall within the scope of the humanities. Subject matter alone may not determine the placing of a field within the somewhat artificial divisions of the liberal arts college, but given such items as the French Novel of the Nineteenth Century, Empiricism in Seventeenth Century England, or the Religion of the Hebrew People, the presumption is overwhelmingly in favor of their being placed within the humanities rather than the social sciences, regardless of the manner in which they may be taught.

Obviously, the same interplay between content and approach applies to religion. A survey of the last several decades of undergraduate instruction in religion would provide examples of course materials (biblical, historical, ethical, philosophical, or theological) which have been so treated as to yield little support to the liberalizing aims of higher education, but examples would also appear of the same materials handled in a way that promoted the critical appreciation of human existence to which humanistic studies aspire.

There has been religion instruction, probably most often found in church-related colleges, where the explicit aim has been to lead students into closer alliance with a particular religious tradition or church, and such instruction may even have produced, within those limits, an emancipative and enlightening understanding of that tradition or church's viewpoints. Or again one could find instruction offered with an eye less to the service of the student body generally than to the development of potential candidates for the clergy. Even where this consideration is paramount, it does not follow in any rigorous fashion that instruction is necessarily "illiberal" or even directly professional. Much depends in this case, as with preprofessional studies in other fields, on the way in which the department construes the nature of desirable preprofessional training.

Another pattern discernible in the teaching of religion has been a posture of "objectivity," widely regarded as the *sine qua non* of academic respectability. Instruction carried out in this key is moved by an extreme sensitivity to the possibility of a charge of "indoctrination," a charge from which, strangely enough, other members of the academic community seem exempt. The laudable purposes of this type of instruction, however, may sometimes interfere with the education of the student when it denies to him the opportunity of sensing the vitality and relevance of religious faiths. Attempts to avoid the danger of indoctrination, which constantly hovers over religion instruction, may prevent a just appreciation of religious beliefs and attitudes; a stringent objectivity may prove to be a deterrent to a genuine engagement with the vitalities of religious experience. The just aims of a humanistic education which among other things purports to develop both critical appreciation and standards of value are thus negated.

That the actual practice of teaching in religion may be checkered in respect to truly humanizing goals need not preclude its acceptance among the humanities. Religion as a phase of human experience, whether it be reckoned for good or ill, has had a profound and decisive effect on man's conception of himself, his destiny, and his actions. It is fruitless to talk of humanistic aims without listening both to the contributions and to the criticisms of those aims which specific religious traditions offer. To attempt to understand man without reference to the systems of belief and insight within which he has attempted to understand himself is to reduce and distort his images of himself by which humanistic education at its best tries to direct its steps.

If scholarship and instruction in religion is a necessary component of humanistic education, so also are the humanities necessary to religion. This must be true in at least two ways. First, there is ever the need for recognizing the interplay between the religious dimension itself and the other humanistic fields. Specialist scholars may jealously guard their preserves from the intrusions of others, but in the last analysis the material itself evades control; religion probably overlaps other fields more than any other one field in the curriculum. And this fact makes it more imperative than ever that there be specialists in religion who at the same time see the importance of their work in relation to the total humanistic enterprise.

The second reason for the relevance of the humanities to religion is derivative from the first. Religion teaching and scholarship themselves profit from their engagement with rather than isolation from other disciplines, where scholars often operate from different presuppositions. For many teachers and scholars in religion, the most attractive possibilities for both instruction and scholarly work occur where the give and take of diverse and sometimes antagonistic viewpoints sharpen and focus thought. The rigor and the vigor of academic interchange are desirable stimuli for the production of work of a higher degree of precision and relevance than that which emerges from a more cloistered atmosphere. A. D. Nock has pointed out: "The serious study of religion is a part of humanistic study in general, and for its well-being needs to be conducted in a community where history, language, and philosophy receive the full service of scholars who have integrity, competence and zeal." [Quoted in *The Changing Humanities*, pp. 132-33.] As religion needs constant confrontation with other humanistic studies, so they in turn require the challenge and supplementation which religion provides when it enters fully into the academic atmosphere of the college and university.

◄§ III §►

UNDERGRADUATE INSTRUCTION

⥼ 4 ⥽

GROWTH IN RELIGION INSTRUCTION

By mid-twentieth century a remarkable upsurge in the teaching of religion in colleges and universities had taken place. New departments or chairs of religion were established, and older departments were revived and expanded. Religion was "in the air" so far as popular culture was concerned, but more importantly, the earnest efforts of competent teachers and interpreters of the relations of higher education and religion had begun to bear fruit. Not only private or church-related colleges had taken up the challenge of relating religion in a significant academic fashion to higher education, but the state-supported universities showed uncommon openness to the possible establishment of courses, chairs, or departments in religion. In 1947, C. P. Shedd had observed that about sixty out of one hundred state universities and land grant colleges offered instruction of some kind in religion on an academic credit basis. [C. P. Shedd, *Religion in the State University,* Hazen Pamphlet No. 16, p. 20.] Recent estimates show that 60 per cent of all colleges, 100 per cent of all church-related colleges, and 45 per cent of state colleges and universities have religion departments or chairs, to say nothing of various alternative arrangements for academic work in religion. [Huston Smith, "The Interdepartmental Approach to Religious Studies," *Journal of Higher Education,* XXXI, 2 (February 1960), 62.] To the astonished pleasure of some and the dismay of others, it was discovered that greater legal latitude existed in state university charters for the inclusion of academic work in religion than had commonly been supposed. This freedom soon began to be exploited, and its manifestations have been watched with interest by those who recognize the potential contributions of state universities to the liberal arts and the humanities.

Even an incomplete list of universities and colleges which have established, re-established, or enlarged programs of instruction in religion is an impressive one: Boston, Columbia, Connecticut, Denison, Florida, Georgia, Louisiana State, Miami of Ohio, Michigan, Michigan State, North Carolina, North Carolina State, Oberlin, Oregon, Oregon State, Pennsylvania, Pittsburgh, Princeton, South Carolina, Stanford, Virginia, Virginia Polytechnic Institute, Washington University of St. Louis, and Yale. A study in depth of the work carried on at these institutions would provide ample justification for C. P. Shedd's observation that a steady increase has occurred in the number of colleges offering religion courses. He also recognizes that a constant broadening in the types of courses, a raising of their academic standards and increased enrollments in them has been taking place. [Shedd, *op. cit.*, pp. 16-17.] These judgments in the main have been supported by the studies of Merrimon Cuninggim [*The College Seeks Religion;* see. esp. pp. 144-45], G. F. Thomas [*Religious Perspectives in College Teaching;* see esp. p. 10], and J. M. Moore [*The Place of Moral and Religious Values in Programs of General Education*].

Not only has there been substantial growth in attention to religion in the academic area, but in the eyes of some observers a kind of religious revolution has been occurring on campuses, which offsets the image of "the godless campus" which church leaders have often lamented. Thus, G. W. Edwards, with an exuberance which outruns the evidence, concludes that the campus is not only more "religious" than its detractors assume, but that it bids fair to become "the rallying ground for a religious renaissance." ["How Is't with Thy Religion?" *Journal of*

Higher Education, XXIV, 9 (December 1953), 460, 600.]

The upsurge in concern over religion in higher education has been guided by and reflected in the volume of literature which the issue has raised. Articles and books discussing the college's responsibility in this area have been flooding the market for at least the past twenty-five years. Studies of student, faculty, and administration attitudes toward religion; studies of curriculums and projected plans for religion departments; interpretive essays on the nature of religion studies and their defense; efforts to define a Christian college, a Christian teacher; pamphlets on the religious dimensions of other disciplines; avowals of alleged contributions which the study of religion would make to liberal education; examinations of the treatment of the religious dimension in typical college textbooks; surveys of the thinking of college teachers of religion—these and many more subjects have made more than a five-foot shelf of readings.[1]

The twentieth century has also seen the rise and growth of

[1] Without prejudice as to the question of the worth of much of this literary output, a few of the more influential titles may be offered in evidence: Howard Lowry, *The Mind's Adventure;* H. P. Van Dusen, *God in Education;* Christian Gauss, ed., *The Teaching of Religion in American Higher Education;* A. S. Nash, *The University in the Modern World;* G. A. Buttrick, *Faith and Education;* A. N. Wilder, ed., *Liberal Learning and Religion;* H. N. Fairchild, ed., *Religious Perspectives in College Teaching;* Walter Moberly, *Crisis in the University;* Huston Smith, *The Purposes of Higher Education;* Merrimon Cuninggim, *The College Seeks Religion;* C. P. Shedd, *The Church Follows Its Students;* K. I. Brown, *Not Minds Alone.* From an enormous periodical and pamphlet literature a number of items may be selected: the Hazen Pamphlets on various aspects of religion and higher education; G. F. Thomas's inaugural address "Religion in an Age of Secularism"; A. J. Coleman, "The Christian in the University"; C. A. Holbrook, "What Is a Christian College?" *Social Action* (September 1949); Gould Wickey and R. A. Eckhart, "A National Survey of Courses in Bible and Religion in American Universities and Colleges." The *Christian Scholar,* the

organizations and foundations which have explicitly encouraged and supported the study of religion, the preparation of teachers for the field, or in fields where religious perspectives have been regarded as relevant. Among the most outstanding organizations in terms of prestige and experience has been the National Council on Religion in Higher Education, founded by Charles Foster Kent of Yale in the late 1920's. His purpose was that of lifting the level of undergraduate instruction in religion by encouraging adequate and specifically vocational preparation for the teachers of religion and allied fields. This group has provided fellowships for graduate training in various fields, including religion, a consultative service for establishing and evaluating religion departments and programs, and a placement service. The Hazen Foundation, often working in close connection with the Council, has also provided support and encouragement for the study of projects bearing on the relations between religion and higher education. A more recent and highly influential impact has been made by the Danforth Foundation, which offers substantial fellowships for graduate work leading to teaching in all fields taught in the liberal arts curriculum. The purpose of the grants is to bring men of high competence into college and university teaching who, from their own religious traditions, are aware of the religious dimension of their fields and who show signs of growing religious maturity. No doctrinal basis for the acceptance of candidates has been established by the Foundation. The recent union of some phases of the work of the National Council on Religion in Higher Education, now known as the Society for Religion in Higher Education, and the Danforth Foundation will un-

---

Journal of Bible and Religion, Religious Education, and the *Journal of Higher Education* have offered informed commentary on religion and higher education.

doubtedly strengthen the work of both groups, and new programs will be forthcoming. The Lilly Foundation, among other encouraging benefactions, has responded to needs among religion professors by establishing research and study grants, which are handled by the Hazen Foundation. And one hardly need mention those aspects of the Rockefeller, Woodrow Wilson, Seaatlantic, and Ford foundations which at graduate school, seminary, or undergraduate levels of instruction have reflected marked interest in the role of religion in higher education.

Professional societies, as well as different types more informally arranged, have arisen and flourished during the first half of the century. The Society for Biblical Literature, founded in the late nineteenth century, has continued to grow. The National Association of Biblical Instructors—a patent misnomer, since many of its members are undergraduate instructors in phases of religion which are not specifically biblical—provides a common meeting place for the majority of religion teachers of the country. College teachers of religion will also be found in the American Philosophical Association, the American Society of Church History, and the recently formed Society for the Scientific Study of Religion and the Society for the History of Religions. In 1953 the Society of Catholic College Teachers of Sound Doctrine was also formed, the purpose of which is "to assist teachers in imparting to college students adequate religious instruction well integrated with the rest of the curriculum." [*Shaping the Christian Message,* ed. G. S. Sloyan (Macmillan, 1958), p. 183.] The continuing relation of recipients of Danforth and Kent Fellowships to their respective foundations, by means of regional and national conferences, provides yet another means of invigorating discussion and study of the relations of religion to the realm of higher education.

With this general rise in interest in religion in higher education there has gone hand in hand a notable growth in graduate education in theology and religion. Although most graduate theological education continues to aim at the production of clergy and personnel for other church vocations, a marked rise in the training of scholars and teachers of religion has taken place, beginning in 1920, at such institutions as Chicago, Duke, Union-Columbia, and Yale. And it is not without interest that, although the opportunities for college and graduate teachers of religion are relatively few compared with the fields of history, literature, or the sciences, the most recent analysis of teacher supply and demand estimates that by 1970 five hundred new teachers of religion will be needed for colleges, universities, and junior colleges. [*Teacher Supply and Demand in Universities, Colleges, and Junior Colleges, 1959-60 and 1960-61* (Research Division, NEA, 1961), p. 55.]

It is notoriously difficult to identify and assess causes of cultural changes, but insofar as such a procedure is ever successful, the following factors may be suggested as having played a significant part in the invigoration of religion in higher education. Whereas sectarianism and secularism seemed to have effectively closed the doors to any substantial advance in making religion a part of a liberal education in the early part of the twentieth century, the much heralded impact of the "moral and spiritual crisis" had its effects on higher education. Horrifyingly spelled out by two world wars among supposedly highly cultured nations, and by an unusually pernicious form of moral relativism in Western culture, the crisis alerted some educators to the unacceptability of an education which failed to deal trenchantly and convincingly with the foundations of human values. The sectarian emphases of churches and church-related college education had been ineffective in meeting the crisis, and in some cases their influence had been provincializing. The secularistic reading of human experience at its worst dogmatically denied man's spiritual nature and fervently preached the necessity of accepting at face value the dictates of "objectivity" and a "value-free" approach to the human enterprise. It did provide, if not an explicit philosophy of education, at least an atmosphere of opinion which made it difficult for both the religious dimensions of life and the field of religion itself to gain fair hearings. Even at its best, prevalent secularistic attitudes had refused, in the name of emancipation from Christian or Jewish dogmatism, to consider the depths as well as the heights of human life. Certain ideas born of the Enlightenment and the Renaissance had seemingly indelibly impressed the university mind with their universal validity. Not a few educators as well as professionals in the predominant religious faiths of American culture questioned anew the validity of both sectarianism and secularism.

The futuristic optimism upon which secularism had prodigally drawn for motivation and justification, and the rigidities within which denominations attempted to interpret and change the world, simply could not stand up to the brutally compelling facts of twentieth century life. And generations of students, leaving colleges and universities with the gloss of learning but lacking in religious and ethical convictions, were viewed as semi-educated barbarians poured into a common pool of humanity which was already dispirited and purposeless. As if drawn by some vague but irresistible lure, influential opinion began to swing to the notion that religion in some equally vague sense could check the drift to social and moral chaos.

This illusory hope has not been realized. What the churches had not done, the introduction of religion into the curriculum could not be expected to accomplish. Except in those institutions where something close to indoctrination serves as an academic philosophy, religion has had to settle for a modest place among the humanities or, in some cases, the social sciences. It has had to accept its role on common humanistic grounds, as do other fields in which man studies himself. It has not been in a position to serve as an integrative center to offset the sprawling, divisive specializations of even the smallest college. Neither has it arrived on campuses, some authorities to the contrary notwithstanding, with a readily adoptable value system by which to end the apparent ethical anarchism of our society.

This is not to say that effective transitions in campus attitudes toward religion have not taken place in many cases. In fact the re-entry and reinvigoration of the academic study of religion on campuses have often provided the first glimpses these institutions have had of scholarly methods and presentations which made religious phenomena something besides a butt of flippancies or crude caricature. Nor can it be denied that the return of religion to the curriculum in many cases enlivened the intellectual life of the campus generally, even going so far as to raise questions concerning the purposes and nature of education itself. But it must also be insisted that many who pressed for the return of religion on the grounds that it would be a major agent in checking secularism, relativism, scientism, and other academic ills created a burden of responsibility which could not be borne by any department or group of courses. Wherever the re-entry of religion was launched on these assumptions, an atmosphere of misunderstanding was created. Some administrators were disappointed that a few courses in religion did not markedly stem the tide, or that faculty and students only grudgingly admitted the presence of religion. Thus when publicly cast in the role of a remedy for social, educational, and religious ills, and proclaimed as coming upon the campus with scarcely concealed polemical interests, religion has been regarded with suspicion. Launched into the academic arena with nonacademic intentions, it has been regarded as a threat to the assumptions of liberal education. The most talented and perceptive professors of religion have been struggling to extricate themselves from the unbearable burden of these false expectations, and to educate others—administrators, colleagues, students, and churchmen—to the opinion that they come to the campus to cast into the common treasury such knowledge and insight as they possess rather than as messiahs bent on establishing domination over other provinces of learning or singlehandedly saving the spiritual substance of Western civilization.

However, the mood created by what G. F. Thomas and J. M. Moore have called "the turn in the tide" against secularism, value-neutralism, and sectarianism helped to give religion the opportunity to return and prove itself on many campuses. It has been able so largely to vindicate its return because it has met the challenge with a continuing and enlarging stream of well-prepared instructors who had been developing in the 1930's and 1940's, many of whom had undergone longer, broader, and in some cases, more rigorous training than colleagues in other fields.

Furthermore, certain trends in religious philosophy, social ethics, theology, and biblical studies current in these decades provided unusually helpful and even exciting means for coping with the prevailing ignorance about religion and the secularistic climate of the campus. The late Twenties and Thirties found religious liberalism regnant in the seminaries and graduate schools of religion. The effect of liberal criticism on stereotyped views of the Bible broke the lances of those whose conception and interest in that book ended with the Scopes trial and Bryan's benighted attempts to make the Bible read like a geology and biology text. The openhanded spirit of liberalism in dealing with philosophical and religious questions further opened the way for fresh understandings of man's religious nature. Nontheistic humanism, which in many quarters had attracted an earnest and sophisticated following, could be met on its own ground and matched, if not overcome, by the extreme and novel forms of religious liberalism of an empirical cast represented by Wieman at Chicago and Macintosh at Yale. The strong appeal of the social gospel, with its liberal advocates, similarly helped to counteract the impressions of those who saw religion largely in reactionary and individualistic terms.

In the 1940's and 1950's the trends of graduate education took another turn which severely challenged the liberal influence which had to a great degree won its way on many campuses by accommodating itself to the currents of Enlightenment thought. No one term catches up the full flavor of what has been called the theological renaissance. Probably the least appropriate but most often used term is *neo-orthodoxy,* though scarcely an influential figure in the movement would accept the term. Some have called it neo-Protestantism or neo-Reformation theology, because there was in Protestant circles a return to the Augustinian insights about man and a fresh appraisal of the reformers. Yet the movement was broader than Protestantism itself, finding in men like Berdyaev of the Orthodox Church, Buber in Judaism, and Maritain in the Roman Catholic Church fresh and exciting interpretations of the sources of these faiths. So far as preparation for college teaching was concerned, however, the Protestant movement by virtue of sheer numbers has been most influential.

The notes struck in the movement were dissonant to the religious liberals, and to those who by inclination and training were drawn to the Enlightenment view of man. The word *sin,* in no simple moralistic sense, came back into at least a muted respectability; arguments for God's existence based on human experience of the natural world gave way to talk of revelation and the centrality of Jesus Christ. Criticisms of man's optimistic view of himself and his capacities to realize even his most beneficent aims within historical time were launched, showing how inextricably in personal, social, and political life good and egoistic pride were intertwined. The Bible, once relegated to textual scholars and courses in literature, was discovered to have a unity of purpose and was viewed as a salvation history portrayed in dynamic categories presumably more or less unique to the biblical or Hebraic mind and distinct from the more static modes of Greek thought in which the Western mind has been amply drenched. Biblical theology instead of the religion of the Bible came into its own as a discipline. An existential, participative stance was advocated as the proper manner in which knowledge of the divine came to man. This attitude was found to be predominant among the biblical authors, and it was underwritten by new interest in the insights of Kierkegaard and Buber. The wide influence of Paul Tillich's philosophical theology, which has caught up many of these elements into a synthesis, and Tillich's openness to the interplay of religious faith with various cultural forms, has added another ingredient to the ferment of religious ideas.

If the advantage of religion scholars trained in the 1920's and 1930's lay in their having a position which was congenial to the best of secular thought, and if they taught to show that the best in religion thought was but an extension or a completion of the most highly respected values of the human mind and spirit, those who came up in the late Thirties, Forties, and Fifties increasingly found themselves enjoying the advantage of a posture from which to criticize the assumptions of the whole enterprise of religious liberalism. Instead of the accommodation of religious learning to secular opinion, more recent crops of graduates were convinced of the folly of attempts to reduce the rugged uniqueness of Christianity. They refused to limit Christian faith to the proportions of those views which confidently regarded man as a supremely rational being whose efforts to acquire virtue were frustrated occasionally by ignorance or immature emotionalism. Without surrendering the validity of biblical perspectives, or insights of traditional theology, religion professors looked increasingly to contemporary life, literature, and art for the evidences of what they were saying about the human condition. Writers such as T. S. Eliot, W. H. Auden, Albert Camus, and Jean-Paul Sartre provided illustrative commentaries on the human possibility; on the other hand, books on the reconciliation of science and theology were less highly regarded. The art of Picasso and Rouault and the plays of Tennessee Williams yielded hitherto unexpected dividends of insight, while the more "realistic" interpreters of international relations were as commonly referred to in religion classrooms as the Bible, Augustine, or Calvin.

The fresh excitement in the religion classroom, therefore, often has come not from insistence upon traditional "humane" virtues or from an invitation to flee to otherworldliness, the medieval or Renaissance past. It has arisen from the kind of teaching that challenges the polite gentilities of liberalism by speaking of the spiritual and moral ambiguities of man's historic and contemporary experience, made especially serious by the contemporary summons to weighty choices to be made in a chancy world. The type of religious insight which speaks out of and to this kind of situation has had a lively impressiveness beside which the blandness of former liberalism shows only the more sharply. The advantage of teachers who have been thus persuaded is that they show religious values in a new exciting light, and act as disquieting agents within the serenities, if such there still be, of the intellectual life of the campus.

Undoubtedly one of the most persuasive reasons offered for the resurgence of interest in religion in the academic world was the overdue realization by all but the most prejudiced opponents that religious phenomena constitute so large a segment of human experience that without specialized study and instruction in it, a college or university could scarcely be regarded as offering a liberalizing education. On this ground, if no other, religion has found its place in academic curriculums as a field where not only the principal cultural forms of man's religious experience may be studied, but where opportunity also is afforded for that growth in sensitivity, understanding, and appreciation which these studies ideally share with all humanistic learning. The recognition that secularistic and sectarian interests have too long robbed the educative process of the contributions which competent studies in religion could bring to it has been emerging into full clarity. The genuinely favorable response of students to these studies continues to show the wisdom of the return. So long as men are curious about the ends of living and continue to ask the perennial questions which religions raise and attempt to answer, the religious dimension will continue to demand informed consideration. Thus the vital pull of the questions themselves seems to have drawn sensitive educators to accept religion into the university not simply as an extracurricular option, or as a morale booster, but as a necessary and substantive contribution to liberal education itself. As Huston Smith has ably put it: "The strongest force returning religion to the curriculum has been the pull of the vacuum created by its removal." ["The Interdepartmental Approach . . . ," *op. cit.,* p. 61.]

‹§ 5 §›

PURPOSES OF RELIGION INSTRUCTION

The vigorous rise in interest in religion in the academic world
has demanded a serious reappraisal of the purposes for which
it is to be taught. On the one hand, it has been necessary to
tone down the earlier exuberant expectations which anticipated
an overthrow of secularism, the overcoming of the curricular
fragmentation, and the development of spirituality and moral
virtues. A decade or two of experience has showed that returns
are less than satisfying and that expectations may have been
wrongly conceived at the outset. On the other hand, the hard
experience of teaching religion in secular-minded institutions
where suspicion or opposition was based on fear of subversion
of a truly liberalizing education has also pressed for a restate-
ment of ends. After all, certain forms of "theology" had in the
past triumphed over science or attempted to control the freedom of the mind, and the academic memory is long in such
matters. That memory rises to haunt the religion teacher at
many turns and rankles in the minds of his opponents. Consequently, statements of goals have had to be wrought out in an
area defined so as to limit the more extravagant expectations
of some educators and churchmen, and the often no less extravagant fears of those opposed to instruction in religion. In
the last analysis, in relative independence of both groups the
specific purposes of religion teaching have been developed in
accordance with the religion professor's understanding of what
constitutes a liberal and humane education in religion.

Obviously, without an exhaustive survey of the expressed purposes of all who teach religion at the undergraduate level, it

would be impossible to speak in universally valid terms. Although no all-inclusive survey is here attempted, the formulations offered below do not seem to distort drastically the convictions with which many work in the field. To be sure, departments and courses all too often appear on campuses without much conscious planning as to their contributions to the wider aims of higher education. Courses often linger in the curriculum because of inertia or the private interest of an instructor, thus contradicting the purposes which ostensibly govern the offerings of a given department. However, when allowance has been made for the creaky machinery by which execution is laggardly conjoined to ideal academic ends, there remain representative purposes and objectives in the teaching of religion. These, of course, are to be stated in the context of liberal education, whether such education is carried on by college or university, private, state, or church-related. Discussion of the preprofessional aims of religion instruction will be found in a later chapter.

The purposes of religion instruction cluster about two centers: on the one hand, the materials and the methods which constitute the field itself, and on the other, the student and his needs. Teaching which emphasizes the first of these has as its initial purpose that of acquainting students with religious phenomena, to show man in his characteristic religious postures. In doing so the nature of the field is set forth, and the student is enabled to recognize the variant forms which the religious dimension assumes. This objective may be formulated more precisely: to acquaint the student with the perennial questions which men have raised and attempted to answer concerning their meaning and destiny as these are reflected in systems of thought, cultic acts, and characteristic attitudes and beliefs. To accomplish this end, the instructor brings before the student the relevant literatures, scholarly studies, technical vocabulary and methods of critical study which the field involves. No attempt will be made here to specify the courses which implement this purpose, but a survey of the types of questions with which religions deal may be helpful in exhibiting the structure and content of the field. Certain religions may place more or less stress upon these questions, but religion, when taken in its broadest span as a human activity, embraces the majority of them.

Every religious system or outlook is in some sense a scheme of salvation, whether or not the term appears in its literature. It is concerned with the identification of the source, nature, and the appropriate methods of removal of some evil believed to afflict human life. It is equally concerned with the achievement, or the reception of the gift of some "blessedness," release, or fulfillment which transcends the evil in either this world or the next, and possibly both. In technical jargon this central issue is called the *soteriological* question. Unlike philosophies, religions arise out of the practical side of man's nature rather than the theoretical, which plays its part in religion at a greater remove from this dynamic center. It should also be noted that religions are not first of all concerned with theories about gods or God, but with responses to concrete practical needs and powers which are believed to have determinative influence over evils, and ways of escape from them. Even if, as in some religions, there be no conception of deity, the religious quality of the system of belief and practice is determined by the concern with which the soteriological question is formulated and answered in its theoretical, ethical, or cultic forms.

About this central soteriological question, with varying degrees of emphasis, there circle other basic questions. The *theological* question, understood in its literal and therefore broadest sense, deals with the issue of the nature of supreme beings or being, or whatever functions in the system as the supreme validity in place of more conventional conceptions of deity or deities.

The religious attitude, properly understood, is not first of all concerned with arguments for or against the existence of such beings or being. Rather gods or God are the experienced objects of religious devotion and practice and only secondarily are regarded as conceptions or hypothetical entities, to be treated with speculative interest. To understand a particular religious outlook calls for a knowledge and an appreciation of the way its adherents relate belief and practice to supremely important beings. The religious dimension as a datum may thus be distinguished from philosophical and theological methods which take over the tasks of explication, defense, and evaluation. To deal properly with the theological question means then that the instructor and student must look as fairly as possible at the manner in which men understand their relation to the object or objects of devotion and at the systems of thought in which this relationship is expressed.

Of equal importance with the theological question is the *anthropological* question, that of the nature and possibilities of man. Obviously this query is intertwined with the soteriological question, since in many religious systems, such as Christianity, Hinduism, and Buddhism, man's nature sets the problem of evil and decisively affects the ways in which to escape from it. Deep meditation on one's nature in upanishadic Hinduism may become a method of salvation, whereas in orthodox Christianity sin deeply embedded in man's nature sets the stage for salvation by divine grace. Even a humanism of a nontheistic form raises its edifice of rational virtue on a prior conception of man's capacities for its achievement, and thereby connects the anthropological with the soteriological question by offering a way out of the evils of superstition, ignorance, and prejudice in the direction of the fulfillment of a richer life.

In those religious systems where deity plays a decisive part, the issue of knowledge of the divine will arises. This question

73

may be labeled the *epistemological* question, though it should be construed in broad enough terms to include those religious systems which, like Judaism, Christianity, and Islam, prize revelation. Consideration of this area of religion calls for an understanding of how devotees believe themselves able to communicate with deity, and how deity makes known its will to them, as through prayer, vision, sacred literature, intuition, or reason.

The *ethical* question plays an important part in most religions, for it raises the issue of appropriate forms of conduct toward the deity and fellowmen, often stated in terms of codes, norms, or laws. It allows also for the consideration of the interplay with social structures. Although to some students the issues raised by this question may seem most central to religious phenomena, it is important to see them as usually subordinate to the central dynamic of the religious system as expressed in worship and the quest for salvation in some form. Another typical question familiar to many religions is the *eschatological* question, which in its sociohistorical form deals with the end or limits of history, culture, and time, and in its individualistic form with death and the possibility of immortality.

When the *cultic* question arises, it refers primarily to the nature and meaning of those acts by which a religious faith assumes public embodiment. In its broad scope the cultic question treats the social organization of the religious community, the functions of personnel set apart for specified religious duties, the modes of worship by which members of the cultus approach the sacred dimension, and the devices used to guarantee proper group and individual conduct. Often, since the cultus offers the assurance of salvation to its members, the acts of worship themselves are regarded as sacred or at least as necessary steps to the goal of salvation. The examination of religious phenomena under the rubric of cultus may lead to consideration of the place of symbols, characteristic gestures, and forms of speech, and even to the effects of religious belief upon architectural and art forms.

Perhaps of somewhat less significance than other questions, but of great interest to certain religious systems, is the *cosmological* question, which refers to man's theories and visions of the creation, nature, and form of the world and his place in it. The conflict of science and theology (rather than religion) has often been connected with this question, arising when both parties to the dispute have assumed that particular religious orientations are inseparable from fixed readings of the nature of the universe.

The foregoing schematic analysis of religious phenomena not only gives a major clue to some of the issues with which the study of religion deals, but also strongly suggests the purpose of those studies which are primarily descriptive or phenomenological. They show that one dimension of the instructor's task is to bring the student face to face with the concrete materials of the field. This may be done in a variety of ways, such as courses in introduction to religion, primitive or world religions, or by taking as subject matter the narrower scope of Western religious orientations found in Judaism and Christianity. Biblical and historical courses have been the normal means for doing this. What the instructor aims to do is to help the student see in as vivid a way as possible the issues with which religions deal, to inspire him to recognize the need for a breadth of comprehension in respect to viewpoints hitherto unknown to him and to insist on a precision of observation and descriptive analysis commensurate with the complexity of the material.

A second aim of instruction moves from the descriptive phase to the evaluative and critical emphasis. Here stress falls upon the ability to distinguish and to assess the various forms of religious, philosophical, and theological statements, such as arguments, presuppositions, convictional utterances, myth, symbol, and the like. It involves naturally the raising of appropriate critical questions by which religious phenomena are evaluated. Not a little of the difficulty experienced at this level is due to a lack of clarity in the use of norms appropriate to particular religious systems or less systematically formed orientations. What passes for criticism of religious ideas and practices sometimes dissolves into triviality when meaningless questions are asked, such as "Is religion itself true or false, valuable or valueless?" or "Is a particular religion as a whole true or false, valuable or valueless?" One of the first tasks of the instructor in the evaluative area is to show that questions of this type do not permit any reasonable answers in the context of phenomenological analysis and logic. He must go further, of course, to show that there are recognizable differences between evaluative judgments reached on the basis of criteria which the religion itself accepts, and those which are derived from criteria more widely accepted but which may be alien to the professed aims and methods of the religion in question. On the one hand, it is proper to evaluate a religious position in part in terms of its internal consistency, so far as it expresses itself in the forms of tenets, statements, creeds, and propositions. It is equally valid to evaluate a religion by its ethical or social consequences in accordance with what it has taught and preached. On the other hand, the critic passes judgment at a quite different level if he forms his evaluations on the basis of, say, the "democratic" ideal or the intrinsic value of individual personality if neither of these is a constituent part of the religion's professed aims. To insist that Judaism is superior to mystical Hinduism because the former stresses moral responsibility of men and the value of individual personality, while the latter has historically tended to withdraw men from the world of external events to seek a culminative union of Atman and Brahman in which individual differentiations vanish, is a judgment passed not on the basis of universally valid

76

criteria to which all religions must bow. It represents an importation of standards initially inconsistent with the aims valued by this form of Hinduism. The point of this illustration, of course, is not that this kind of judgment, when intelligently and carefully worked out, is invalid a priori. The point is that discrimination must be used in assessing presuppositions which give validity to the criteria themselves, and care must be exercised in recognizing at what level of investigation the criteria are employed.

Other factors also enter into the making of evaluations. It is fitting to evaluate religious systems on the grounds of their capacity to do justice to the actual complexities of man's relations to himself, nature, and the superhuman. Some religious perspectives may be regarded as inadequate because they place excessive emphasis upon the welfare or the salvation of the individual, or upon cultic acts to the detriment of social action, or upon ethical actions at the expense of man's yearning for aesthetic satisfaction or the experience of worship. Or again purity of doctrine may be stressed at the expense of depth of devotion or inclusiveness of concern for mankind. In these instances the criterion used is the adequacy with which the religion treats the manifold dimensions of human existence, presupposing the value or importance of comprehensiveness. It is equally important, however, for evaluation to do justice to the variety of phases which a particular religion exhibits in its own right. For example, there are not only conservative elements to be found in Christianity but also the sources of revolutionary social movements. To interpret Christianity only in terms of one or the other of these aspects would be to pass a one-sided judgment upon it. Christianity embodies rational and volitional as well as emotional elements. Intellectual formulations stand side by side with symbolic acts which delineate and express religious convictions. Any substantive and accurate evaluation of the Chris-

77

tian movement demands that these various facets be given serious consideration.

It need not be assumed that a neat classification of courses separates the evaluative purposes of religion instruction from the descriptive and historical ones. Although ideally a reasonably sure grasp of the descriptive aspects of religion studies should be presupposed for evaluation, it is more common to find these two purposes mingled in religion courses. Biblical and historical materials repeatedly call for evaluative approaches which cannot be shunted aside to courses specifically designed for that purpose. Courses have been developed, however, which are primarily evaluative in purpose. Among these there may be mentioned advanced courses in world religions, philosophy of religion, theology, Christian ethics, and modern or contemporary religious thought.[1]

The purposes of teaching religion are both informational and evaluative (a term which includes the appreciative element as well), but correlated with these purposes is another which partakes of both, yet which is sufficiently distinctive to call for further comment. Religion has been studied and taught in a broader dimension by relating it to cultural forces which themselves are either not directly religious in intent or which have cast religious convictions in more vividly appealing forms than sober discursive prose, propositions, and creeds can achieve. In some instances an attempt has been made to use religious values to integrate survey courses in Western culture or to serve as the basis of a general humanities course. In these courses religious beliefs and outlooks are seen as shaping and being shaped by

---

[1] It is regrettable that courses in the philosophy of religion, in spite of their pretentious title, are often limited to Christian thought. In many cases "philosophizing" is also carried on at such a far remove from careful phenomenological or descriptive work that a student may leave these courses thinking that arguments about God's existence or about epistemological theories lie at the center of religion.

different cultures or aspects of Western civilization. Reports on the successes and failures of these courses suggest the advantages of treating religious phenomena in their cultural milieux, but also indicate the dangers of superficial treatment. The effectiveness of courses of this type is diluted if they are taught at the introductory level, where students are likely to have insufficient acquaintance with religions and other areas of thought. Apparently such courses are more successful in doing justice to the rich complexity of cultural interplay after students have some semblance of mastery of the principal cultural elements. Other methods of showing the relation of religion to civilization are those in which personnel schooled in the field of religion and in another discipline are attached to departments where they are to show, where relevant, the religious factors involved in these disciplines, or where courses are offered within these departments serving the same purpose.

In spite of the practical problems involved in the various methods by which this purpose has been worked out, there seems little doubt that there result a considerable enrichment and advancement in understanding not only of the role of religion in culture but of the nature of culture itself. When materials from the study of history, economics, sociology, and government are brought into significant relation with religious belief and behavior the effect can be one of mutual illumination.

One of the most important places at which the study and teaching of religion in relation to culture has been developed is in the area of literature, drama, and the fine arts. In recent years there has been a serious attempt made to bring these fields into closer union with that of religion. This has been due in part to reconceptions of the field of religion itself and in part to the increasing realization by scholars in other fields that the study of religion is highly relevant to their work. Henri Peyre, speaking

79

of studies in French literature, frankly admits that "the scholar's equipment is frequently deficient today since theology has been a closed book to many researchers since the Fathers of the Church are seldom consulted and scholasticism is known but to a very few." [*Proceedings of the Second Conference,* Frank L. Weil Institute for Studies in Religion and the Humanities, chap. 5 (1961), p. 23.] Courses offered within and outside departments of religion have moved in the direction of bridging gaps between the study of religion and the study of literature, drama, or art. Camus, Sartre, Kafka, Rouault, and Picasso have become familiar classroom figures in courses bearing the title *religion.* Even as the *Confessions* of Augustine has been a staple of history courses in Western civilization, the book of Job a part of comparative literature, or the study of Gothic cathedrals a component of art history, so now in turn Euripides, Sophocles, Shakespeare, Dostoevsky, Hawthorne, Joyce, Yeats, Fra Angelico, El Greco, Rembrandt, and Jackson Pollock are likely to turn up in religion courses or in books written by theologians.

There are those who may complain at this breakdown of traditional provinces over which history, philosophy, art, or literature departments have long held sway, but their complaints are somewhat hollow. For years intracurricular "poaching" of this kind has been going on. Plato, for example, has long been taught in philosophy, classics, history, government, and world literature, as well as in religion. For decades, religion departments have watched the Bible disappear into literature courses, philosophy of religion into philosophy departments, Christian ethics into general ethics courses, and world religions into history courses of Eastern cultures. It is understandable that the "loss" of materials long held as a kind of private preserve by certain departments may be resented, and that the competence of the "poaching" department may be questioned. Yet clearly, so long as there are specific religious concerns expressed in literatures and art, and there are those who are competent to interpret them, no ironclad divisions for their treatment can be devised.

The second focus for the purposes of instruction in religion is the student himself. Unquestionably, the majority of religion professors would agree that one of the motives which has drawn them to teach has been the opportunity to work with young men and women at an impressionable and creative period in their lives, and to bring them into a significant engagement with religion studies. This general purpose has normally moved in two directions: that of enlightening the general run of students whose attitudes may range from apathy or downright antipathy to that of extreme piety, and, secondarily, that of finding and helping to train those who may be committed to a religious vocation or to the teaching of religion.

There is little doubt in the minds of religion teachers that the general student beginning studies in religion represents both a challenge and a source of frustration. He is abysmally ignorant. In spite of what churches, synagogues, preparatory schools, and summer camps have attempted, he enters the college classroom at a level of preparation which if found in English, mathematics, or history would consign him to pre-high school levels. He is usually ignorant of the Bible's content or any intelligible way of understanding it; he is ignorant of the teachings of his own religious tradition if any; he has the scantest and vaguest notions of religious groups other than his own, and of world religions he has perhaps the slightest acquaintance by virtue of travel or some unusually good history course. He may have either closed his mind to religion on the basis of an unpleasant experience in family or church or opened it so widely that a jumble of ideas about the Bible, clergymen, the Ten Commandments, God, sacraments, and whatnot jostle each other about in his head. He has seldom seen religious ideas or literatures dealt with in a systematic manner in an academic setting. His identification of religion has normally been with the institution of the church and its personnel, rather than the academic world. Since he has seldom had any rigorous education in religious matters, as distinct from preaching or indoctrination, he is surprised if not shocked to discover that scholars have been at work for centuries, producing books and interpreting ideas about religion, and that he is now expected to learn something of all this in a situation where piety or the lack thereof is no compensation for knowledge and the ability to think critically. The redeeming feature of this admittedly dark picture is the amazing quickness with which, given a normally healthy attitude toward other academic fields and native intelligence and curiosity, the student picks up competence and interest in the field. Sometimes its very novelty, in comparison with other subjects well worn with long handling in preparatory and high schools, proves a spur to achievement.

If the most explicit purpose in teaching religion is simply to dispel ignorance, another purpose which the religion instructor pursues is a more "existential" one. This may be formulated in statements of this type: "To assist the student in coming to an understanding of himself in the light of a broadened and deepened understanding of the nature of religious orientations as found in his own and others' cultures" or "To encourage the student to think with fairness and discrimination about his own religious beliefs and those of others, thus enabling him to formulate a comprehensive view of life which is not only intellectually defensible, and emotionally and ethically satisfying, but also possessed of the openness requisite for further growth in knowledge and appreciations." This purpose has also been expressed as that of stimulating and calling forth appreciative understanding of religious sensibilities so that "students may either participate or refuse to participate in religious institutions and experiences without defensiveness, irrationality, or dogmatism." In all these statements the underlying assumption is that a student is not properly at grips with the study of religion unless he also, in a manner conformable to the aims of a liberalizing education, has confronted himself in some phase of the religious posture, whether it be influenced by Christian, Jewish, humanistic, or Oriental insights. Furthermore, it is presupposed that attitudes toward religion are educable, that a person can change his mind by new insights, new information, and criticism. In brief, it is assumed that religious convictions are not adamant, ingrown structures of the self.

It is eventually pointless to defend any form of education pertaining to valuation which does not assume that the person being educated can in fact grow in discrimination and self-understanding. This is as true of poetry, art, or music as it is of religion. At last the learner must, and in fact does, make his own decisions in matters of religious faith. Even when explicit efforts are made to convince or persuade a student to certain religious viewpoints he does finally decide for himself. Hence the question is one of whether his instruction has presented him a sufficiently wide range of viable options and their criticisms to provide a context for intelligent commitment, and whether the instruction has provided an atmosphere of openness within which the student has been free to exercise his option in an unabashed and public fashion. The teaching of religion presupposes as the basis for this aspect of its work that whatever the content of belief may be, some posture of belief, conviction, or loyalty moves and directs men as they try to make sense of or find value in human experience. No matter how transient, fragmentary, or inexplicit the loyalties or commitments may be, they in fact constitute the living stuff of religions. They express themselves through social structures and movements which in turn play back into the intimate subjectivity of personal convictions. Without this presupposition, the teaching of religion is in large measure impeded, for in its absence teaching would have no paradigmatic experiences to which to refer, for understanding the religious behavior of others or oneself.

The science teacher may "do" science in the laboratory; the literature professor may have his students write a poem and thus in a sense "do" literature; the language instructor may have his class "do" a language by using it; the philosopher may have his students "do" philosophy by practicing philosophizing; but the religion teacher finds that he and his students cannot "do" religion in the same sense. He cannot turn the classroom into a laboratory in worship or a studio of prayer. These characteristic forms of religious conviction must be left outside the academic gate. Visits to churches, synagogues, or studies of religious conditions in a community, or occasional lectures by competent representatives of various religious faiths at best only provide the most meager of opportunities for a participative knowledge of diverse religious traditions and practices. The only recognizably legitimate parallel to the scientists' laboratory or field trip, or to the practice of literature, language, or philosophy, is an opportunity, provided at some point in the religion curriculum, for the student to come to grips with his own life posture, to identify to the best of his ability what he believes, to evaluate and defend what he believes in the light of increased knowledge and evaluative techniques developed by the study of religious concepts and practice. So long as the student deals with his own deepest concerns and not those which he believes to be agreeable to the instructor, and so long as the instructor's aim is that of assisting the student to clarify and enrich *his own beliefs,* the purposes of liberal education are served. Even as sensitive instructors of humane letters or philosophy do not feel their task is done by teaching about their fields without effort to engage the student in the excitingly informative task of personal evalua-

84

tion and appreciation, so the religion teacher claims equal rights to do the same in his area. If interiorizing as well as criticism of values be an aim of humanistic learning, and most defenses of the humanities play this tune incessantly, then the teaching of religion legitimately may provide for these practices within its own territory. The question is less whether such instruction is compatible with a liberal, humanistic education than it is whether an education which purports to be liberal can exclude this dimension of religion instruction. At this juncture the vexing and complex issue of "indoctrination" is bound to appear.

◆§ 6 §◆

THE PROBLEM OF INDOCTRINATION

The highly charged issue of indoctrination is one that the religion professor meets perhaps more often than members of any other department of the university. Departments of economics, government, sociology, and philosophy have been subjected to the charge, but these attacks have seldom been sustained nor have they often been mounted from within the university itself. The religion professor, on the other hand, frequently finds himself from the outset looked upon as the only faculty member who by virtue of his field alone is likely to indoctrinate students. Efforts to dominate education by the state and secular pressure groups even in the recent past, abroad and in this country, have been forgotten or overlooked, but past interference with the intellectual life by religious authorities continues to be regarded as a lively threat by the academic community.

Even when historical precedent has not initiated suspicion, confused notions about the character of religion itself and the methods by which instruction and scholarship can be carried on in the field have engendered antagonism to its incorporation into liberal education. Those who maintain that instruction in religion automatically involves indoctrination in specific religious beliefs and attitudes consequently regard religion as totally incompatible with the purposes of a liberal arts education.

Indoctrination is not a simple idea; in the university setting, it appears in at least three forms. The first of these immediately springs to mind when the word is mentioned: a conscious attempt to bypass critical judgment in order to elicit a desired re-

86

sponse to certain ideas, beliefs, and attitudes. The essential methods of this form of indoctrination are the studied effort by the instructor to produce predetermined effects and the use of deliberate techniques for evasion of a critical response in the student. The instructor must know, of course, what specific result he wishes to produce and he must seek it inflexibly. The means he devises may be various: limiting discussion, disregarding views opposed to his own, restricting reading lists to those books which support his purposes, adopting an excessively polemical or authoritarian manner of presentation, or using ridicule or deprecating remarks about positions other than his own. It would seem that indoctrination of this type could be easily detected, but there are a number of accompanying features which stand in the way. The privacy of the classroom, one of the safeguards of the professor's academic freedom, makes difficult the discovery of what a professor actually does when teaching. Furthermore, in a liberal arts college or university it would be rare indeed if anyone would confess that he is indoctrinating. The presumption is that no one, unless it be the religion professor, is indoctrinating. Few faculty members would admit that indoctrination takes place when ideas congenial to their own points of view are in question. Usually indoctrination is supposed to be taking place only when ideas distasteful to those making the charge are under consideration. Thus in some cases the ideas themselves as well as the manner of presentation may play a part in determining what is considered to be indoctrination. In view of these difficulties it is all the more remarkable that there are those in the academic community who suppose that indoctrination is so obvious a fact that it can be detected without ever entering the classroom of the presumed offender.

Indoctrination in the form described above, whatever the difficulties of its detection, constitutes a major evil in the university. The instructor who practices this kind of brainwashing

87

has failed to abide by the claims of the ethos of the free university which he is assumed as a man of moral integrity to have accepted when he entered upon a teaching career. His is a moral shortcoming which has infected not only his own university but the academic world at large, a tacit admission before his colleagues that he and his field cannot stand the contest among ideas freely and honestly expressed in the arena provided by the university. And as important as any consideration is the fact that he has broken contract with the student's legitimate demand for intellectual growth, which is shortchanged even when inherently valid ideas are introduced by means of indoctrination. If indoctrination of this type is a betrayal of the ground rules of the university, opposition to it is the responsibility of every member of the faculty. No exceptions or privileges can be granted to any field, and the possibility of its occurrence must be as sternly watched in philosophy, literature, or economics as in religion.

Indoctrination in another form assumes a more subtle guise, recognition of which reveals how ambiguous the term itself is. The characteristic feature of all indoctrination remains that of bypassing the critical judgment of the student. But this can be done without forethought. Unconscious indoctrination consists of the impression the instructor makes upon the student by his personal characteristics or unspoken attitudes toward course materials. Any professor worth his salt presumably exudes a respect and enthusiasm for his whole field. He will probably, however, respond with more vitality and interest to some features of it than to others and, through his own preference for a particular viewpoint, he may unwittingly lead the student to attach unjustified significance to it. Conversely, by the brevity of treatment or dullness of presentation he gives to some periods of history or philosopher's ideas, he may, without conscious intent, fasten in the student's mind the notion that they are unworthy of serious treatment. Thus the instructor's personal response to materials may decisively affect the student's understanding and appreciation of them although no conscious effort has been made to influence the student in a certain direction.

Other variations of unconscious indoctrination occur. The materials studied may prove so engaging to the student that in spite of the professor's efforts to preserve an evenhanded treatment of them the student uncritically accepts them and identifies himself emotionally with their viewpoints. A professor studying the writings of Kierkegaard or Kafka with his class may even be overtly unsympathetic to the intense subjectivity found in their pages, but the writing itself may so deeply enter into the student's consciousness that no amount of criticism will dislodge the impression made. Or again, the very status of the professor may lend such an air of authority to his comments that even his most trivial observations may determine the student's conception of the field or influence him in his vocational choices.[1]

This type of indoctrination seems inescapable, and some feel that its effects in the form of attracting students to various fields and courses which they may otherwise have put aside is not altogether baneful. By the same token, however, students may avoid studies which have great value. Undoubtedly ideas gain impressive power when they seep into the undergraduate's mind unchallenged at the time by critical assessment and when no conscious effort is being made for indoctrination. It is also probably true that attempts to deny faculty members the right to be themselves in the classroom are futile and wrongheaded. Indoctrination carried on in this way will probably remain a

---

[1] See D. D. O'Dowd and D. C. Bearslee, "The Image of the College Professor," *Bulletin of the American Association of University Professors* (September 1961), pp. 216-21. This article shows the college professor as an attractive and influential figure for students.

feature of university life whether for good or ill. All that can be asked is that professors not use their status or personal characteristics as a way of unduly shortcircuiting the critical process and that all self-conscious cultivation of mannerisms and attitudinizing be treated with the scorn it deserves.

A third form of indoctrination involves paradox. The publicly professed aims of liberal education usually include reference to values—not only knowledge of them, but the incorporation of them as habits of mind and outlook for the students. Resounding statements on the purpose of education as the training of the mind are paralleled by announcements of equally compelling goals which relate the human person to definite roles desired by society. We educate for citizenship in a democracy rather than in an autocracy, for knowledgeable participation in a complex, mixed economic system rather than in a government-controlled economy. In the humanities we seek to develop discriminating tastes in literature, the arts, and music, and reflective practice in philosophy and religion. Much of what is said and written about the appreciative aspect of education is another way of affirming that the educational task cannot approach finality until the student has come to some value commitments which have emerged out of doubts, confusion, questionings, and debate. It is assumed as a goal and in practice that education can take place in the area of value discrimination, and that it must develop in the depth of the human personality. However, doubt persists about an education which moves in these directions because it is not clear how value formation and commitments can come about without running the dangers pointed out in connection with the two types of indoctrination mentioned above. Values seem to be both taught and caught, as the expression runs. Thus we find the curious circumstance that even with the loftiest aims of an education which seeks liberalization of the mind there also runs the explicit goal of influencing the student by some fairly definite preferences which the academic community holds to be desirable. In a sense, these preferences are not debatable, since they form the essential context in which any debate about educational purpose is placed. That freedom of the mind is better than a closed mind, that knowledge is superior to ignorance, that informed rather than emotional, snap judgments are to be sought, that free contests of conflicting ideas are preferable to rigidly prescribed conclusions, that scrupulous attention to facts is needed rather than slanted presentations of opinion, that honesty rather than deceit is the basis of the academic enterprise—such preferences are the subsoil of education known at its best, and to the development of them education directs its energies.

But is the inculcation of these preferences and the largely tacit acceptance of them as goals a form of indoctrination? Some undoubtedly would deny that the word *indoctrination* can be properly used in this connection. They would point out that the goals or presuppositions are in clear contradiction to the nature of indoctrination as understood in its first form and that no process of inculcating them can be regarded as indoctrination. So long as free debate goes on about these goals and presuppositions and so long as the achievement of them as aims is carried on without resort to methods which bypass critical assessment, the question of indoctrination does not arise. On the other hand, there are some indications that indoctrination is involved. True, these preferences may be debated openly, but success in justifying them ultimately depends upon presupposing them in order for the debate to continue in any significant way. Their validity is made clear in the debate rather than by its conclusion. They are accepted as the basis of the debate rather than its end. They are open to debate only in terms of themselves and as such are not seriously in question at any point. As in the case of indoctrination of the first type, the presuppositions and goals to be achieved are accepted or known in advance. They are not the results of a free-for-all discussion, but the preferred values of a community which defines itself by reference to them. They cannot be disputed except on some other ground which by definition is unacceptable to that community. Thus, for example, indoctrination in its most obvious form is counted to be wrong although the viewpoint for which the indoctrination takes place may itself be valid. But the method of indoctrination itself acts against the accepted principle of the free encounter of ideas which is one of the norms of the academic community. This observation, incidentally, enables us to understand that indoctrination has no inherent attachment to any one field or to erroneous opinions alone. It can freely attach itself to any field and any shade of opinion or knowledge.

Here then another aspect of indoctrination shows itself. If we take seriously the announced aims of most colleges, discussion about values is not the sole goal of education. The achievement of certain value attitudes by the student is given high priority. But are not the achievements of these preferences in fact carried out often by means which do bypass the critical functions of the student? Are they not inculcated, and intended to be so, not simply by talking about them and lecturing upon their advantages but by the "spirit" of the campus and by the behavior and attitudes of faculty members who are committed to them? These preferences in some way it is hoped and expected will be internalized by the student, and not a little academic effort is expended, if only in an extracurricular manner, to this end. The adoption of these preferences may come as a by-product of the educational process, but it may also come because someone makes it his business to set the preferences persuasively before the student. Sometimes deliberate intent, a characteristic of indoctrination, may be lacking, but it is not uncommon to find even this feature in the educative process. Education in any recognizable form therefore seems to involve something more than the acquisition of knowledge. It publicly announces that decision, commitment, or acceptance of values which enter into the very texture of the student's life are also its concern. But this is to say again that education necessarily treads close to the shadowy line which divides it from indoctrination.

The preceding analysis may give pause to the facile use of the term *indoctrination*. Indoctrination is not a simple idea; it does not have peculiar affinities only with certain viewpoints or fields; it is less easily detected and proved than some have assumed; it is not easily eradicated in any of its forms from the university; it enjoys an anomalous connection with the valuational goals and presuppositions of education; and it is a term which itself too easily may become indoctrinational when used as a "smear" word with which to attack opinions about which men disagree. The university mind is at one in repudiating it in its most patent form, but normally lives in relative peace with its less obvious but no less pervasive forms. Consequently the issue for religion is usually posed as one of indoctrination of the type first mentioned rather than the second and third types.

The virtue opposed to the vice of indoctrination is customarily called objectivity. It carries with it a sense of openness to all points of view, a refusal to distort evidence willfully or to twist arguments to preconceived ends. It suggests a resolute neutralism as to the value of what is being taught and a disengaged, nonparticipative attitude on the part of the instructor. It is the safeguard against bias and prejudice, and as such ranks very high in the hierarchy of values accepted by the university. It is often praised as the prime requisite of a liberal education. It brings before the university mind the image of the scientist in the laboratory, his mind freed of all preconceptions, simply following the evidence whithersoever it leads, and as such it hovers over the academic scene as an abstract model.

As a rule of thumb, objectivity in this rather straightforward sense is the obvious and effective counteragent to indoctrination. As the opponent of conscious efforts to bend students' minds to that of the instructor, the value of objectivity cannot be overestimated. It safeguards younger, more impressionable minds from the tyranny of older and more prestigious ones. When expressed in the form of "teaching about" the subject, it represents the absolute, minimal requirement of instruction in any field.

The ideal of objectivity, however, may cloak pitfalls of its own. Since in its pure form objectivity is extraordinarily difficult to achieve, it may appear on the academic scene as a pose without substance. In a specious form it may cover the timidity or the unwillingness of the instructor to show his own engagement with the materials at hand. At a deeper level it may be a posture consciously assumed to hide intellectual laziness or to defend the validity of the instructor's presuppositions from forthright challenge. Nor is objectivity even in its ideal form necessarily a virtue which blankets all education. There are some aspects of human knowledge, especially to be found among the humanities, which derive only from a participative attitude on the part of the instructor and the student. The place of what may be called subjective understanding, or understanding from "within" a position, constitutes no less an important element in liberal education than does objective understanding in the narrower sense. To place oneself, if only imaginatively and temporarily, within a particular philosophical perspective, religious system, artistic or literary viewpoint may be the only way to come truly to intellectual grips with these positions. Some of the most exciting teaching which has been done has been carried through in this manner, and certainly if evaluative

94

work of any substantial worth is to be encouraged, the role of subjective understanding cannot be dismissed on the grounds that it fails to accord with an abstract model of objectivity.

A genuinely effective objectivity would seem to call not for an uncommitted professor without worthwhile convictions of his own to share, a kind of lackluster neuter whose posturing seldom deceives students in any case, but one who with as full recognition of his commitments and presuppositions as human nature permits is willing to place them in the public arena and to change them in the light of the insights he receives in the battle of ideas which is bound to ensue. Then education takes on life and becomes surcharged with enthusiasm about issues which are held by someone in particular rather than by some faceless author of a text or a remote historical personage. Certainly, one of the great experiences to which every student is entitled is to hear a first-rate mind at work on a subject of which it is master and about which it has profound convictions. Equally important should be the opportunity provided for the meeting with a mind which vigorously but without rancor disputes the passage of the student's ideas rather than lets them pass with bland permissiveness. Objectivity should not mean in all cases a disengaged approach to materials and issues of importance. Rather it should make place for the expression of ideas and commitments which cut to the heart of human life itself. So long as there is no attempt made, intellectually or psychologically, to cudgel the student into conformity with the beliefs held by the professor, the threat of indoctrination is fully met by an objectivity so conceived.

The pertinence of the preceding discussion to the question of religion instruction should be clear. The charge of indoctrination as made against religion as an academic field reveals the same ambiguities of meaning as it does when made against any field of study. But in the case of religion there seems to be an uncommon virulence in the charge, making it less easily swept aside by the defender than when it is lodged against other fields. Furthermore, it is a charge which not only arises within the precincts of the university but also among leaders and members of religious groups.

The teaching of religion in the university is not greeted with universal approval by churchmen. Some think that religion instruction is destructive of the distinctive tenets of their faith as taught to their young people, and they see this destructive tendency as a form of indoctrination against religion as understood in their terms. The typical grounds alleged for the charge of indoctrination as made by this group are these: Students have returned from college skeptical of the viewpoints, doctrines, and practices of their home church or synagogue. They have been demoralized personally by the loss of their faith, and nothing positive has been put in its place. Instructors in religion have taken unfair advantage of the innocence, ignorance, and gullibility of students by influencing them toward non-Christian or non-Jewish ideas and have undercut their belief in God, the Bible, Jesus Christ, and the church. By their unceasing analysis of the Bible and religious notions, they have left the student adrift. In their practice of an "objective" or "neutral" attitude toward religious matters, professors have left the impression that all religious options are equally valid or equally invalid. Religion instructors are not themselves convinced Christians or Jews and are therefore unsympathetic to the readings of Christian or Jewish faith. Therefore, it would be better if churches and synagogues alone did their own religious teaching—a judgment often concurred in by the more secular-minded on other grounds—since only distortion can be expected when instruction takes place within the general academic world. In brief, indoctrination against Christianity or Judaism has been taking place under the guise of scholarly instruction.

Except in rigidly controlled denominational colleges, charges of this kind probably bear less weight with the religion professor than those made by his secular colleagues. Nevertheless, answers have been offered. While it may be admitted that a certain amount of teaching does indulge in iconoclasm for its own sake, the majority of teachers would probably hotly deny that they have intentionally been engaged in indoctrinating students against family and church religious traditions. They would assert that change and development in religious ideas is desirable, and that although some of that change may come through taking religion courses, some of it comes from the campus atmosphere and other courses. Responsibility for the student's faith, they feel, cannot properly be placed on the religion professor. After all, the student psychologically is in a questing and questioning period, and the confrontation from whatever source with ideas at variance with his former beliefs is apt to be unsettling. Nor is it evident that beliefs held by the student when he comes to the classroom are inherently valid or sacrosanct or that churches have the right to attempt to forestall criticism of them. Furthermore, the instructor may insist that his is not the function of the preacher or pastor, but that of the teacher, and that, in the open market of ideas provided by the university, religious beliefs must take their chances along with other beliefs. He may point to those instances where he is convinced that students have deepened and broadened their religious convictions rather than lost them. And in the last analysis, he may argue that if indoctrination has been charged against him the charge is supportable only by evaluation of his work on academic grounds, not by tests established by religious bodies external to the institution where he does his work. The question is solely one of academic or educational competence, not one of ecclesiastical affiliation or effect.

The charge of indoctrination which bears the most painful

sting is that made by certain members of the academic community. No one word accurately and fully describes the attitudes of this group, but in the main it is composed of those who are confident that they possess a fair degree of objectivity in their own work, who are dedicated to the preservation of the intellectual freedom of the university, and whose conceptions of religion are deeply infected by ideas current in the Enlightenment. They may be called secularists—although some religion professors covet this term for their own approach to the study of religion and are not inclined to use it in a pejorative sense. A fair example of a moderate statement of the secularist position may be found in Professor Morton White's book, *Religion, Politics and the Higher Learning.* Professor White opposes instruction *in* religion in a secular undergraduate college because it involves the danger of special pleading. He sees a place for teaching *about* religion, although apparently he also has some reservations on this score. Commitment to a religious position, in his view, does not inevitably lead to indoctrination by the instructor, and he does not suppose that all religion professors will misuse their classrooms. But he suggests that other types of commitment are less likely to lead to indoctrination than those of a religious nature. [*Religion, Politics and the Higher Learning,* chaps. 8 and 9 (Harvard, 1959); see also John A. Hutchison's review of White's book and the author's reply, *Union Seminary Quarterly Review,* XVI, 4, 397 ff.] White's distinction between teaching in religion and teaching about religion is plausible but it is one which, although simple and attractive, may prove misleading and as difficult to maintain as it is in philosophy, art, or literature. It validly represents one aspect of the religion professor's task, but it fails as a neat and comprehensive solution of the problem of indoctrination.

A more severe expression of the charge of indoctrination is one which regards all teaching of religion as necessarily involved, even when conscious intent is lacking, with the inculcation of values and attitudes which its proponents feel cannot stand the rigorous test of intellectual conflict in the university. In an even more suspicious mood, there are some who charge the teaching of religion with being an illicit smuggling into the academic world of ideas and attitudes which will ultimately subvert the free intercourse of ideas for which liberal education stands. Instruction in or about religion, in their opinion, is a method of accomplishing for the churches what they have failed to do for themselves, namely, to indoctrinate their young people with their beliefs, in this case, under the guise of a respectable college education. Unfortunately, critics of this type seldom seem to be aware that religious groups may be equally suspicious of religion professors for precisely the opposite reasons.

Innumerable disclaimers of intent to indoctrinate have been made by religion professors and those who support their position. Father Thomas C. Donlan writes: "A supine acceptance of indoctrination has no more to do with virtue than it has to do with learning, and that is nothing at all." [*Theology in the Catholic College,* ed. Reginald Masterson, O. P. (Priory, 1961), p. 36.] John C. Meng, also a Roman Catholic, insists on the need for objectivity in scholarship and in the university. "Remove objectivity from scholarship," he writes, "and you kill scholarship. Objectivity—the cold, hard, unbiased assessment of an idea or a fact for what it is worth—is the soul of scholarship. . . . No Catholic scholar and no Catholic university worthy of its title should place denominational fences around the flow of ideas or facts." ["American Thought: Contribution of Catholic Thought and Thinkers," *Bulletin of the National Catholic Educational Association,* LIII (August 1956).] Similar vigorous protests against indoctrination and defenses of university standards have been made by Protestants and those sympathetic to their tradition. Professor Virginia Corwin attempts carefully to mark the difference between education and indoctrination when she suggests that "religion by its very nature may involve the student in that further step of becoming a participant, committed to religious faith and action whether within one of the great traditions or outside them. But he must take this further step by himself. . . . This must be a by-product of classroom teaching, not its end." ["The Teaching of Religion" in *Liberal Learning and Religion,* ed. A. N. Wilder (Harper, 1951), pp. 183-84.] Statements in this vein have been published for the last three decades at least, but apparently they have yet to be accepted at face value.

The notion that religion instruction is irremediably biased still seems to rule the minds of many of the secularistic group. They apparently find it well-nigh impossible to understand the simple distinction between the two uses of the term *religion,* employed in the university setting as a referent to the field of study and commonly applied in nonacademic circles to a system of belief and practice, the activity itself. The confusion of the words *religion* and *religious* causes the critic to convert the idea of teaching religion into the notion of religious teaching. Yet the field of religion involves numerous courses which call for mastery of languages and historical, sociological, philosophical methods as demanding and objective as anything found in other fields. Even when this is brought to the critic's attention, he may still insist that the ultimate object of these accessory disciplines is somehow to persuade students of the validity of certain religious ideas without recourse to critical, objective considerations. Or he appeals to what seems to him to permit no successful contradiction, namely, that there are several major religious traditions in the world, and that consequently the teaching of them, if it is to be done well, must be done by a partisan of each. If it be asserted on the contrary that the religion instructor is as capable of presenting in an academically respectable fashion more than one viewpoint or tradition, as is a professor of government, history, or economics, the comment may be met with a knowing look and the observation that "after all, religion is different." This seems to be a way of saying that the critic, who may never have studied religion in a scholarly way, knows better what is involved in religion instruction and the field than the trained instructor himself.[2]

Thus, the charge of indoctrination may expand into questions of competence or, at worst, questions of the motives of the religion professor.

In replying to these charges the religion professor finds himself at a disadvantage at several points. He must admit at the outset that there are instructors who see their task as that of indoctrination, of bringing students around to certain religious beliefs and attitudes regarded as indispensable. They may not call their work indoctrination, but in one way or another this is the way they conceive their function as agents of a religious tradition or body. The professor who denies the charges further realizes that some of his materials deal with dimensions of human experience which easily lend themselves to the bypassing of the critical faculties. He also knows that to answer the charge of indoctrination he cannot violate professional etiquette by inviting his critic into his classroom to see how in fact he does treat differing religious viewpoints critically and constructively. Furthermore, he feels that he has so often been unfairly singled out of the faculty as the one most likely to be

---

[2] It is curious that so perceptive a critic as Professor White should confidently refer to his conception of religion as one which "rightly regards" it as a total way of life [Religion, Politics and the Higher Learning, p. 86], while insisting that those in the field who recognize the value of religion instruction are in error in construing religion in other terms. A firmly established academic principle would seem to hold that those who work a field are those who determine its nature and limits.

guilty of indoctrination that out of sheer weariness with the charge he may be tempted to retire to the ground of the "tu quoque" argument, evidence for which is no more difficult to gather than that used against him.[3] But this would only be to admit the charge rather than to answer it. He might take the position, which is not without validity, that indoctrination against the teaching and study of religion rather than candid examination of its claims is often found in the university, since indoctrination, as we have seen, can work in the interest of more than one opinion. But this also might prove to be a fruitless debate because of the ambiguous character of indoctrination itself. In the final instance he patently must exhibit in his own professional conduct a high respect for the ideal of the free spirit of the university, and he must turn aside the charge of indoctrination as a blanket accusation by substantial argument.

In analyzing the critic's charge, one is struck by the fact that the critic often conducts his case without benefit of information as to what has been going on in the field of religion. He may be ignorant of the quality of graduate training through which the instructor has passed, a training which generally does not suffer by comparison in either breadth or depth with that of other fields.[4] He may seldom, if ever, read the journals

---

[3] An extreme and therefore presumably untypical example of indoctrination may be suggested by the following course description: "Comparative Government II. Exposes the fallacious doctrines of Marx-Engels, and Lenin-Stalin, and reveals the dangerous infiltration of Communist thought into the institutions of this nation. This course exposes the dictatorial nature of the government of the USSR and gives the student a greater appreciation of the blessings of the democratic government of the United States. 1 hour. Offered 1956-57." [*Catalogue of Louisiana Southern College,* LXX, 1, 146.] If this course description were to be translated into the idiom of Protestantism versus Judaism or Roman Catholicism or any variation thereof it is not difficult to imagine the uproar which would rightly ensue!

[4] For further discussion of this issue see Part IV.

and books in the field where the give and take of scholarly debate goes on across and within denominational lines. He is often unacquainted with the professional societies in which many religious viewpoints are presented and where interchange seldom follows the lines of religious affiliation. He may be unaware of the degree to which scholars cooperate across religious lines or of the way in which religion studies progress in various areas and how positions change or are surrendered under the impact of new insights.

Several years ago, a careful study of representative textbooks in various fields indicated how limited and how inaccurate were the portrayals of religion in these books, and how often consideration of religious dimensions was neglected when it was called for by the context. The editor of the study commented: "The lightness of touch and even ignorance with which intellectual issues having a religious bearing of import are dealt with would seem little less than astonishing when the expansion of scholarship in general is taken into account. Moreover, the hostility to religion revealed in some of the textbooks described becomes perhaps most effective when it is implied or suggested through the aggressive development of a positivistic attitude." [College Reading and Religion: A Survey of College Reading Materials (Yale, 1948), p. x.] A series of consultations with faculty members also revealed a dreary picture of the lack of intellectual sophistication respecting religion in the academic world. Dr. Howard Jefferson was moved to conclude that "the reports of the consultants make abundantly clear that a substantial number of college teachers are religiously naive and in some cases they hover on the brink of religious illiteracy." [The Teaching of Religion in American Higher Education, ed. Christian Gauss (Ronald, 1951), p. 65.] In a similar vein, Dr. Helen C. White comments that "we still have in intellectual circles a widespread suspicion of theology with an equally widespread ignorance of what it is all about." [*Religion and the State University,* ed. E. A. Walter (U. of Michigan, 1958), p. 90.]

These judgments are not examples of "name calling," but represent the sober opinion of those who have for a considerable period of time dealt with the problems of religion in higher education.

Moreover, it should be made clear to the critics that much goes on within the field which is not essentially religious in character. The study of the prophet Isaiah, for example, calls for attention to the political and military aspirations of Assyria, Syria, and Egypt; the study of the religious life of America calls for as much attention to industrialization, emigration, and urbanization as any similar course in history; a course in New Testament calls for the use of the methods of textual and higher criticism as applicable to other bodies of literature as to this; a course in the philosophy of religion or contemporary theological trends demands as much discriminating and concentrated attention as courses offered in philosophy proper; a course in Christian ethics calls for understanding of sociological, economic, and political factors. The point to be insisted upon is simply that the religion instructor is not at all times handling volatile materials which are ever ready to explode into indoctrination. It is also important to note that since no one instructor can effectively teach all the areas which the designation *religion* encompasses, there are some professors who seldom get close to potentially indoctrinational materials.

When course materials do involve value considerations, especially those of a philosophical and theological type, it has not been impossible to treat them objectively and descriptively and the value judgments made in these courses have not been notably marked by bias and prejudice. As one commentator has put it: "It has been demonstrated that it is possible to treat the materials of religion in such a way as to produce in students a genuine growth of their understanding, a deepening of their convictions with regard to their own faiths, and an intelligent tolerance of others." [*The Teaching of Religion in American Higher Education,* p. 71.] Indeed, precisely because the threat of indoctrination lowers over the religion instructor he may fall into the opposite danger of "leaning over backwards" to be as objective as possible both in descriptive presentation and in evaluation. Nor should it be forgotten that there is no simple and direct relation between the study of materials weighted with value considerations and the appropriation of these values by the student mind. Many a professor of literature can testify that the study of great literature does not guarantee that its ennobling visions will become the possession of students. And the case is no different in the teaching of the literary deposits of man's religious consciousness such as the Bible, the Upanishads, the *Analects* of Confucius, the *Confessions* of Augustine, the *Summa*s of Aquinas, the writings of mystics, or the *Dogmatics* of Barth. It might even be said that the dangers of indoctrination are considerably lessened because of the skepticism which today is easily evoked in students when matters of religious import are discussed, the possibility of which is heightened by the fact that few student bodies are monolithic in religious persuasion.[5]

Insofar as the charge of indoctrination is based upon simple ignorance or oversight of what is being done in teaching and scholarship in religion, the accusation is without merit. If the idea that "everyone" knows what religion is, and is therefore competent to pass judgment on the nature and limitations of

[5] Roman Catholic colleges and universities as well as state universities report increased enrollments of students from many religious traditions. [See *The Shaping of the Christian Message,* ed. G. S. Sloyan (Macmillan, 1958), p. 185.]

religion instruction and scholarship, were used in reference to any other academic area, it would be laughed off the boards. The notion that, since religious belief and practice are widespread, the knowledge of religion and its disciplined study are equally widespread has for too long dominated certain academic circles in their approach to the problem of indoctrination.

The charge of indoctrination does not always stem from ignorance or oversight. The crux of indoctrination for some critics lies in the problem of commitment itself. With ample justification it is urged that religion, the activity itself, involves dedication. When this dedication relates to superhuman beings or a being, the danger of a closed mind appears in the form of what is glibly known as "dogmatism." The teacher of religion who holds such a point of view, it is contended, inevitably will fail to approach his studies with the same candor and fairness that mark the secularist's approach to his materials.

Stated in these plain terms, there is no question about the desirability of excluding religion from higher education. But there is another aspect of the problem which carries beyond that of the threat of a biased or closed mind. Certainly religious commitment on the part of a professor need not be an unmitigated evil if at the same time he is able to conduct his work within the intellectual framework laid out by the university. But an additional danger does appear when any attempt is made to make one form of religious commitment the precondition for instruction in religion or when a certain type of commitment is enforced in some way upon the college or university as a whole. Thus it is not commitment as such which threatens the educational system, but the insistence by some authority that only a certain kind of religious commitment be admitted to the institution.

Professor White has stated this problem of commitment most clearly. "Creative work in any field is impossible without the adoption of a set of beliefs and attitudes and therefore it is not likely that a man who has no firmly held convictions or deep feelings about the problems of his field will come to anything whether he be a theologian, philosopher or historian." White goes on to suggest that theology by historical precedent has often insisted upon certain beliefs which must be held. "The history of scholarship and teaching, especially in theology, has shown the danger of codifying and calcifying the doctrines that a man must hold." He concludes: "Every creative scholar does and should begin with certain basic beliefs and commitments, but any attempt to legislate what they should be is bound to imperil our scholarly tradition and educational system." [Morton White, *op. cit.,* p. 109.] It is difficult to take objection to this point of view. The crucial importance of Professor White's remarks lies in his understanding that commitment as such is no barrier to academic excellence, and that in fact it is the *sine qua non* of competence in scholarship and teaching. Whether the pressure to uniformity of belief in theology is as great a threat as he implies, however, might fairly be questioned.

If commitment as such is not a danger to the university, why then has it often been placed at the center of the problem of indoctrination in respect to religion? In part because statements by church leaders have made the university suspicious of their motives in introducing religion into the curriculum. It has been previously noted that the rise in interest for offering religion studies was due partially to the desire to offset secularism, fragmentation of curriculums, and to strengthen the moral and spiritual fiber of America. But this is to say that religion then comes to the university not as an intellectual enterprise among others sharing the responsibilities of the institution, but as a foreign agent bent on using the university to promote ends which are peculiar to its own conceptions of the meanings of human life. It represents social groups outside the university.

107

Distrust of the purposes with which religion is proposed as an academic subject also arises when reputable scholars insist that it can only be taught by representatives of Roman Catholicism, Protestantism, and Judaism—as though religion as an academic field were coterminous with these three traditions or that religious commitment necessarily is to be identified with commitment to an institution.[6]

Nor is concern about the motives of religion instruction alleviated when interpretations of the relation of religion and education in denominational institutions are set forth so as to suggest that certain religious bodies alone possess a truth which is incompatible with the spirit of other institutions of higher learning. Thus Thomas J. Higgins, S. J., argues that Catholic leaders can only come from Catholic colleges and reminds his readers that Canon 1374 of his church "forbids under pain of mortal sin the attendance of a Catholic at a non-Catholic school, without explicit permission of his Ordinary." "Since we possess the truth concerning the whole of man's nature," he adds, "it will be our own fault if we fail to breed leaders." [Quoted in *American Catholicism and the Intellectual Ideal*, ed. F. L. Christ and G. E. Sherry (Appleton, 1961), p. 107.] In a more liberal mood, Edward B. Rooney, S. J., observes that "the only limitations that Catholics will put on freedom, research, publication and teaching are the limitations of truth itself and sound moral principles." [*Ibid.*, p. 124.] But even in this statement one detects the influence of a religious commitment which by determining the "limitations of truth and sound moral principles" might block out the freedom which the university cherishes. Protestant authorities may not have been as

[6] Although the problems of commitment and sectarianism are interrelated, it has seemed preferable to treat them separately, since commitment is a broader issue than sectarianism. Discussion of sectarianism will be found in Chapter 9.

forthright in their statements about the relation of religion to education in their institutions, but conformity in belief or adherence to a particular ecclesiastical body is not an unknown ideal in some of their colleges. The question is not whether a religious body is free to inculcate certain religious beliefs through its educational institutions. Their freedom to do so is part of American religious freedom. Whether such institutions should be recognized as liberal arts colleges is another question about which many would have doubts. What is significant in the present context is the impression made upon the university world at large when religious authorities and educators offer interpretations which, although they may be acceptable within their own institutions, confirm the worst fears about religion instruction when it is proposed that such instruction be offered in private, secular, or state institutions. Commitment on the part of an instructor in religion then becomes a focal point of concern.

Whatever threat commitment offers to the university seems to lie in two intertwined factors, the content of the commitment and the manner in which the commitment is held. Some religious commitments generally regarded as narrow may be held with such intensity as to make impossible the fair treatment of other viewpoints, especially those of an agnostic or atheist. Similar ideas, on the other hand, may be held in ways that illuminate opposing viewpoints and come into fruitful contact with them without the exercise of an authoritarian spirit. Some holding extremely liberal views maintain them with a rigidity which makes it impossible for their holder to understand views of a narrower compass, while others accepting the same beliefs maintain a spirit of openness which invites the freest possible communication. It would seem then that it is not simply the narrowness or breadth of the content of belief which determines the possible danger of indoctrination, but the manner in which such views are held. It is possible—to take an overly simple example—to believe in a supernatural deity whose power and knowledge are absolute and unlimited except by the principle of noncontradiction. The person holding this belief may maintain it against all comers with fanatical zeal; he may regard every doubt expressed about its existence as a personal affront not only to the god in which he believes but to himself; his manner of teaching becomes infected with a defensiveness which staves off all rational inquiry, and he may feel the day wasted which does not see another student won to his point of view. Yet a similar conception of deity may be the focus of another instructor's commitment, but his interpretations and reactions may be quite different. His is a notion of deity whose absoluteness renders relative all knowledge and earthly realities including religious knowledge itself; he is less concerned to defend his conception of deity than to explain it, to entertain questions and arguments about it, and to show how his view of deity better illuminates other beliefs and viewpoints than its alternatives. He is able to enter fully into the academic enterprise not as a propagandist but as one who from a particular vantage point can contribute understanding of the meaning of human existence. He finds a freedom for his own intellectual endeavors both by virtue of his view of god and the acceptance of the standards of the university community to which his commitment has led him. His motives for the acceptance of the free spirit of the university may be different from those of his secular colleague, but his adherence and defense of it are as firm and resolute. From such a commitment there need be no fear of indoctrination.

It need not be assumed, however, that every religion professor holds religious convictions of the type referred to. There are instructors whose interest in various aspects of the field of religion is ruled not by religious but by intellectual motivations.

The field is one which holds interest for them in the same way as history or philosophy does for others. They find satisfaction in the study of it and in the sharing of their insights with others. Their commitment is only to the general goals of humanistic education, and their private convictions may be reserved to a separate compartment of their lives just in the same degree as they are by scholars in other fields. Probably the number of such instructors is small and it is no more likely that their convictions at all points are rigidly prevented from entering into contact with their materials than are those of a similar persuasion in other fields. But professors of this type are to be found in the field of religion serving as successful teachers and scholars. Again, the threat of indoctrination by them would seem to be minimal.

In sum it has been admitted that the charge of indoctrination can be sustained against religion teachers in some instances, but it has also been pointed out that indoctrination is not a danger inherent in the teaching or study of religion itself. The supposition that the religion instructors may justly be singled out as more prone to indoctrinate than other faculty members is gratuitous, since suspicion of motive is neither evidence nor proof of the charge. There is enough evidence to show that religion professors are able to handle without distortion and prejudicial treatment controversial subjects upon which they may have the deepest convictions. By virtue of training and sensitivity to their position as faculty members they have been able to show their allegiance to the ideal of free intellectual interchange. Although the professor cannot insist on a preferred position because of the high importance he attributes to his field, he must insist that he be free to handle his materials even in their valuational aspects and to function as a teacher to the fullest range of his abilities without the constrictive pressures of some dominant campus ideology.

It has been said that freedom of religion in American society is promised to individuals because they are citizens, not because they are members of this or that church. [*Religion and American Society* (The Fund for the Republic, Inc., 1961), p. 18.] So the religion professor derives his freedom to teach because of his "citizenship" in the academic community, not because of his adherence to certain religious ideas or membership in a religious body. His right to challenge alternative positions within the bounds of that citizenship cannot properly be disputed. His commitments as a religious person cannot be used as the grounds for barring him from the university. All that is at stake is his competence and his faithful observation of those principles which govern the treatment of evidence and argument within the academic community. If his religious commitments are demonstrably at odds with those of the university, he has no place in it. But it may be that his religious convictions, when introduced into the pattern of academic discourse, will provide rich contributions to the unending search for human significance.

STRUCTURES OF RELIGION INSTRUCTION
AND THEIR EVALUATION

The modern university or college builds its educational program on the departmental system. Various rationales have been offered for this arrangement. It provides an orderliness to human learning without which the administration of higher education would become more unwieldy and cumbersome than it already is. It makes possible, as no other system can, the concentration of study and teaching in a particular area in the absence of which specialization and its rewards would flag and the entire field of higher education would be a confused and amateurish affair guided by men who were jacks of all trades and masters of none. Moreover, the system has behind it the power of tradition.

Critics from time to time have challenged its effectiveness and the arbitrary limits which it places upon subject matter, but departments seem to be a fixed feature of the academic scene. Seldom is the existence of departments of classics, literature, or philosophy challenged, although the materials with which they deal touch upon a wide range of human experiences which tend to merge into each other. But the complex interrelations of human concerns and the materials arising from them are not taken as a guide to the organization of the modern university. The departmental system, whatever its faults, remains the principal method by which educational purposes are carried out.

Other humanistic disciplines are stabilized as departments, but religion is in an anomalous position. In the main it is taught within a department, usually within the division of the humanities, less often in the social sciences. It has been estimated that all church-related colleges, over half of all colleges, and about 45 per cent of state colleges and universities employ the departmental method for teaching religion. Judged solely on the basis of numbers of departments, religion would seem to have found its place in the collegiate structure. But it is also taught by other arrangements, and from this state of affairs arises doubt about the validity of the departmental approach.

In earlier days special responsibility for instruction in religion and morals often rested upon the president and Bible instructors in the college. The teaching of religion was regarded less as an academic subject, the mastery of which was necessary to a liberal education, than as a means of lifting and maintaining the religious tone of the campus. The early decades of the twentieth century saw the beginnings of a trend which separated the practice of religion from instruction in it. This transition, by no means as yet complete, was marked by a more resolute and self-conscious effort to set the teaching of religion within the departmental structure. Sometimes joint departments of religion and philosophy were developed on the supposition that both offered culminative insights into life's meaning and that they shared certain methods and content. This alliance, once so fruitful, still is to be found in some colleges, but in more recent days it has become noticeably frayed. Each field has emphasized certain technical features of its respective provinces and both have declined increasingly to serve as campus morale agencies. Philosophy, under the impact of analytical and positivistic views, has moved away from the development of world or life orientations and in some quarters shows dwindling enthusiasm, if not outright animosity, toward the perennial quests of traditional philosophy and theology. Similarly, religion has increased its emphasis on the technicalities of biblical study and has stressed the importance of historical subjects. Often its theological insights have moved in directions diametrically opposed to those found in philosophy, and the result has been a mutual divorce of the two fields which is now lamented by many.

The increasing autonomy of the religion department has also reflected the desire of religion professors and administrators to establish the study and teaching of religion on grounds of independent, intellectual equality with other disciplines. It has come to be understood that religion cannot be satisfactorily treated as a mere addendum to other fields of inquiry, but must be taken seriously as a province of intellectual inquiry in its own right. Thus, for example, a committee at Princeton University, in recommending the establishment of religion studies in that institution stated: "It [religion] is an independent power, the study of which is worthy of an independent place in the curriculum along with the other humanities." ["Report of the Special Committee of the Faculty on Religious Education" (Princeton, 1935), p. 2.] To execute this purpose at any institution has called for trained specialists in the various subdivisions of the field. Thus the development of religion in the departmental form has in turn given new impetus to the development of highly trained personnel to staff religion departments.

The teaching of religion is not confined to religion departments. Probably no other field appears at so many places in the curriculum and in so many arrangements as does religion. Certainly its right to departmental treatment is anything but settled. Some educators and professors of religion argue that religious attitudes and beliefs are so closely intertwined with other human concerns that it should be taught only in connection with those departments where these concerns are treated. Any other manner of instruction would distort the vital relationship of religion to life interests. Thus as a matter of academic policy the components which ordinarily constitute the offerings of a religion department are parceled out to other departments and are sometimes controlled by them. A committee serves to provide whatever structure is needed for the administration of the work in some cases. The practice of teaching religion through other departments sometimes has been resorted to on grounds of expediency or because legal restrictions forbid the establishment of a religion department. This approach most naturally is employed in publicly supported institutions. As a whole, this approach to the teaching of religion might be called nondepartmental, since a religion department is not involved, but since other departments do take up the task it is preferable to refer to it as the diffusionist approach.

Instruction in religion also takes place in the university even when there is no conscious planning. Courses which in some instances would be grouped within a religion department are often offered in other departments. Courses in Hindu or Buddhist thought may be taught in a department of Oriental studies; courses in the literature of the Bible appear in English literature departments; courses in medieval and Reformation thought are not uncommon in history departments. Thus certain aspects of the field may be taught without benefit of title or department. Furthermore in certain institutions, as for example Roman Catholic colleges, courses offered in the philosophy curriculum might, if placed within a private or Protestant-related college, be counted as religion courses.[1]

The diffusionist method of teaching religion then falls roughly into two categories: the structured form in which instruction is carried out for reasons of academic policy or on the

---

[1] See Barry McGannon, "The Philosophy Curriculum in Catholic Colleges," *Journal of Higher Education,* XXIV, 2, 85ff. Also, R. G. Simonovitsch, *Religious Instruction in Catholic Colleges for Men* (Catholic U., 1952), pp. 15ff.

basis of legal restriction, and the unstructured form in which teaching occurs because it naturally arises out of the materials treated in a department. The former method, with certain variations, is used at Stanford University, the University of Michigan, and Washington University in St. Louis. The latter may be found in many state universities.

The departmental and diffusionist approaches presuppose that religion is an integral part of the university structure. The teaching is done from a nonsectarian position, and credit is granted for the work. But there are still other structures which have been used in religion instruction, largely due to sectarian and legal pressures. The first of these is the cooperative pattern in which a school of religion is established in connection with a university, but is not a completely integral feature of the university. The school is largely, if not entirely, supported by private funds, manned by teachers from the several religious traditions, and supervised by a joint board composed of representatives of these religious faiths. Courses offered by the several faiths are given credit in the university, which may retain academic supervision, and may, as in the case of the School of Religion at the State University of Iowa, even finance certain aspects of the program. At this institution the school operates essentially as a department of the college of liberal arts, although it is not in all respects an integral part of the university. In some universities, majors are offered, and at Iowa graduate work has been developed. Sometimes faculty members are accepted in full standing in the university, but in other cases they are not.

In variant forms, this general pattern has also been developed at the state universities of Kansas, Montana, Missouri, and Tennessee. Although sectarian interest has been accepted as basic to such schools, the principle which justifies their connection with the university is that the best teacher is one who is a competent and articulate interpreter of the religious tradition which he represents. As corporate entities these schools are not sectarian in the sense that they attempt to indoctrinate in the tenets of a particular religious faith, although the selection of faculty would seem to presuppose sectarianism. They represent serious and quite successful attempts to link the religious pluralism of American culture to the free atmosphere of the university world.

Finally, there are cooperative programs which are financed, administered, and sponsored by denominational groups, but which have some recognized standing with the university near whose campus they operate. Religious foundations, chairs, and institutes provide courses taught by their representatives, who meet certain standards established by or in conjunction with university authorities. Although the personnel of these arrangements are not part of the university as such, usually their appointment and the courses offered by them are approved by the appropriate bodies within the university. Usually the number of hours of credit accepted by the university is limited. Allowing for certain varieties of procedure, the universities of Alabama, Idaho, Illinois, North Dakota, and Texas may be singled out as representative of this type of cooperative program.

Programs of this type, whatever the intrinsic merit may be of their courses, are burdened by the yoke of sectarianism and legal restrictions. They represent the churches' attempt to place worthy representatives in the environs of a center of higher learning, as well as to make contributions to the educational fulfillment of students. They are sometimes hopefully regarded as temporary arrangements to be admitted later into the university on grounds of academic and legal respectability. In any event, they do provide the possibility of faithful presentations of the various religious traditions and enjoy a certain freedom in instruction not always found in the colleges and universities themselves.

Legal restrictions have made it difficult to assess satisfactorily the merits and demerits of some of these structural types. Whereas, for example, a judgment made solely on academic grounds might find it preferable to have a department of religion in a publicly supported institution, a legal prohibition in the university charter or a state law forbidding this arrangement would make fruitless efforts to do more than argue the desirability of the departmental arrangement without much hope that under present circumstances the conditions will be changed. The evaluation offered here must then be confined to a major problem concerning the organizational placement of religion on grounds of academic validity alone, and leave to another context the issues raised by legal restrictions, or other non-academic factors.

In recent years a rather warm but friendly debate has been carried on between those who contend for the desirability of a department of religion and those who insist that the study of religion be carried on in connection with other departments where religious issues arise naturally. The question as to whether the present system of departments in higher education is a desirable one is not at stake here. To be sure, there may be good reasons to question the departmental pattern as a whole, but it is highly unrealistic to carry on the debate concerning departments of religion without reference to the departmental pattern.

We are best introduced to the contention by listening to the arguments for and against the diffusionist method. Two of the ablest among several advocates of diffusion have been the late Alexander Miller of Stanford University and Dr. Huston Smith, formerly of Washington University, St. Louis, and now of the Massachusetts Institute of Technology.[2] Both men possessed experience in experimental programs which they helped to inaugurate and direct in the formative period. Both held the most earnest concern for education and religious values, although Miller, by virtue of his theological posture, disdained what he considered to be the vapid neutralism implied by the latter term. Miller was explicitly concerned with introducing what he called the theological dimension into as many areas of the curriculum as properly could benefit from its presence. Smith maintains the relevance of the religious dimension to several of the fields within the humanities and social sciences. Both agree that a department of religion will not do the job of showing the theological or religious dimension in those fields where it most naturally appears, since religion departments, in their opinion, separate religion or theology from those areas of human experience with which the already constituted departments of the university deal. It is important to notice that neither argues against the departmental system as a feature of the university as such. Both recognize the need of "housing" those who carry out the teaching of religion or theology in some department.

Miller's argument runs as follows. There are two communities in tension in the educational world, the Community of Christian Faith and the Community of Learning. The problem he sets himself is that of relating each to the other without diminution of the authenticity of either. A tension first arises from the side of the Community of Learning, because it holds to two basic images of man, the Enlightenment-Renaissance idea of the rational man, whose mature freedom would consist in

[2] See Alexander Miller, *Faith and Learning: Christian Faith and Higher Education in Twentieth Century America* (Assn. Pr., 1960), and Huston Smith, "The Interdepartmental Approach to Religious Studies," *Journal of Higher Education,* XXXI, 2 (February 1960), 61ff.

the mastery of reason over all the parts of the self and its passions, and the technological-manipulative notion of man as an adjustable organism, the aim of whose education is that of a successful adjustment to society. But Christian faith, in Miller's view, which is deeply influenced by Reinhold Niebuhr and Paul Tillich, "does not believe that the fullness of personal being is constituted by the enhancement of rational and contemplative power or by the improvement of environmental adjustment." It challenges these basic ruling images not for the purpose of substituting another image, but to protest the limitation of options offered and the truncation of heritage expressed by contemporary higher education.

Christian theology will not be expected to give answers to the many enormously perplexing questions which human experience meets, but it will be relevant to the university scene when it raises in depth the questions which some disciplines now bypass.

Theology is needed in the curriculum, but not as set apart in a religion department. In supporting this idea, S. E. Ahlstrom adds a warning of the effects of establishing religion departments: "drastic departmentalization can have the same secularizing effects as the founding of seminaries did." ["Toward the Idea of a Church College," *Christian Scholar*, XLIII, 1 (1960), 34.] The Christian revelation should be seen as illuminating those aspects of life where it is most needed, the fields of politics, psychology, business administration. But since it is "the nature of theology that it cannot be dealt with as one intellectual discipline among others," arising as it does from a particular community of faith, it cannot be housed in a department of religion, and it must be taught "only by those who share the faith and belong to the community."

Why, then, cannot this theological work be carried on from within the structure of a department? Miller apparently felt his

most convincing arguments were these. Religion is not a separate dimension of human experience, but a dimension of all life
and therefore should not be corralled in a distinct department,
but should be taught as conjoined with existing disciplines.
Furthermore, and here he speaks from a distinctively theological posture, Christianity is not a religion! Religion for him
signifies what man makes for himself out of his fears, hopes, and
projections of imagination, whereas "the gospel" witnesses to
what God would make of man and criticizes even man's religious idolatries.[3] Christianity is not simply one among the
several religious options available to man; it is a distinct form of
God's revelation to faith, the explication, systematization, and
clarification of which theology carries out. Therefore since religion departments, Miller assumed, could only deal with Christian faith and theology as instances of some generic phenomenon called religion, the tendency would be to emphasize
elements which Christianity had in common with other religions and "to manufacture affinities where they do not exist."
The distinctiveness of Christian faith would then be lost. But
Christian or biblical faith has nothing in common with other
world religions such as, for example, Buddhism. It has nothing

---

[3] This disjunction between Christian faith and religion and the subse-
quent structures and devaluations placed on "religion" and "the religious" has become quite popular and intellectually confusing. C. C.
West makes the distinction; Dietrich Bonhoeffer gave it currency.
Joseph Sittler spells it out as fully as any when he writes: "Religion is
always a way by which man operates upon a malleable Ultimate in order
to affirm, realize, give meaning to himself, save himself. Both Judaism
and Christianity deny this anthropocentrism and affirm an utter the-
ocentricism. . . . Neither is a religion. The terms *covenant* and *election*
in Judaism and the terms *called* and *grace* in Christianity point to an
entirely non-religious structure of the God-man relationship—and no
single feature in the multitudinous data of that structure, either in word
or in the central symbols of the cultus, is clearly exposed under the categories of religion." [*Religious Education*, LIII, 2, 139.]

otherworldly about it; it rejects any notion of the end of life as contemplation; it has a profound preoccupation with time and history, and does not seek to escape from the world, but to order it righteously. Thus if it be true that Christian faith is distinctive, and if religion is practically coextensive with all experience, the study of Christian faith or religion, in the best sense, does not belong in a department. It (or they) should have "the concentrated attention of as many major departments as can bring their methodologies to bear on it."

The case for diffusion is then largely built on the case against a religion department. A religion department "for the sake of minimum cohesion . . . tends to settle for a definition of religion which does not do justice to the endless variety of its manifestations, to the myriad ways in which man's ultimate concern may express itself." Or else "it will tend to corral an unconscionable amount of material to cover an inordinate amount of ground" and thereby exempt other disciplines from dealing with the religious or theological dimension.

How then shall the teaching of religion (theology) be structured? The Stanford plan is one which centers the program in an administrative unit called Special Programs in Humanities. A number of courses are offered, mainly centering on Christian elements. Interestingly enough, to the time of Miller's writing, only two interdepartmental courses were offered, although he had hopes of more to be developed in the future.[4]

The justifications offered by Miller are sufficiently different in extent and content from Smith's to warrant an independent and substantial critique of them. Miller's argument for diffusion and against departments of religion rests in large part on the notion, derived probably from Tillich, that religion is or may be a pervasive dimension of all human experience. Even if this

[4] All quotations and references are from *Faith and Learning*, chap. 5. See also Miller's *The Renewal of Man*, chaps. 2 and 3 (Doubleday, 1956).

assumption, which itself rests upon a certain conception of the nature of religion, be accepted, it does not follow that a particular way to study or teach that dimension has been determined by the assumption itself. One cannot pass so easily from the nature of the experience of religion, art, or our psychical natures to a conclusion about methodology and organizational arrangements. Religion as a dimension of human existence does not yield by any coercive logic a determinative evaluation, either for or against a departmental program in religion. In the one case we use the word *religion* to refer to the concrete experience itself, which even on Miller's ground is distinct from Christianity, and in the second case we use the word *religion* to refer to an area of study organized in a certain fashion. The categories are obviously different, but Miller confuses the two uses of the term. Because religion is diffused in human experience, it does not follow that it should be diffused in the curriculum.

The impressiveness of the criticism is heightened when we notice certain implications of Miller's position to which he failed to pay sufficient attention. If religion as a dimension of human experience, rather than a separable substantive factor, is to be taught in connection with various disciplines, then other dimensions call for similar treatment, since according to Miller's professed philosophy of education, religion or theology cannot hope for a preferred position in the curriculum. There are psychological, zoological, political, and historical dimensions to human experience. Should these not also be taught in a diffused fashion? Or why should not they be taught in connection with religion itself as the central focus, rather than to make the teaching of religion adjunctive to these disciplines? Are they more substantive than religion as fields of study? Do they possess bodies of material, information, and methodologies lacking in religion which automatically put them in places of academic priority, compared to religion? Thus Miller's logic seems to head toward the elimination of most departments of the university, not just religion, since the interpretation of many dimensions among disciplines would call, on his basis, for the representation of these dimensions in practically all the existing fields of study. Although he would not presumably have accepted this line of reasoning, in terms of his own argument there is no built-in principle by which to forestall this conclusion. After all, no university tries to represent in its curriculum or organization the whole of social experience. It consciously selects such experiences as it thinks are worthy and in that selection inevitably distorts the living flow of experience.

Another line of argument can be pressed against Miller's argument from the dimensional view of religion. Religion may be a universal dimension of human experience, but Christianity is not. If his argument moves from the universality of religion, conceived as "ultimate concern," to the conclusion of a diffused treatment of it, this argument does not at the same time provide the ground for his further contention that Christian theology should also be treated as an aspect of other disciplines. Since he has set apart Christian faith and theology from religion in general, which he sometimes seems to have regarded as "idolatry," he cannot gain profit from his argument for the dimensional view of religion without at the same time admitting that Christian faith and theology are forms of religion, and as such are options among many which the religious consciousness of man has developed.

Obviously, he cannot have it both ways; either religion is a dimension of all experience inclusive of Christian faith, or the two are quite distinct, as he also argues. Therefore Christian faith must make its case for diffused treatment on other grounds. However, if the latter option is accepted, the justification for its place in the university curriculum, under any type of structure, must be on humanistic not revelational or theological grounds, since Christianity and theology do not justify their presence by asserting their truth over all other alternatives.[5]

It would therefore seem clear that Christian theology can maintain its posture among the university disciplines only by arguing for its relevance, by its contribution to what Miller called "the prerequisite of real manhood," its illuminative, informational, and critical contributions to man's understanding of his situation. By these tokens alone it takes its place among the humanistic fields of the university world, where it must give an account of itself in accordance with the standards that there apply.

This turn in the discussion makes necessary reconsideration of Miller's insistence that Christian faith or biblical faith and theology cannot be subsumed under the category of religion. This contention has provided major support for his argument that Christian faith or theology should not be housed in a department of religion, where it could only be treated as one among several instances of religiosity. There seems to be no reason whatsoever for assuming that teaching courses in theology or the Christian faith in a department of religion inevitably distorts Christian faith, whereas teaching it in the context of other departments escapes this danger. If anything, it might be thought that this peril lies in instruction so intimately related to other fields that it has lost all distinctiveness for the sake of relevance. And it may be asked with equal fairness why the threat to Christian faith is any greater when taught departmentally than it is when Hinduism or Islam is taught departmentally—a possibility which Miller would seem to have been more ready to accept.

[5] "Of course, the case for letting the voice of the theologian be heard in the scholarly debate cannot be based on the proposition that the Christian faith is true. The church is committed to that proposition, but the university is not." [*Faith and Learning,* p. 118.] This concession seems extremely damaging to Miller's case; "truth" is obviously an appropriate issue to be raised in the university.

How these are taught rather than where they are taught seems the essential point, and experience shows they have been taught in departments of religion without the dire consequences which Miller conjured up for himself.

The more basic question, however, is whether Christian faith and theology have similarities structurally and phenomenologically with other religions, as well as differences. Miller suggested that Christian faith, compared with Buddhism, has nothing otherworldly about it, and that it rejects the idea of contemplation as the goal of life. What then of the concern for immortality in practically all forms of Christianity, as picturesquely represented on the façades of medieval cathedrals by carvings of the resurrection of the righteous and the damnation of evildoers? What of the mystical element in Roman Catholic piety, Augustine, Luther, the Quakers, and even Calvin? Are these not part of the phenomenon of Christianity? What of those theological treatises which exalt the vision of God as the goal of human existence? [See K. E. Kirk, *The Vision of God* (Longmans, 1931).] True, as Miller asserted, Christian and biblical faith emphasize time and history and the righteous ordering of this world, but so do Judaism, aspects of Islam, and even certain schools of Hindu and Buddhist thought. There is scarcely a term (e.g., *covenant, grace*), practice, or thought form which although used distinctively in Christian faith does not also have its roots in the broader backgrounds of religions and cultures. Few if any are original with Christianity, or with other latecomers on the scene of man's religious consciousness.

The purpose of pointing out these caveats and omissions is not to deny the distinctiveness of Christian faith and theology, or to deny that genuine tensions exist among religious perspectives. It is to show that certain problems and considerations are common to religion as such. The content of ideas about immortality, for example, may be different in Buddhism and Christianity, but their structures or form agree to the degree that both do have doctrines about life after death. On grounds such as these Christian faith may be studied comparatively, historically, and critically with other religions without denying its uniqueness and the uniqueness of other religious perspectives. Nor does the diluting of Christian faith to an innocuous religiosity necessarily result.

What is perplexing, if not dangerous, in Miller's position at this juncture is the selectivity he exercised in respect to the Christian tradition itself, a selectivity which in turn he employed as an argument against the department of religion and for the diffusion method. The uniqueness he found in Christian or biblical faith seems to have been arrived at less by taking into account the whole breadth of the biblical and Christian tradition than by his adoption of one theological stance, which he counted as normative for the uniqueness of Christianity.

But there are also other Christian theological postures and interpretations of "biblical faith" which do not necessarily lead to setting Christian faith in so rigid an opposition to "religion" and which correspondingly do not necessitate the withdrawal of theological studies from a department of religion. It seems that Miller's adoption of a partial or sectarian view of Christian faith would reintroduce into the curriculum the same kind of sectarian bias that the secularist and other Christians may fear, and which he in fact was attempting to overcome. Instead of contributing to the cooperative function of Christian faith with other disciplines which he espoused, he would seem to have headed, logically if not in fact, toward a further fragmentation of curriculum, organization, and perspectives.

In any case an ambiguity exists in his argument at this point. He treated one interpretation of Christian and biblical faith as authoritatively Christian and biblical for the sake of doing justice to the distinctiveness of Christian faith, and insisted on these grounds that theology could not be dealt with as one intellectual discipline among others. At the same time he urged that theological studies be taught in conjunction with other disciplines. If theology were as distinctive as Miller suggests, there would be an abyss so deep between it and other fields that it would be practically impossible for theology to build bridges of any kind to these fields which would not endanger both the distinctiveness of Christian faith and its theological foundations and the autonomy of the disciplines themselves. Furthermore, if theology, in his sense of the term, could not or ought not to be taught within a department—an assumption contrary to fact, many think—it is doubtful that it has at any point a legitimate place in the curriculum.

The strongest argument against the department of religion rests less on theological considerations than on the more general thesis that religion, when studied in a departmental arrangement, is cut off from other aspects of human culture where its presence is felt. Not only Miller and Smith but also defenders of the departmental program press this argument. G. F. Thomas points out that if most of the curriculum of higher education is taught from an explicit or implicit secularistic viewpoint, or if religion is neglected entirely, and if students take only one or two courses in religion, where there is a department of religion, the result for a student is that religion is either regarded as nonessential or is understood in a highly abstract fashion. Therefore Thomas argues that religion should be taught not only in a department, but also should be dealt with fully and honestly wherever it properly and naturally appears in other disciplines. It can be seen then both as a distinctive kind of human experience and also as a fermenting force in the shaping of culture. [See Thomas, in *Religious Perspectives in College Teaching,* ed. H. N. Fairchild (Ronald, 1952), pp. 11-13.] C. P. Shedd, also a strong advocate of the departmental view, has advanced a similar conviction.

Certainly the danger persists that if there is a department of religion, some instructors in other fields will feel that religion is taken care of "over there" and will neglect their own academic responsibility in this area. However, the same risk pertains to every other dimension of man's experience, insofar as it is represented in the curriculum, and religion will probably have to continue to accept that risk. Furthermore, the presence of a religion department may do as much to stimulate interest in the relation of religion to other fields as would the diffusionist alternative. The advantages and disadvantages are about even in balance.

Several practical difficulties may also be briefly noted in the diffusionist's case. Where does one find the personnel trained adequately to deal with both theology and the fields with which Christian faith and theology are supposed to be related? The problem, as Smith has seen it, is that men trained in theology seldom have the necessary training in, say, art or government to give an academically respectable account of themselves, whereas men trained in these fields are even less likely to have adequate training in theological or religion studies. The answer may lie in learning by doing, given the good will, openness of mind, and scholarly acumen on both sides.

In both the Stanford and Washington University plans a series of courses is offered which in fact, with few exceptions, are exactly those offered by many departments of religion. At Washington University they are taught by selected individuals attached to various departments; at Stanford they are taught within a curriculum in religious studies, but the courses, so far as their titles are concerned, are at least roughly paralleled in innumerable departments of religion across the country.[6] Even the two interdepartmental courses offered at Stanford are not without parallels so far as content, if not title, is concerned. One could entertain doubt that the conduct of these courses contributes substantially to the overcoming of the compartmentalization of knowledge, which they purport to overcome, although obviously any final judgment on this score would have to await further experience with the practice. It appears that in all but name, both at Stanford and at Washington, there are programs which in fact operate as departments.

The remaining question put by the critic of the diffusionist attempt is simply whether there is anything now being done in these programs which cannot be done in a departmental arrangement. There would seem to be no serious difference of opinion between upholders of both sides of the argument on the desirability of a type of teaching which cuts across departmental lines. Proponents of the departmental program, however, would insist that true interdepartmental courses in which the religion department joined on a basis of equality with other established departments are desirable and are able to do the integrative job as well, if not better, than any alternative so far offered.

Smith's handling of the case for diffusion rests on a different rationale from that of Miller, although in certain features of their thought they agree. Smith, whose work has been primarily in philosophy, the philosophy of religion, and world religions, has not been distracted by theological issues. He recognized the educational value of relating religion studies to their natural allies in the curriculum. The manner of accomplishing this end was to institute a program which introduced into particular departments or disciplines personnel well trained in the disci-

[6] Cf. *Faith and Learning*, pp. 133-35; Smith, "The Interdepartmental Approach . . . ," *op. cit.*, pp. 64-65.

pline and also in religion studies appropriate to it. The plan called for the cooperation of nine departments, each to have one "specialist" as a bridge between religion and the department, who would teach one or two one-semester courses.[7] An inter-departmental committee discussed together the formation and goals of the program under Dr. Smith's leadership. The project was underwritten by a sizeable grant from the Danforth Foundation for a period of four years. Simply put, the purposes of the program and its justification were the mutual illuminations it afforded for religion and the disciplines involved, and the possibility of providing a "vision of unity" for large sectors of the field of humane learning, now lacking in the compartmentalized teaching of the university. From Smith's report, it appears that the program has been highly successful. The departments cooperated, student enrollments climbed steadily, and evaluation of the teacher's work and the courses themselves were most encouraging.

In spite of its successes in the formative, experimental period, there are difficulties, which Smith recognized, in the program. There are marked omissions in the courses offered and an uneven coverage of the field of religion. It could be asked whether time at present spent on courses in biblical archaeology, hymnology, and liturgical music could better have been expended on more basic courses, now omitted, such as the History of Christianity from the Middle Ages to the Present, Theology, Contemporary or Modern Religious Thought, Postbiblical Judaistic Thought, American Religious Institutions and Culture. Notably missing are courses which relate religion and

---

[7] Miller criticized Smith's program at this point on grounds that there was something invidious in the notion of specialists in religion, "as if any cultural materials could be adequately studied by anyone without reference to that dimension of depth which is implicit everywhere, whether or not it finds expression in religious phenomena." [*Faith and Learning*, p. 112.]

political science or government. The strong impression is left that since the disciplines themselves largely determine what courses of a religious nature may be offered, the result has been that large tracts of the field of religion are left untouched, which might have been dealt with in a well-rounded religion department. Many of the courses, regardless of the department in which they now are offered, could as well constitute departmental offerings in religion.

Smith has also seen the problems of recruitment of staff for the future. Not only is it difficult to find trained personnel, but since the initial financial support of the program has now expired, it is doubtful that qualified personnel can be given the security of salary and tenure necessary to attract them. Smith felt that the program should be put on a permanent basis and that a director with a Ph.D. in theology should be appointed who would either occupy an independent chair or, if his training and experience were sufficient, be placed in an existing department.

One of the inherent difficulties of any transdepartmental arrangement comes to the foreground in Smith's evaluations and recommendations, namely, the instability of programs which are not securely lodged in a departmental structure. Without centralization of budgetary considerations, a degree of autonomy over the offerings and the recruitment of faculty, a certain suspense lurks over the fate of such programs. While being largely sympathetic to the Washington University program, C. P. Shedd nevertheless commented: "I am inclined . . . to feel that the subject matter in the modern university that doesn't have reasonably independent departmental status is not likely to have a chance to grow in such a way as to meet the expanding need in the field." [Quoted in Smith, "The Interdepartmental Approach . . . ," *op. cit.,* p. 67 n.]

One may also raise the question whether it is even tactically wise in the present overwhelmingly departmental structure of the modern university and college for religion to settle for only a transdepartmental status. The inadequate knowledge of the field of religion by faculty and students alike can be easily converted into the impression that instruction in religion calls for little specialization in training and that the religious dimension itself is a kind of extraneous addendum to other more basic disciplines, to which religion weakly appeals for acceptance. In the last analysis, as with the Stanford program, the Washington University program in its interdepartmental committee appears to function as a department in all but name and authority.

We may briefly take note of two other arguments advanced for the interdepartmental method of teaching and against the departmental arrangement. It has been suggested that a department of religion, especially in a state university, would be peculiarly subject to religious pressures from outside the university, and that scholars trained in religion are not usually well enough grounded in such fields as psychology or philosophy of religion to teach courses in them. The first of these charges Dr. Virginia Corwin turns aside by pointing out that there is no reason to think a department would be more susceptible than an individual to "outside" influences. Economics departments, for example, seem to have survived the pressures which have played upon them from outside. The second charge Professor Corwin finds insufficiently discriminating. A person trained in theology is not necessarily prepared to teach psychology of religion, but neither is a specialist in abnormal psychology. Furthermore, even a person well trained in religion studies may also have carried on some specialized work in fields that impinge upon his main area of concentration. [See Corwin, "The Teaching of Religion" in *Liberal Learning and Religion,* ed. A. N. Wilder (Harper, 1951), pp. 190-91.]

The advocate of the department of religion is not usually content to allow the argument to be carried on in a manner which puts him on the defensive. He feels there are positive arguments to be advanced in favor of his theory. Although he must make allowance for all the difficulties involved in the widespread practice of departmentalization, he nevertheless embraces it as the most workable and relevant option wherever law or campus ethos permits.

He notes that the absence of a department and the presence of various schemes of diffusion may indicate not only that religion or Christianity touches many phases of human experience, but also, and with more likelihood, that this state of affairs may be taken to signify that religion is unworthy of a place among the offerings of the university. He remembers the times and places at which the battle for the inclusion of instruction in religion in any form has been fought and won, often by the establishment of a department. This gain he does not want to see jeopardized by the sweeping educational plans of influential spokesmen in the field. He recalls those instances when the omission of religion instruction served notice on students that this area was unworthy of serious study and unimportant as a means for understanding life. Christian Gauss once remarked, in an earlier period of the debate over the inclusion of religion among liberal arts subjects: "When the college excludes a subject it is telling the student that in its opinion the subject is not important and not an essential component in any over-all conception of the truth." [Gauss, ed., *The Teaching of Religion in American Higher Education* (Ronald, 1951), p. 13.] Now that we are for the most part past this stage and there are many departments of religion firmly anchored in American colleges and universities, the spokesman for the departmental arrangement is not likely to see much virtue in surrendering what in some quarters have been hard-won gains. If departmental status is the sign of academic prestige, and it seems to be in American higher education, then suggestions which make more difficult the establishment of departments in institutions which do not at present have them or plans which by their logic call for the dissolution of present departments are clearly not to be greeted sympathetically by those supporting a religion department.

The presence of a religion department, whatever shortcomings it may have, ensures the possibility of serious consideration of religion in higher learning by giving it a habitation within the prevailing structure of higher education. Religion cannot so easily be overlooked if it has an established locus in that context. The allegation that the existence of a religion department isolates the study of that field from other areas seems of dubious validity. The existence of any department does not by any rigid necessity of educational philosophy result in isolation of effect. Its influence, if properly manned, may be felt throughout a university, for dynamic departments are seldom without repercussions in other parts of a campus climate of opinion. Furthermore, the presence of a department of religion makes clear to skeptically minded colleagues that there are definite limits to the range of subjects to be taught and that no attempt is being made to establish some kind of domination over other areas of study or to infringe upon their relative autonomy. The study of religion is not simply the study of a religious dimension wherever it pops up; it confines itself to certain avenues of investigation where bodies of materials and methods have been developed and which in turn afford access to the most representative expressions of the religious consciousness. The realization that the religious dimension is exceedingly complex and pervasive does not prevent a religion department from dealing with it comprehensively, yet without grandiose anticipation that its treatment will ever be inclusive of all domains in which religious phenomena appear.

The religion department is not then set upon the task of

penetrating all disciplines nor is it content to play the part of a kind of jack of all trades. By its presence it represents the fact that in the enormous range of conceivable religious phenomena responsible specialists have carved out an area in which disciplined study and instruction can take place. Thereby it provides both focus and balance for these studies and instruction in them, which under alternative plans seem lacking.

In a similar vein the special committee at Princeton University approached the problem of establishing studies in religion at that university. The rationale offered in the committee's report is not unlike that which undergirds many departments of religion. "It is true that the effects of religious forces can be studied in all the humanities and also in the sciences. But the sum total of the knowledge of these various effects is no substitute for, although a great aid to, an understanding of what the religious forces themselves are, how they come to be, and how they have developed. It is a fact that many courses in the university already deal in some manner or other with religion, and many of them, no doubt, deal with it in a very effective way from their own several points of view. But it is an equal and contemporary fact that the confusion of the student mind with regard to what religion actually is, falls little short of a phenomenon in itself. . . . The remedy for it here and at large is surely to give some focus to this variety of notions and to place that focus in the study of religion itself." ["Report of the Special Committee of the Faculty on Religious Education," p. 2.]

The importance of focus and balance in the course offered by a department having a certain autonomy is seriously urged by proponents of the departmental arrangement. They are quick to point out the inadequate coverage found in diffusionist programs and in those offered by denominational groups functioning outside the university structure. In turn, they argue that a department can better provide courses ranging from biblical and historical to philosophical and theological studies since it retains control over its courses and the appointment of competent instructors. Richness and variety of courses, as well as assistance to the student in integrating his work in other courses with that in religion, can better be accomplished by a department than by either of the strategies offered by diffusionist or extra-university programs. The student is more likely to see the field of religion as a whole, even if he is unable to take all the religion courses announced in the college catalog, when there is a clear-cut distinction between religion and other fields.

A certain advantage also accrues to the departmental faculty itself. The mutual intellectual stimulation of a group of men working in the proximity of a department encourages scholarly productivity in specific areas of the field in a way that the more loosely organized committee system may not. After all, it is pointed out, one of the principal reasons offered for the diffusionists' position is that it provides a superior method of teaching religion. The emphasis therefore falls not upon scholarship in any of the recognized disciplines within the field of religion, but almost solely upon the method of instruction. The committees which oversee these programs therefore have a mainly administrative function; when that function is carried out, the committee's work is done. The rest depends upon the instructor's ability and competence. Furthermore, whatever literary productivity emerges from the stimulus of the committee often may turn out to be writing about the program, methods and justifications for it, rather than substantial, scholarly contributions to the disciplines which make up the field of religion itself. If scholarly production is forthcoming from those engaged in the diffusionist program, it owes its origin less to the method than to the return of the scholar to some one of those distinct disciplines in which he has been previously trained and in which he has retained interest and competence. These disciplines, the advocate of the department reminds us, are those which the department safeguards and in which it tends to encourage research and publication.[8]

Another point at which the proponent of a department of religion finds advantage is the possibility of establishing a program for majors. Whereas advocates of the diffusionist position emphasize the service of their program to the general student and even discourage students from majoring in religion when such opportunity exists, the defender of the department sees definite advantage in a major program which centers in but may not be totally restricted to the department. The student, whether or not professionally interested in the field, may "dig deeper" into the area, rather than be left with a superficial acquaintance with it. The existence of a major program likewise stimulates the instructor. If the student expects to advance to graduate work, his instructors are moved to offer work at levels which will commend themselves to graduate faculties. This in turn means that the instructor will be pressed to keep up in his own specialty, so as to offer the best possible preparation. In a few cases where undergraduate faculties of religion also serve as part or the whole of a graduate faculty, the results presumably are similar to those mentioned above. Instructors are kept intellectually alive by working at both levels. Even when the student does not expect to pursue postgraduate work in the field, the opportunity to provide experience in depth of the field may be expected to have salutary effects upon the instructor's work. Without a department and without the major program which a

[8] Whatever impressiveness this line of thought possesses is somewhat reduced when one recognizes how difficult it is for a member of one of the many small religion departments to find opportunity for research and productivity. The common practice of teaching several separate courses constitutes an exhausting burden which often prevents the instructor from following up work in his own disciplines. However, the main thrust of the argument is not thereby nullified.

department makes possible, the teacher of religion is reduced to a general service function which may derogate from his dignity as a teacher and eventually deaden his own intellectual growth.

At last the advocate of the religion department argues that the departmental arrangement has worked as satisfactorily in the case of religion as it has in any other field. It has incorporated any advantages which the diffusionist experiment has discovered without running the dangers of that method where it has failed. Any failures of the departmental system lie less in the system than in the lack of personnel or in the limited educational imagination of departmental members. Defenders of the departmental system maintain that the criticisms of it—isolation, fragmentation, and even secularism—are grotesquely exaggerated, existing more in the realm of possibility than of fact, and that a thorough, widespread examination of the actual practices of departments would show that in many cases these charges are simply baseless. Moreover, given the departmental structure of the college and university, the departmental arrangement for religion is the only realistic alternative. Hence, only with the firm base of a department can steps be taken which are mutually advantageous to both instruction in religion and the total educational enterprise. Or as Dr. Kenneth Morgan puts it: "On the basis of the practice of several of our leading colleges, it is clear that, when there is no specific department or division responsible for instruction in religion, it [instruction in religion] is likely to play a less significant part in the pattern of undergraduate education." [Quoted in *The Teaching of Religion in American Higher Education,* pp. 117-18.]

It is possible, however, that the question of organizational structure itself is not of paramount importance in meeting the difficulties in the departmental position to which the diffusionist directs attention. Questions of organization, after all, do not per se determine whether or not religion is pigeonholed and isolated from fruitful contact with other fields. The crucial issue, rather, is the question of what is taught and how it is taught, regardless of the broader but less immediately relevant issue of organizational structure. No amount of toying with problems of structure can ever be proved to be decisive in determining the actual impact which particular courses of religion instruction have on the student or even on the campus as a whole. Consequently, for persons of this opinion the debate as a whole is less important than it is for members of the two camps.

The exposition of the details of this dispute sets forth the contrasting evaluations of both proposals. Neither system may be said to have won a clear-cut victory, but probably, on grounds of educational policy, the departmental system has the advantage. Neither system will command universal assent on American campuses by virtue of the superiority of its arguments alone. Too many other factors operate as weighty deterrents in deciding the types of structure in which religion shall be taught. As we have previously noticed, legal restrictions usually based upon fear of sectarianism and indoctrination or antireligious sentiments moulding faculty opinion have sometimes forced the instruction in religion out of the university proper into programs labeled "cooperative." In these cases the arguments between diffusionists and departmentalists are wide of the mark, for no option for organization seems to exist except those of a school of religion affiliated with a university or denominational chairs of religion.

Whatever the academic success achieved in these patterns, it has still been argued that these arrangements in themselves are faulty from the standpoint of the integrity of both the university and the field of religion itself. Nonacademic rather than academic considerations have largely determined the placement and organization of these programs. They are blatant evidences to the public and the university that religion is not a full and respected partner in the academic enterprise. This impression is not in the least alleviated either by the actual academic success of the program or by the concessions or sympathetic treatment offered to them by the university. These structures merely reflect the religious pluralism in American culture, which has too easily been accepted as the base line for all these operations, and they do not meet or surmount it by appointment of men solely on the basis of academic competence. Rather they fortify sectarianism by insisting that the additional qualification for faculty appointment be that of membership in one of the several dominant religious groups in our culture. Thus they give explicit structural form to the ever-present conviction that religion is a field calling less for academic competence than for a series of personal convictional options. Even the vaunted opportunity afforded in these programs for interfaith understanding, sometimes urged as one of their peculiar benefits, bespeaks the ultimate acceptance and the irresolvable character of subjective attitudes. On other grounds, it has been pointed out that standards of academic excellence are difficult to establish and maintain in these programs without full university supervision. But if academic standards are fully met, and they are met more often than the outsider may surmise, then why should not the courses offered be included within the university proper? If credit is granted or transferred for these courses by the university, and it usually is, why then should not the teaching and the teachers be accepted in full into the university?

The problem of faculty recruitment and retention for "cooperative" programs is often a troublesome one. In those programs which employ denominational representatives who stand outside the regular university system, the questions of proper academic qualification and continuity of program are extremely bothersome. Since the teacher under this system, except for the director, seldom holds a full-time or lifetime position, his work may suffer not only from lack of adequate preparation for the teaching field, but also from the confusion of multiple roles which he is called upon to play—pastor of a church, counselor to students, administrative head of a foundation, for example. Even the "school of religion" structure has problems in this area in spite of its genuine achievements. The aura of "experimentation" clings to these projects in spite of the length of time some of them have existed. Frequent changes of faculty and program indicate that the securities of the academic life normally provided for those teaching within the college or university have not operated to the advantage of either the faculty member or the program itself. Nor is it inconsequential, in the eyes of the critics of cooperative plans, that special, expensive, complicated, and time-consuming administrative machinery has had to be established and maintained by denominational and university authorities to sustain these programs.

Defenders of these cooperative arrangements admit some of these difficulties, but point out that, despite the legal limitations within which they must operate, certain benefits have also accrued to these procedures. High quality academic work is being done at the best of these schools of religion, and at Iowa State, graduate work has won its place. Opportunity for exploring interfaith perspectives and the building of fuller understanding among faculty members as well as students of differing faiths is afforded. The genius of the American pattern of religious freedom and mutual respect without loss of conviction is therefore being exhibited in its finest form. The work of instruction in religion is being accomplished; what more may reasonably be asked of these programs, inquire their defenders.

The critics, however, are not happy with the structure itself, regardless of whatever measure of success has been achieved in the teaching. They press the point that many state universities and publicly supported institutions of learning have been able to establish departments of religion or to make provision within the university structure for religion instruction. Their judgment is that more legal latitude exists in many cases than at present is being utilized by either the exponents of religion instruction or the universities themselves. And they believe more daring steps should be taken, in the name of academic freedom and for the sake of a more defensible portrayal of the field of religion, by which religion as an academic subject could be freed from the sectarian mould into which it has been cast by public sentiment and the denominational mind. Religious sectarianism may rightfully exist outside the university, but there is no invincible reason why it should be given academic respectability by including it in the curriculum or structure of the university itself.[9]

---

[9] For further discussion of the problems of sectarianism with special reference to the state university, see Chapter 9.

144

◅§ 8 §►

CURRICULAR CONTENT AND EVALUATION

The difficulties encountered in establishing the position of religion in relation to the departmental structure of the university stem in part from uncertainties about the dimensions of the field itself. Attention has been drawn in Chapter 5 to the purposes of religion teaching and the types of problems with which it deals, but it is now necessary to indicate with more precision the nature of the field by reference to the types of courses which ordinarily are assumed to constitute it. Wide variation exists in the titles of these courses, and differences of emphasis are to be expected among institutions, but the types themselves are widely recognized and accepted.

Biblical courses include studies in the literature and the religion of the Bible. Among these usually are found the literature of the Bible, the motifs of Hebraic-Christian thought, the life and teachings of Jesus and Paul, the teachings of the prophets, the life and thought of the early Christian church. The centrality of the Bible is understandable. It has been a principal formative element in Western culture. Its imagery permeates our literature and art. It has conveyed to us dimensions of the religioethical foundations of Western civilization without which we would be immeasurably impoverished spiritually. "If it is the Greek element . . . that has chiefly bred our art and science and philosophy, we owe chiefly to the Hebrew the religious and moral elements of our civilization." ["Report of the Special Committee of the Faculty on Religious Education," (Princeton, 1935), p. 3.] The study of the Bible keeps alive in the complex of Western thought and life the noncyclical view

145

of time and history, the importance of individual dignity and social justice, and the awesome character of the transcendent which defies all efforts of men to harness its power and authority to their finite ends. Appreciation of a biblical (Hebraic-Christian) understanding of human life and destiny serves as a counterpoise to the predominantly Greco-Roman constituent of our culture. In the Bible's pages one finds the primary sources of the rise of three great world religions, Judaism, Christianity, and Islam, as well as interpretive patterns of human existence applicable to contemporary life.

In recent years, biblical courses have retained the position of centrality accorded them in much earlier periods when the term *religion* was virtually identified with them. However, changes in emphasis have occurred. Whereas in earlier days the Bible, especially in Protestant institutions, was regarded as the basic source of all religion instruction, its study later turned in the period of liberalism to an increased historical and literary analysis of content and text. Heavy emphasis was placed upon the similarity of its content to other historical and religious forces contemporaneous with its origins. The wide diversity of its insights was stressed. The analytical study of the Bible has continued, but recently weight has shifted to a consideration of its unity and uniqueness of insight as compared to other bodies of religious or philosophical material. Although interest in the literary study of the Bible has slackened in favor of what has been called biblical theology, there are some indications that courses in the literature of the Bible may once more find their place in the curriculum. In any case, biblical courses retain their importance and are often used as introductions to other religion courses and to the field itself.

Historical courses are diverse. Those most commonly taught are the history of the Christian church; the history of Christian thought and action; postbiblical Judaism; religions in American culture; specialized courses in the Middle Ages, the Reformation, Puritanism; early American religious thought; biographies of religious leaders; the relation of religious phenomenology to cultural anthropology; and world religions—Hinduism, Buddhism, Islam, and Confucianism especially.

Increasing attention has been given to courses exploring the relation of religion and culture in America, a study which borders upon both sociology of religion and Christian ethics. Interest in courses in religious phenomenology seems also to have increased, especially when they are employed as introductions to the field of religion offering greater breadth than that provided by biblical courses. This small beginning, it is hoped, may grow, serving not only to provide an enlarged view of religion itself, but also to offset the stigma of a narrow concern with Western religions and particularly Christianity. World religion courses apparently have not kept pace with the development of courses in historical Christianity. [See J. Edward Dirks, "Trends in Teaching Religion in Independent and Church-Related Colleges and Universities," *Religious Education,* LIV, 3, 167.] This is surprising in view of a general interest in world conditions, in which non-Western cultures, with their traditional involvement with religion, play so large a part. A recent partial survey of courses in all fields where non-Western materials might be expected to appear indicates that opportunities for study in these areas are minimal for the general student. The survey does indicate, however, that religion courses along with art, anthropology, and history courses have made some contributions to the understanding of Eastern cultures. [American Council of Learned Societies *Newsletter,* XII, 7 (September 1961).] Unfortunately, courses in world religions seldom permit the depth and particularity of study which is possible in courses on Christianity and Judaism, for several non-Hebraic-Christian religions are normally grouped in one course. This condition, however, is not simply due to an American or Christian provincialism. The plain fact is that it is difficult to find men adequately trained in these religions, possessing a command of the languages of their religious literatures.[1] World religion courses are also affected by the fact that in most colleges the student is confronted with heavy major requirements and an abundance of riches in the form of electives. He may well choose courses closer to his existing interest in religion rather than venture afar into more exotic intellectual fields. Where lack of interest exists, the resultant small enrollments affect budgetary considerations, thus placing a further limitation upon course expansions. Nevertheless, any department which bears the title *Religion* rather than *Bible* or *Christianity* must continue to offer, if only in a minimal fashion, courses in world religions and religious phenomenology, and where possible, to expand its offerings in that area in order to develop a better balanced view of the field itself.

A third group of courses may be broadly designated as philosophical and theological. In this category one customarily finds courses in philosophy of religion or philosophy of Christianity, modern or contemporary religious issues, Christian ethics, religion and science, and studies in great Christian and Jewish thinkers ranging from Augustine, Aquinas, Maimonides, and Schleiermacher to Barth, Brunner, Maritain, Gilson, Wieman, and the Niebuhrs.

For some years the philosophy of religion course held a prestige position in the religion curriculum. Its title suggested breadth of understanding and depth of analytical clarity. The

[1] Thomas Berry, C.P., points out the failure of producing Orientalists among Catholics. But his interest seems mainly to lie in the evangelistic purpose that trained Orientalists could serve. [*American Catholicism and the Intellectual Ideal,* ed. F. L. Christ and G. E. Sherry (Appleton, 1960), pp. 205-06.]

148

assumption of purely rational inquiry left unasked, or so it seemed to some, the question of the place and validity of reason itself. Was it possible to offer a course in which a kind of disinterested, rationalistic, and even value-free approach could be maintained? Was it possible to be a philosopher of religion without in fact maintaining certain antecedent value judgments which in turn would color the direction of the course itself? It came to be doubted by some that a philosophy of religion course could be offered that was not at the same time a more or less covert appeal to value positions. Thus the possibility of a purely rational approach was seriously questioned. There grew up in turn an increasing emphasis upon the value-laden nature of all human thinking. This emphasis expressed itself in courses which took more seriously than did the traditional philosophy of religion course the convictional basis from which both philosophy and theology operate. The term *theology* which once stood for a peculiar narrowness and dogmatism of outlook, began once more to be heard in the halls of undergraduate education, for it increasingly was regarded as a more accurate and realistic way of describing the thought procedures of the instructor and the nature of the course. If, in traditional terms, it could be said that philosophy of religion tended to move from reason to faith, now the relation was reversed and the movement was from faith to rational explication, criticism, and defense. Today on many campuses, regardless of course title, the movement in religion instruction in the area of philosophy of religion has been toward investigation of the presuppositions or valuational stances of various authors and positions and away from the earlier avowed, purely rationalistic approach to the questions of God's existence, the comparison of religions, freedom of will, mysticism, and religious epistemology. On the other hand, the impact of analytical philosophy has been widely felt, both in courses in philosophy of religion and in courses of more explicitly theological bent. The traditional course in philosophy of religion has often been converted into an examination of the vexing problems of the religious consciousness in terms of how words and concepts are employed. Hence, for example, the question of the existence of God is less often treated as a problem concerning the existence of a definite kind of being than as an inquiry into the ways in which the word *God* may be significantly employed in sentences about him.

Christian ethics courses exhibit even more diversity of treatment than do courses in the philosophy of religion. Once courses of a moralistic nature, largely based on "the ethics of Jesus," were offered, but these have now proliferated into courses on the meaning of history or culture; the relation of revelation to power structures; analyses of race relations, war, sexual morality, economic struggles, Marxism, and other "culture religions" of Western civilization—all carried out in the light of Christian assumptions about the nature of man. The deposit of social awareness left in the American religious consciousness by the social gospel has not been dissipated. Rather, through the influence of the Niebuhrs, it has been informed by a new relevance. In place of the more abstract speculations about values or ethical principles, there has emerged an awareness of the necessity of a hard-headed analysis of the power relations in the context of which ethical judgments are to be formed and policies developed. Where the influence of the Niebuhrean school of theological and social realism has been felt, courses in Christian ethics tend to include both technical information drawn from the social sciences and insights into the nature of man and God found in the Christian tradition. The wide variety of problems and methods of approach which can appropriately be considered in this context have made this type of course a "capstone" course in some departments. There are indications, however, that undergraduate student interest in Christian ethics courses is not as high as that of instructors who have studied the subject under the tutelage of leading theologians and social analysts. In part this seems due to the fact that Christian ethics courses call into play acquaintance with the principal Christian traditions, the Bible, problems of philosophical ethics and relevant information drawn from the fields of government, economics, and sociology. The extensive subject matter, as well as doubts of the validity of a Christian approach to these subjects, may tend to discourage the general student from entering a course of this type.

The three categories of courses mentioned to this point—biblical, historical, and philosophical and theological—comprise the stock in trade of the field of religion. However, another type of course has now appeared which bids fair to become as important to the field as the more traditional ones. This is the transdepartmental course. Interest has burgeoned in the development of courses in religion and art and religion and literature. Here we see an explicit attempt to join fruitfully aesthetic appreciations and religious or theological insights. It is important to notice that work in this area is not oriented to the study of so-called religious art or literature as such. Thus, for example, attention is not solely focused on art objects or literature with an explicit religious content—e.g., madonnas, or the *Divine Comedy*. Rather the products of the secular, humane spirit of man are studied with an eye to what is there reflected concerning man's self-understanding and interpretation of human existence—e.g., *Guernica, View of Toledo,* or writings of Yeats, Blake, or Camus. [Cf. W. T. Noon, *Joyce and Aquinas* (Yale, 1957).] Formidable problems are met in such courses, for the instructor must not only be knowledgeable in theological modes of thinking, but must also show himself to be sufficiently skilled in the practice of literary and art criticism to avoid the charge of dilettantism. Furthermore, the very popularity which often greets courses of this type suggests that their appeal may lie less in interest in penetrating the religious depth of the literature or art than in the aesthetic dimension or in the broad opportunity which they offer for unbounded discussion in which the resolution of controversial issues can seldom be brought about. On the other hand, the entry into significant religious understanding apparently comes to many students through these channels precisely because the formal approaches elsewhere found within the curriculum and the approaches to religion offered by the churches have seemed to lack novelty and dramatic power. The vividness of poetic, fictional, and visual imagery may bring into sharper focus the issues of human destiny than many pages of Aquinas, Calvin, or Edwards. The additional value obtained is the enriching opportunity afforded the student of appreciating the intimate association between religious values and aesthetic creativity, even when these are met in secular contexts.

Within the category of the miscellaneous, a variety of courses may be placed. Courses in religious education are sometimes offered, although these are frowned upon by the liberal arts purists among religion professors as smacking too much of the semiprofessional. Dirks reports, however, that they are reappearing in Midwestern church-related colleges. The psychology of religion is still taught, although it appears to have lost its former popular position of the 1930's and 1940's. A few departments of religion offer courses in the biblical languages. This has apparently been done to offset the decline in some quarters of classics departments and to make good the absence of Hebrew, which has largely and unfortunately been confined to theological schools. Instruction in languages may not conform to the conception which some may have of the proper function of a department of religion, but the teaching of these languages, at least by historic precedent, has its place among humanistic subjects, as does the teaching of other language skills, even though in their initial stages there is little of a peculiarly humanistic quality about it. Sociology of religion has recently appeared more often in religion or sociology departments, but as yet has not won a sure place in the curriculum. Work done in this area, however, usually finds its way into courses in Christian or religious ethics or courses dealing with the problems of the relation of religion to culture.

For the most part the field of religion, as presently understood, is reasonably well defined. It is composed of subjects which fall under the rubric of liberalizing arts or humanistic studies, and seldom verges into the area of professional service. It has an identifiable body of primary and secondary source materials; it draws upon a long and distinguished tradition of scholarship; and it employs techniques of scholarship and instruction common to the main body of humane studies and appropriate to the subject matter at hand.

The foregoing analysis of the field in terms of types of curricular offerings poses two major questions, that of balance among certain types of courses and that of the academic propriety of courses in the theological category.

The first of these questions may be most sharply defined by citing a series of polarities detectable in the formulation of the field. Courses in Western religions are more widely offered than those in Eastern religions; biblical courses make up more of the curriculum than do courses in religious phenomenology as such; Protestant orientations are more common in religion courses than are other forms of American religious traditions. Although discussion of these obvious polarities will not serve to eliminate them, it may illuminate the distortions by showing their basis and the possible grounds for relaxing the tensions which they engender.

The lack of balance between Western and Eastern religion

courses is symptomatic of a certain limitation of vision from which religion suffers, as does much of the curriculum in the American college and university. Although we live in a world of constant cultural conflict and assimilation, American education has been slow to recognize the advantages of a deeper understanding of alien cultures. In a manner somewhat similar to that of our laggard performance in learning foreign languages, we have continued to treat Orientalia as a step-child of Western history, economics, government, philosophy, and religion.

It may even be said that religion's record in this respect is better than that of some other fields, although this observation provides no excuse for continuation of present practice. However, a justification is offered for this practice of relative cultural isolation, namely, that the student in a university of the Western world, as the student in the East, should first of all be as fully cognizant and appreciative as possible of the processes and values of his own tradition before attempting the serious study of those of other lands.[2] In short, the argument is one from immediate relevance, rather than from any sense of devaluation of other religious traditions and cultures.

Although this explanation is not without merit as it applies across the whole field of higher education, it is by no means clear that so great an emphasis on Western modes of thought as now obtains can long be justified. Courses and studies in Western culture seem to have an irresistible tendency to proliferate, until little space in already overcrowded curriculums is left for more than a relatively superficial glance at forms of thought and life which lie outside our own culture. Until some more

---

[2] Edwin M. Good states this position: "I am not arguing that the university should pay no attention to world religions, but rather that the study of these other religions is only peripherally related to the examination of the western cultural traditions, which is the central point of the university's concern." [*Journal of General Education*, XIII, 3, 187.] Good's idea of the university's concern is unnecessarily limited.

equitable balance across the entire field of higher education has been achieved, a balance to which religion must make its contribution, it is not likely that the particular imbalance within the fields of religion will be markedly redressed.

A particular onus of guilt does lie upon religion for failure to make more of Oriental religions. Many who teach and have framed the undergraduate curriculum in religion have received their graduate training in theological seminaries, which themselves, whether by explicit policy or by default, have seldom emphasized work in world religions. The so-called theological renaissance in Protestant seminaries helped to inundate whatever minimal work was then going on, with the result that it is exceedingly difficult today to find men trained in more than undergraduate fashion in the field. Many who have developed at least a modicum of competence have done so by their own efforts after formal graduate work has been completed.

As usual, the first suggestion made for remedying the situation is the intensification of training of scholars and teachers at the graduate level, and a rigorous reconstruction of present religion curriculums as these teachers appear in the colleges and universities. As yet, however, there seems to be little indication that significant numbers of men entering graduate religion study have been drawn to the field. This, in turn, may be the result of an undergraduate training in religion and other fields in which Eastern cultures have been largely overlooked. Furthermore, not only is high competence in Oriental religions difficult to achieve, but the available market for professors specializing in this discipline is not large, although some institutions still find it difficult to fill openings which call for at least some graduate preparation in the area.

The imbalance between biblical and phenomenological studies owes its existence to similar factors. The Bible has long been a central feature of the field of religion, for obvious reasons: its study preceded in point of time any other discipline within religion curriculums, and seminaries and graduate schools place heavy importance on it. Naturally, it holds a long established position, criticism of which evokes amazement if not anger on the part of its proponents. Sometimes suggestions that it take a more modest place are greeted less by arguments advanced on grounds of academic validity than by resort to a defense of tradition. Arguments in favor of its privileged position have already been presented, and its presence obviously calls for no extended defense. It has been noticed, however, that biblical courses which are often used as introductions to the field of religion provides a relatively narrow door through which the student may pass into other areas within the field, and that the relatively larger number of courses in biblical subjects in many colleges implies a weighting of the departments' offerings in the direction of Christianity, or at most the Judeo-Christian ethos.

These two objections are turned aside first by contending that biblical studies do not narrow the opportunity for the student's introduction to the field. Biblical materials provide a relatively manageable body of material, the nature of which itself serves as an introduction to the many facets of religious phenomena with which the student may be expected already to have at least passing acquaintance.

The question then is not whether the student is limited by a certain body of literature, but whether that body of literature, properly taught, offers a breadth of understanding as the basis for further studies in Christianity, Judaism, and other religions. The defenders of biblical courses as introductions to religion maintain that it does. The second objection is answered along lines similar to those used to defend the predominance of courses in Christianity and Judaism vis-à-vis other religions. As the Bible is one of the mainstays of the principal Western religious tradition, and that tradition lays first claim upon a cultured man's understanding of himself and his world, so the relatively heavier offerings in Bible are justified.

There are those who would maintain that no introduction to religion is completely justified on academic grounds that fails to place Christianity or Judaism in the broader context of religious phenomenology as such. After all, these religions did not develop in a vacuum. To understand one of these religious traditions calls for more than immersion in its particular reading of man's nature and destiny. Every religion, as we have urged, for all its specific uniqueness, also shares with others such items as rituals, myths, legends, sacred literatures, sites, personnel, ethical codes, certain ways of conceiving and approaching the holy, etc. Therefore an impressive case can be made for courses, especially on the introductory level, which attempt to set forth the nature of these religious phenomena as the context for further advanced work even in biblical subjects. The studies of Eliade, Otto, Wach, and van der Leeuw constitute a not inconsiderable resource upon which to draw for this purpose. The fact that the field of the history of religions, for some time in eclipse, has apparently begun to find its way back among scholars of note should be a further stimulus to advances in the direction of the establishment of courses which by the descriptive and comparative method make clear the domain of religion itself.

A protest often lodged against efforts to redress this imbalance in religion represents the recent and still vigorous opposition to the history of religions approach regnant in the late nineteenth and early twentieth centuries. Of late it has been customary to insist that attempts to study religious phenomena as such either stress the similarities of all religions at the expense of their individual distinctiveness or turn out to be weak distillations of subject matter, called religion in general, which cannot be identified with any known religion, past or present. Since there is no such thing as a general religion, but only distinctive religions or theological traditions, any attempt to deal with religion in these terms is largely an effort to analyze a mere hypothetical construct, a fallacious approach engendered by the deistic and rationalistic thought of the late seventeenth and eighteenth centuries.

The positive aspect of this protest seems incontrovertible, since there is no such thing as religion in general. Studies and courses in religious phenomenology, however, do not take as their subject matter this hypothetical entity. Rather they turn attention to the structural elements, motifs, and categories which are discoverable in specific religious traditions in a wide diversity of cultural milieux. [Harland E. Hogue, "Three Levels of Value in Religious Education," *Religious Education,* L, 4 (1955), 248.] The advantage of this approach is that it widens the scope of intellectual understanding and appreciation of specific religious traditions without necessarily diminishing their uniqueness. So long as the emphasis falls, as it properly should, upon a descriptive and nonvaluational approach to the data, it is difficult to see on what grounds this discipline should be denied an important place within the field or in the curriculum. The terms *religion* and *the religious dimension* cannot properly be identified, as in fact they are in some departments of religion, with Christianity or the Judeo-Christian tradition. Religion is a cultural phenomenon, a product of man's historical and creative experience. Thus, without by any means supplanting biblical studies, it can be successfully argued that some lessening of emphasis upon biblical work and a strengthening of the phenomenological approach in college curriculums will more faithfully represent the field of religion in the liberal arts program.[3]

[3] Although I have discussed this problem primarily in terms of curricular revision in religion, it should not be forgotten that in most colleges religious phenomenology does appear in one form or another, not only

The third of the persistent imbalances within the field of religion pertains to the apparent emphasis upon Protestant religious orientations at the expense of other American religious traditions. The field of religion as represented in the curriculums of most colleges and universities does bear the impress of a Protestant ethos. This is due to many factors, the most important of which are the facts that the majority of our colleges and universities have been founded and for long periods developed from a Protestant interest in higher education and that religion departments have been staffed normally by men who have received their training in Protestant institutions and have therefore developed the field in terms of the emphases provided by their training. The courses offered are normally those found in Protestant seminaries and graduate schools rather than in Catholic or Jewish seminaries. Perhaps even more important as a pragmatic matter is the fact that Protestantism by virtue of the very diversity of its beliefs and the varieties of preparation its institutions have provided has proved capable of establishing a liberal context more congenial to dealing with other religious traditions than have alternative postures. It has proved itself able to work within the free university situation of even so-called secular colleges and universities with a freedom and lack of doctrinal rigidity which can incorporate the study of various religious positions which on other grounds now available would be difficult if not impossible. It is also true that neither Catholicism nor Judaism has as yet prepared men specifically for teaching and scholarship at the undergraduate level to the degree to which Protestantism has. It has sometimes appeared that well-prepared Catholic instructors have not been permitted by ecclesiastical authorities to participate in college teaching outside

---

within the religion department when world religions are taught, but also in courses in cultural anthropology, history, and sociology of religion.

Catholic institutions except as *ad hoc* representatives of the Roman Catholic faith. Protestant and Jewish instructors are less affected by ecclesiastical authority and influence in respect to scholarship and instructional purposes. Under these conditions it is natural that the field of religion should take on a Protestant cast within the university.

These considerations, important as they are, may explain but do not justify the preponderance of courses organized around Protestant thought. Although the appearance of courses in American religious traditions, medieval thought, Old Testament, and in a few cases postbiblical Judaism has served to redress the balance to some degree, the areas of Catholic and Jewish thought remain largely unplowed. The answer lies not in introducing on grounds of expediency faculty members of the Roman Catholic or Jewish faith. The focus must rather be on the production of scholars and teachers, regardless of religious affiliation, whose competence meets the highest standards of the best colleges and universities. If the field of religion is to be faithfully represented as an integral ingredient in liberal education and not a mere meeting place provided for the exposition of sectarian tenets, then both as a field and in terms of a curricular structure, it must make provision for the study of Catholicism and Judaism without regard to the denominational affiliations of the instructors. Protestants, in spite of a certain vested interest in the development of the field, must avoid the temptation to treat it as a private preserve.

The problem raised by the appearance of specifically theological subjects in the field of religion may easily be overrated as a danger to the free intellectual intercourse of the university. The arguments adduced in opposition to their incorporation traverse familiar grounds: that theology is a technical subject which properly belongs to seminary or graduate work; that it involves sectarianism and apologetic considerations which forfeit its right to be heard in the general academic milieu; that it can only be taught from a committed or even unyieldingly dogmatic point of view; that its "ultimates" or essential presuppositions, unlike other fields, lie outside the limits of public inspection or validation.[4] References to *revelation, God, Trinity,* etc. clearly suggest that the territory of theology rests upon peculiarly private or esoteric assumptions nowhere else to be found in the university.

The beginnings of understanding this problem lie in drawing several distinctions. First of all we should omit explicit reference to pastoral theology since it deals with practical church disciplines which normally fall outside the range of humanistic studies. The term *theology,* however, may cover historical theology—the study of the doctrinal development of religious traditions—and systematic theology, sometimes designated as dogmatics or constructive theology. The study and teaching of historical theology present few if any problems to the critic since the history of crucial ideas may be taught without bias as a part of the entire cultural tradition. The study and teaching of constructive theology, on the other hand, involve the problems of the kind of theology to be taught and the manner in which it is to be taught.

The traditional identification of systematic theology with the doctrines of the Christian church suggests immediately the dangers of sectarian bias, and much of the opposition to its presentation rises at this point. But even if this traditional identification of theology with the teachings of particular segments of the Christian church be accepted as an accurate statement, nothing

---

[4] "Unlike all other disciplines, religion, as a body of knowledge or information which can be taught, rests on principles that are accepted and held by faith." [Anthony Nemetz, *Journal of Higher Education,* XXX, 4, 196.] The replacement of the word *religion* by *theology* makes the statement a representative charge against teaching of theology. The statement, however, in either form, unfortunately, operates in this context as a conclusion or assumption for which no evidence is offered.

has thereby been decided about the nature of the theology itself beyond the very general designation that it stands in peculiarly close association with a particular kind of institution among many others in culture. For example, questions as to whether "revelation" and "faith" lie at the basis of theology, whether *revelation* is understood in propositional or nonpropositional terms, whether natural theology and revelational theology are necessary components in the church's self-understanding, whether theology is controlled by denominational or interdenominational considerations, and whether creeds are essential to the development of theology remain to be answered not only according to the lines laid down by the Christian church but by the intellectual acumen and creative insights of scholarly theologians. The variety of types of theology generated in the process is evidence that theology as such is no monolithic structure which mysteriously and definitively forecloses intellectual options.

There are those, however, who regard theology as a discipline not primarily directed to the interests of the church. As Dr. Perry D. LeFevre puts it: "Theology deals with man's experience of values; its central theme has to do with what Calvin called 'the fountain of all good.' The theologian's study focusses on that which sustains, nourishes, and creates the good in human life and experience. . . . Religion is the commitment to that which sustains, nourishes and creates the good. Theology is the intellectual interpretation of that to which man commits himself. ["Religion and the Teaching of the Humanities," *Religious Education,* LIII, 6, 501.] The theological enterprise, as this author sees it, strives to get at deeper levels of meaning, to sensitize men to their levels of significance, and to enrich their perception of the world and to confront them with the problem of judgment which itself requires one to discover his own criteria for judgment among values. Theology carried on in this vein is oriented to the whole range of value considerations and conceives its relation to the church in a looser fashion than do more traditional patterns. In fact, there are indications that the term *theology* is coming to have a unique character, as it is used in the college and university outside the theological seminary and the church. There seems to be a tendency to regard theology less as a way of speaking to the church about itself or its relation to the world than as a way of understanding the traditional problems of theology in relative independence of the church's concerns and employing the resultant insights for a critique of the churches and culture. A prophetic element has developed which denies to the church sole rights to the interpretation of revelation. Thus recent efforts to relate Christian insights to art, music, literature, politics, and economics are self-consciously less ecclesiastical or sectarian in orientation, less confined to doctrinal considerations, and less systematically developed than more traditional conceptions of theology demand.[5]

These differences in the conception of the field of theology are connected with its manner of instruction and with the mode of theologizing itself. We may distinguish three modes of approach. The open-end approach derives from what has been called the Protestant principle, which regards no intellectual formulation as having divine sanction or authority, but as ever being open to correction and supplementation by new revelational and rational insights. When the divine is conceived in dynamic terms, and revelation itself is not regarded as providing doctrinal propositions but illuminative configurations for the structuring of knowledge, the direction of thought and instruction tends to lose the aura of "dogmatism." The synthesizing mode of theologizing attempts to bring into one inclusive world view the diverse elements of human experience as seen

[5] The development of an almost secular theology seems to occur more often in secular or Protestant institutions than in Catholic schools.

from the standpoints of certain normative convictions of the Christian tradition. Its purpose is to provide an intelligible organization of experience which will be distinctively Christian, inclusive of genuine diversities of experiences without diminution of their uniqueness, and an outlook which will produce fresh interpretations of experience and a basis for practical action. The point to be emphasized about this mode of theologizing is that although its formulator may consider it to be the "right" way in which to put together the pieces, he does not deny the possibility of alternative readings, both of Christian faith and of the concrete richness of human experience. The third form of carrying on the theologizing enterprise is that in which it is believed that certain doctrines are themselves divinely revealed, in the light of which a deductive system is then constructed, the crucial validities of which are unchangeable because they have the impressive weight of divine authority behind them.[6] All sciences and arts are then to be placed within this unifying and ordering structure, although, its advocates maintain, not necessarily in a despotic manner. The arrangement is more like that of a political domain in which the rights of the fields are respected as part of an organic synthesis yet without cancellation of their autonomy within the whole.

It appears at first glance that whereas the first two modes of carrying on theology as a process of intellectual investigation and as a part of the curriculum can be appropriately incorporated into the university world, the third cannot be accepted, since by definition it refuses to submit its credentials to the open court of free critical inquiry. This conclusion is but a partial

---

[6] This mode of theologizing is not intended to be a covert reference to Roman Catholic theology. It is found among some Protestants and Jews, as well as others. Roman Catholic theology in fact does make place for natural theology as a basis for revealed theology in a way in which some forms of Protestant theology do not.

truth, for everything depends on how its proponents see the-ology's function and purpose in the general academic arena. If theology is regarded as entering to establish itself as "the queen of the sciences," it in fact and principle aims to destroy the very conditions to which it first appeals for entry into the university. Its proper place, if any, is the seminary, not the university. There is nothing in the nature of a free university, however, to forbid the entry of theology as one of the intellectual structures which religion has historically and contemporaneously assumed. It is then subject to the same kinds of rational evaluation and types of evidential criticism as any structure which makes simi-lar types of claims for its authenticity, whether they be in the religious, scientific, political, or aesthetic realms—all of which have some basic assumptions which are not universally accepta-ble even by educated men.

The point then is that the term *theology,* or *theological sub-jects,* is more flexible than is sometimes supposed. Conclusions about the academic validity of courses in this area therefore can-not be arrived at merely by begging the question, by refusing to assess the type of theological content or mode of theologizing involved. Even the assertion that certain theologies deal with data and experiences which are not open to general inspection does not decisively defeat their entry into the curriculum. Any discipline or subdivision of a discipline which purports to deal with ultimate meanings or comprehensive interpretations of human experience similarly involves prerational assumptions, experiences, or "givens" which provide the starting points of normative interpretations.[7] Nor does a theological system neces-

[7] The Roman Catholic answer to this problem is stated by Father Regi-nald Masterson. "One is not generally judged to have scientific knowl-edge concerning matters which he accepts merely on faith, even divine faith. But such reasoning fails to distinguish between the principles of the supernatural order—the object of the virtue of faith—and the virtue of faith itself by which man is enabled to assent to them . . . the

sarily rule out the possibility of a contemporaneous experience of these ultimacies, even though at any given moment neither the instructor nor the student may be experiencing them in his own life. In principle, according to the type of theology in question, one may experience what theology ordinarily speaks of as grace, redemption, the presence of God, revelation, etc. Therefore, since theology is concerned with the rational understanding of these experiences rather than directly with the engendering of them, it, no more or less than other fields in which basic insights are presupposed, maintains a type of esoteric privacy which would make it unfit for a place in the university. Analogies with the fields of art, music, and even mathematics may easily be found to this type of problem. All that is genuinely at stake is whether statements about these experiences are meaningful, and what grounds exist for their acceptance as significant statements. And at this level theology can strike hands with any other discipline which confronts similar problems and continues to abide by the accepted rules of intellectual discourse in the university.

From the standpoint of comprehensiveness of treatment of religion and Christianity in particular, theology properly takes its place within the field of religion. If theology is refused its place both as a descriptive and a normative discipline the field of religion loses the opportunity to study the historical and contemporaneous alternatives which lend distinctive color and illumination to man's existence. Furthermore the treatment of theology serves to enrich and clarify the competing viewpoints which culture spawns while, at the same time, theology is itself brought face to face with secular experiences which challenge its insights. Thus one need not be a devotee of Reinhold

medium by which we assent to them is accidental to their truth and certainty." [Masterson, ed., *Theology in the Catholic College* (Priory, 1961), p. 43.]

166

Niebuhr to appreciate his contributions to political wisdom. One need not be convinced of the validity of Paul Tillich's theological system to find enriching insights in his observations on art, history, and depth psychology. H. R. Niebuhr's perceptive analyses of America's historical development or the relations of Christianity to culture shed light upon man's historical and religious development without demanding total acceptance of his theology. Nor does one necessarily adopt a neo-Thomist position in order to appreciate the wisdom of a J. Courtney Murray or a Jacques Maritain. Yet such benefits as these have emerged from the prosecution of the theological task, carried on not only by these distinguished figures, but also by less influential figures in colleges and universities. Their work has helped to provide the conditions of ferment in the university without which its job is only half done and, at the same time, they have joined this ferment with the persistent quest for the grounds of meaningful and defensible commitment without which humane education itself remains sterile. It would be supremely ironical if studies of world religions continue to include the various "theologies" or systems of thought in which convictional affirmations are spelled out and, at the same time, to set up an unpassable barrier to the study of the theologies of Christianity and Judaism as a deterrent to theologizing itself. To the rational clarification of religious convictions which theology entails, the university is no less dedicated than to rational clarification in other areas. Theology can ask no more nor settle for less. It must negotiate in the open market of competing ideologies, structures of thought, and options for loyalty, but it cannot legitimately be denied access to that market. It has business there not because it is the voice of the church, not because it is based on revelation, but because it is a part of culture and can only be so dealt with in the exchange place of ideas. Theology may be what Alexander Miller called the "articulation of

Revelation," but that articulation is itself a facet of culture, and that is what the university is confronted with and with which it must deal. If theology is to be set outside the pale or restricted entirely to the theological schools, there is only one valid basis: the failure of those who teach it to accept their proper responsibility to the larger world of intellectual commerce.[8]

---

[8] It is ironical that often those who deny the place of theological subjects in the curriculum also argue in the name of religious pluralism and liberalism that only committed personnel be hired to teach the principal religious traditions found in America. Yet this basis for the selection of personnel introduces in turn the very theological differentiation which it is avowed has no place in the university, and tacitly admits that theological partiality is inevitable, a clear reason for the denial of its incorporation into the university in any form.

❧ 9 ❧

SECTARIANISM, PLURALISM, AND TAX-SUPPORTED INSTITUTIONS

Although the notoriously difficult problem of sectarianism appears elsewhere, it comes to full expression in the area of publicly supported institutions of higher learning. Perhaps nowhere in higher education has it been more difficult to maintain the principle that religion is a field of study and scholarship rather than a veiled attempt to introduce the peculiar biases and convictions of religious bodies into the public domain under cover of academic respectability.

As a matter of principle, some would deny to religion any place in the curriculums of tax-supported institutions. Their appeal is to the American principle of separation of church and state or to the specific legal limitations found in state and university constitutions. On several grounds this extreme position is highly questionable. The phrase *separation of church and state* as Paul G. Kauper has indicated, is not a specific rule but a generalized concept which calls for judicial interpretation. It therefore does not by itself resolve any issues. It is an imprecise and elastic idea whose usefulness in part lies in its adaptability to changes in American cultural values and to the pragmatic weighing of competing interests in our society. Neither the principle nor the interpretation of it has reached that final precision of application which would make it an unimpeachable last resort. [See Kauper, "Law and Public Opinion" in *Religion and the State University,* ed. E. A. Walter (U. of Michigan, 1959), pp. 69 ff.] [1] Even had the principle achieved definitive interpretation, it would say nothing, in fact, about the study and teaching of subjects in the field of religion, except by an unwarranted extension of the term *church* to include the academic life itself. The assumption that "sectarianism" is an inevitable concomitant meaning of the term *church* may be legitimate; undoubtedly this assumption had great weight in the original idea of the principle of separation. It is quite another matter, the validity of which has not been established, to construe the academic treatment of religion as necessarily sectarian in nature.

When the case against instruction in religion is made on grounds of specific injunctions found in state constitutions, the issue becomes both more definite and more complex. The definiteness derives from the specificity of statements concerning the use of public funds and property for religious purposes, sometimes including reference to the support of teachers of religion. The complexity stems from the fact that each state has its own constitutional provisions which govern the place of religion in its state universities. Apparently no generalization covering all state-supported institutions can be offered because of the diversity of these provisions. But only three state constitutions (Arizona, Utah, and Washington) prohibit the use of public funds "for any religious worship, exercise, or instruction," without the customary reference to "sectarian" influence. Nevertheless, it is to be noted that the term *religious* used to modify the word *instruction* moves the sense of this prohibition in the direction of sectarianism and intimates the confusion which repeatedly arises when the word *religious* is employed as a synonym for *religion*. As we have previously seen, confusion

[1] For fuller treatment of the phrase *separation of church and state* and related matters, see Kauper, *Civil Liberties and the Constitution,* chap. 1 (U. of Michigan, 1962).

arises whenever religion as an area of study is forced into the category of religious exercises or given ecclesiastical connotations which candid examination of the best of actual practices of instruction and scholarship would dispel.

When the number and diversity of legal restrictions found in state constitutions are considered, it becomes the more remarkable to discover how much instruction in religion actually is carried on. Apparently publicly supported universities have not been content to divorce religion as an academic subject from higher education with the same decisiveness with which the American people have insisted upon its omission in the public schools at lower levels. Dr. Seymour A. Smith in studying religion instruction in state universities found that 76 per cent of the state universities offered instruction in the field in 1933, 80 per cent were doing so by 1940, and, by 1955-56, 97 per cent of these schools were engaged in religion instruction. There appear to be no clearly dominant ideas about the organization of this work. Makeshift curricular and personnel arrangements and *ad hoc* rationales dot the area, and have often been reflected in inferior academic work. [*Religious Education,* vol. LIV, pp. 97, 291.] On the other hand, it is clear that in spite of the mixed scene which Smith's study exposed, much first-class scholarship and teaching is being carried on in state institutions (e.g., University of Michigan, State University of Iowa). In sum, an overwhelming number of institutions are providing academic work in religion, a fact which suggests that legal factors may be less restrictive than customarily is assumed, or that interpretations of state constitutions and university charters have opened ways to legitimize religion instruction in one form or another. [M. D. McLean and H. H. Kimber, *The Teaching of Religion in State Universities* (Office of Religious Affairs, University of Michigan, 1960).]

Professor Kauper has pointed out that the recent increase in academic work in religion has taken place for the most part without being accompanied by changes in the relevant provisions in state constitutions. "It is fair to infer," he suggests, "that constitutional limitations relating to separation of church and state have not been the primary factor in determining the role of religion at the state university." ["Law and Public Opinion," *op. cit.*, p. 79.] Furthermore, some who have studied the problem are convinced that existing legal structures permit more latitude for religion instruction than is being used in a coherent and effective way.

Additional perplexity, however, arises when the procedures of the federal government in respect to higher education are considered. No clear line of demarcation appears to exist for distinguishing between the granting of funds to state universities and to private or church-related institutions. For example, the American Civil Liberties Union declared on August 21, 1961, that it saw "no constitutional bar to the granting of building loans or grants to those church-related colleges and universities which concentrate on higher education rather than inculcation of religious doctrine." The Union drew the line between institutions of higher learning which met what it considered to be desirable educational criteria and church-controlled elementary and secondary schools which served the purposes of nurturing and fortifying the religious faith of certain groups. [*Civil Liberties*, no. 191 (September 1961), p. 3.] The position of the Union appeared to support the case for federal aid to church-related institutions but it did not explicitly address itself to the question of support for tax-supported colleges or universities where religion courses are offered. This latter problem remains unsolved.

Although public pronouncements rehearse the theme of the separation of church and state, federal subsidies in various forms are granted to all forms of institutions whether or not they offer religion instruction or have a religious affiliation. The writers of a recent report on the problem were moved to state flatly that "under present conditions the national government does not know exactly what all its policies with respect to higher education are, not to mention classifying and ordering them." [*The Federal Government and Higher Education,* ed. Douglas M. Knight (Prentice-Hall, 1960), p. 161.] It is little wonder, in view of the confusion of practice by the federal government, that state university administrators sometimes hesitate to commit themselves to policies which might involve their institutions in legal and financial problems for which no clear guidelines at present exist. It would appear, nevertheless, that in this state of affairs no insuperable barrier exists against the possibility of the federal government making grants to state institutions offering instruction in religion so long as grants are given to other institutions where religion is accepted as part of the curriculum.

If legal restraints are less formidable than sometimes is supposed, there remain other restrictive factors which have clouded the issue. The presence of an antireligious bias on a campus, faculty inertia or animosity in respect to the potential contribution which religion can make to a liberal education, or administrative timidity may hinder efforts to place religion within the regular curriculum. Fear of denominational criticisms, possible law suits, and entanglement with off-campus pressure groups may steer administrators away from an area which has proved to be extremely sensitive at the lower levels of public education. On the other hand, some administrators are more ready to enter this controversial area than are faculty groups, which may continue to distrust religion as an academic subject.

The issue of sectarianism and the state university is not one which can be settled simply by appeal to legal measures or historic precedent. Its resolution depends in large part on the suc-

173

cess with which professors and scholars in the field of religion are able to convince policy makers of tax-supported institutions that the study of religion is not necessarily bound to sectarian interests. Until scholars and teachers make a substantial case for the academic respectability of religion among liberal arts subjects and its potential contribution to the enrichment and liberalization of the human mind the fate of religion in the state university will remain in doubt. At the same time, religious bodies must come to a deeper appreciation of the intellectual contribution which such studies may bring to the total development of man even when they are divorced from the context of the church or synagogue. The state university is a *university* and as such should incorporate all major fields of learning germane to the development of man's highest potentialities, among which the study of religion takes a respected place. The purpose of offering instruction in religion and providing opportunities for its scholarly examination is not that of making the university religious, but to assist the university to be itself in the fullest and best sense. If the university is to achieve its own purposes within our culture, the incorporation of religion into its very essence is not a concession to be made to religious pressures but a necessity for the fulfillment of liberal education. Nor should it be overlooked that increasing numbers of students find their way to publicly supported institutions, a fact which makes more imperative the need for providing first-rate opportunities for study of crucially important segments of culture, including, of course, religion.[2]

In view of the opportunities and problems which religion

---

[2] A recent study of enrollments in colleges and universities shows that 60 per cent of all students are to be found in state and municipal institutions; it projects that 80 per cent will be educated in these institutions in the future. [*New York Times,* Education Section (April 29, 1962).]

faces in publicly supported institutions, it is distressing to hear proponents of religion instruction advocating, even as temporary measures, programs which would further crystallize impressions that the nature of the field of religion is sectarian.

Influential voices are heard arguing that because of the religious pluralism of American culture no other option exists for instruction in this area except that of a tripartite arrangement in which the three major religious traditions, Protestant, Roman Catholic, and Judaistic, will be represented either within a religion department recognized as a fullfledged part of the curriculum or as a faculty operating at the circumference of the university.

H. E. Wornam has insisted that there must be "advocates of differing positions who understand and believe in these positions in terms of the integrity and wholeness of their respective systems of thought." Otherwise "dialogue is not genuine with respect to ultimate questions unless the argument for various positions is made by persons who have found truth and reality in those positions." Wornam, however, maintains that the teaching of religion in terms of America's religious pluralism should be carried out not in order to satisfy the interests of the substantially different tenets of faith "held by the three predominant bodies, but for academic reasons." Why these "academic reasons" call for representatives of the three faiths in religion, but do not also call for similar representatives in such fields as economics or government is not clear. ["Critical Issues in Public Higher Education," *Religious Education,* LIV, 2 (1959), 99, 107.] A similar line of thought is expressed by Father J. Courtney Murray, who states that "the possessor of the faith is . . . the proper qualification of the professor who would wish to communicate a critical understanding of it." [*Religion and the State University,* p. 26.]

Will Herberg's analysis of American religious life has convinced him that the teaching of religion in higher education generally does not accord with "the essential requirements of contemporary religious pluralism." He feels that the tripartite teaching arrangement would offset the present predominantly Protestant orientation of departments of religion. By virtue of their common rootage in the Bible, the three faiths could stand together in a common religious framework before the academic world. [*Ibid.,* pp. 37, 40-41.] On the grounds of the disagreement among the three faiths on the question of revelation, Roland Bainton takes an even darker view of the possibilities of teaching religion within state institutions. The only possibility which he would tentatively entertain is the tripartite program, but even that would amount to the inculcation of specific religious traditions by representatives of the three faiths. Consequently even this proposal is an impossibility in a state institution "because of the limitations imposed on education by the separation of church and state." The only alternative left, and one which it must be noted does not avoid the very problem it is intended to meet, is "that religious bodies at their own expense may set up faculties of theology on the university campus and offer courses open to election by all students, for which the university will grant credits toward its own degree." [*Ibid.,* p. 54.] Leo Pfeffer in *Church, State, and Freedom* reaches the conclusion that there is "no legal objection to having three chairs of theology, Protestant, Catholic, Jewish, in the university of any state." The teaching thus provided, he also argues in a strangely incoherent manner, must be objective, multisectarian, nondenominational, and noncompulsory! [Cf. "Critical Issues in Public Higher Education," *op. cit.,* p. 102.] In the interests of objectivity, it would seem we must settle for the admission that the study of religion must be hopelessly rent by sectarian divisions!

The apparent reasonableness of the tripartite proposal must

be challenged, even in the face of experimental efforts which have operated with some measure of success. The assumption of Dr. Herberg and others that the teaching of religion should be determined by the presence of three predominant religious traditions in American culture is highly questionable. Americans in fact do not neatly fall into these three groups. The categories themselves are too broad and porous to do justice to the variations of religious belief within each of the three strands of religious faith, to say nothing of those who count themselves Protestant, Catholic, or Jewish but have only the dimmest of notions about their beliefs or the diversity of beliefs and practices within these traditions. Beyond these three groups there exist significant numbers of agnostics, some of them of great religious sensitivity, atheists, earnest seekers, and members of what are usually called Oriental religions. The threefold pattern may serve as a sociological shorthand for certain purposes of analysis, but it is of dubious worth as a foundation upon which to build a policy for guidance in the employment of religion teachers in a university. It offers a spurious clarity of design by overlooking religious variations within these groups and by omitting sizeable groups that do not conveniently fall within the pattern. Furthermore, when the field of religion itself is understood in breadth, it is obvious that it is no more circumscribed by the existence of Catholicism, Protestantism, and Judaism than the idea of democracy is by the existence of the United States.

The notion that the university's offerings and its employment of personnel should be controlled by the aim of reflecting cultural conditions outside the university is a fallible principle. Nowhere else in higher education does it hold. Not all species of economic or political doctrines, kinds of art, forms of science and pseudo-science, types of professional and technical studies, or classes of literature are deemed worthy of a place in the university simply on the grounds that they exist in society. Rather the university operates on a principle of selectivity, the criteria of which are established by the institution itself. The fact that the university takes account of what goes on in society, responds to its needs in definite ways, and does reflect in its constitution certain aspects of the culture does not in any way contradict the important principle that the university retain in its hands control of the manner in which interactions with culture shall affect its nature and function. Insofar as the university cherishes and makes effective the ideal of serving as the critic and leader of a vital culture, it must retain its autonomy. And this can only be accomplished when the misleading conception of its function as a reflecting agency is completely given over.

In the case of religion this means that no inducement can be given to the university to bring its services into accord with what Herberg called "the essential requirements of contemporary religious pluralism" any more than it can be called upon to bring its teachings into conformity with the essential requirements of economic, artistic, or political pluralism. Sectarian religious groups have no more right to insist upon institutional representation than have government, business, or labor. University professors represent fields of study, not institutions which are found in these fields. What rightly pertains to the nature of the university is the study of religion, government, business, labor, economic policies, art, and literature; the qualifications of those who teach these subjects remain in the hands of university authorities.

The question is not one of whether the university is always wise in deciding what fields shall be studied or who its personnel shall be. Clearly it is possessed of no superhuman wisdom in these matters. The issue is rather that the university, to be true to its own nature, cannot adopt in the case of religion a principle which is at variance with its own character and its practice in other fields. Hence the idea that the teaching of religion must correspond to the religious structure of American life has no more validity than has the notion that departments of economics and government should be staffed by those who are devoted to the maintenance of some particular economic or political opinion.

If the employment of religion instructors were to be guided by the principle of religious pluralism, there is scarcely an identifiable point at which representation in the university of these groups and innumerable subgroups could be stopped. Not only Catholicism, Protestantism, and Judaism would have to be represented, but variations of positions within these groups properly should find their place in the university along with representatives of positions which do not fall within any of them. Even the case of the three major faiths is not simple; the question arises—since none of them is monolithic in belief—of which of their aspects shall be represented. Furthermore if the sectarian principle were adopted in other fields where value orientations are present, even greater confusion in the university would result. Then would appear the spectacle of Milton taught only by one who believes fully in Milton's ideas, Dante only by a Roman Catholic, Aquinas only by a Thomist, Hume only by a skeptic, Blake only by a mystic, Chinese history only by a Chinese historian, problems of taxation by both a Republican and a Democrat, and international relations by both an isolationist and an internationalist! Since sectarianism in its basic sense is not only a peculiarity of religion, but may refer to many subjects about which people hold different ideas with great intensity, nothing could halt the proliferation of viewpoints within a faculty except the good sense of those responsible for the welfare of the whole university. To move in the direction of pluralistic representation as the basis of academic policy would be as destructive of the university as it is unnecessary.

179

The university recognizes diversity of viewpoints within various fields and disciplines. It thrives on the fruitful clash of ideas for which it provides an arena. But it does so by endeavoring to secure instructors who can competently present and evaluate a diversity of viewpoints. It trusts the training and personal integrity of the professor to offset any bias which would so seriously affect the teaching of these trends of thought and perspectives as grossly to misrepresent them. Commitment on the part of faculty members is to be expected and hoped for, but so long as higher learning premises education as distinct from indoctrination, academic competence alone—rather than political, economic, or religious affiliation—determines the professor's right to be a part of the academic community.

When, in the case of religion, sectarian involvement is made a crucial factor in the acceptance of a faculty member, an alien and discriminatory feature is introduced. Competence then includes participation in a religious group, the evaluation of which now must rest with a body or authority outside the university. The question then becomes "Is Professor X a worthy representative of the religious tradition for which he is to speak?" and the answer can only be given by those in the religious group who are in a position to know the individual's religious status. Thereby the university surrenders its right to be master in its own house. Although those who have authority to judge a person's religious attitudes may be watchful of intellectual competence, their principal reason for entering the scene is one of a religious rather than an academic nature, since presumably the university is capable of judging the intellectual competence of the professor.

Moreover, it would appear that those who defend the tripartite proposal lean excessively upon the importance of representation itself. But ability to represent sympathetically a certain position is not the only criterion of a faculty member;

equally important is his capacity to criticize even the viewpoint which he represents. Unfortunately some who advocate sectarian representation give the impression that the sole purpose of their proposal is to ensure that certain religious beliefs and groups shall have a hearing. But the practice of faculty selection only on the basis of ability to represent may omit from consideration the capacity to enter fully into critical discussion. It may also increase the possibility of a defensive attitude, since the faculty member may be tempted to construe his function too largely in the light of his role as a representative of a religious group rather than as a member of the academic community. Although it must be admitted that often certain religious perspectives have not been given a fair hearing in the academic world, the remedy seems to lie not in introducing sectarian considerations into the university, but in the university itself living up to its profession as a liberalizing influence by offering work of a high order in the field of religion, the faculty for which would be recruited from scholars—of whatever religious group or none —who understand their business as educators. Religion is in a profound sense the testing point of the freedom the university professes.

Competence in the academic sense is not dependent on either one's participation in a religious group or lack of it. Anthony Nemetz has validly maintained: "To say that good standing in a religious community is essential to the teacher of religion or that only a practicing member of a religion can teach a course in a given religion is simply inconsistent with the accepted principles of academic freedom." Neither, as he further argues, is lack of religious commitment a criterion of acceptance of the instructor into the academic world. [*Journal of Higher Education,* XXX, 4, 197.] The sole grounds for the reception of the religion instructor are his academic qualifications, his capacity as a scholar and teacher. And this competence, it must again be insisted, should extend over an area larger than that circumscribed by his own personal religious convictions. He appears on the academic scene not to press his peculiar brand of religiosity or simply "to represent" his religious group. The justification for his presence lies in his abilities to engage with all his powers in the give and take of intellectual activity and to present with intellectual acumen and sensitivity those portions of the field in which he has demonstrated ability, whether or not they are all equally congenial to his personal convictions. Ecclesiastical affiliation will not necessarily determine his approach to or his conclusions about religious beliefs. More often than not he may find himself agreeing with those of differing religious persuasions and disagreeing with those of his own religious group, since conflicts about values and truth seldom run according to denominational lines as defined by the religious structure of American culture at large.

Of course, members of the three predominant religious groups in America should rightfully find their places in religion departments, but only for academic reasons. It may be difficult to find a Christian scholar to teach postbiblical or contemporary Judaism, since to date relatively few Christian scholars have been prepared in these areas; similarly it may be difficult to discover a competent Roman Catholic scholar to teach courses in the Protestant Reformation or contemporary Protestantism. But the essential point must not be given over for whatever short-range advantage there may be in seeking "representatives" of the several faiths.

The fact that an insufficient number of teachers and scholars from the major faiths have been trained to carry out work of high quality in areas not directly connected with their own religious predilections cannot be accepted as the basis for an academic policy which would merely support the sectarian principle rather than overcome it on the higher ground of the intellectual community. Rather the lack of trained scholars and teachers underlines the necessity for a type of training for university teaching which is freed from the denominational grooves in which much of the present training for teaching and scholarship has been done. Graduate schools of religion which turn full attention to religion as a field of study and preparation for teaching are very much needed. But in the meantime we do well to notice that eminent scholars of diverse religious traditions produce works which are received with respect by scholars of dissimilar religious persuasions. The avenues of discourse for the most part have been kept open among religious bodies by the scholarly world, and in this realm the criteria of excellence are not established by religious bodies, but by the larger academic community itself.[3] Likewise, competent work is being done by those whose religious affiliations do not intrude upon their instruction and who do not regard their roles as those of representatives of particular religious bodies. As has previously been argued in respect to the problem of indoctrination, there need be no obstruction to teaching religion in any institution of higher learning, so long as the basic rules of the academic community are not violated. So long as the principles of fair and comprehensive presentation of data and the rules of argument and unapologetic, nonpartisan treatment of materials are observed, the field of religion can make a place for itself within the framework of the state-supported university by appeal to the very grounds upon which the university justifies its own existence.

[3] A few examples of this respect for scholarly achievement regardless of religious affiliation: G. F. Moore on Judaism, Joseph Klausner on Jesus and early Christianity, Harry A. Wolfson on the early church fathers, Erwin R. Goodenough on Philo, Ignác Goldziher on Islam, Karl G. Kuhn on the Dead Sea Scrolls, Hans Jonas on Gnosticism, Hans Ur von Balthasar on Karl Barth, Heinrich Zimmer on Hinduism, W. M. Watt on Islam, Jaroslav Pelikan on Roman Catholicism.

There need be no softening or "neutralizing" of the divergences among religious traditions within this context, even though the instructors may not themselves hold the particular viewpoint being presented. The well-trained instructor in religion can give as thoughtful and sensitively sympathetic a reading of views which are at odds with what he personally believes as can his colleague in literature, art, or government. Every field in the humanities probably contains ideas which to a particular instructor are uncongenial, but one of the marks of a good teacher is his capacity to set before his students not only the reasons why some have found worth in such ideas, but also to enable his students to entertain with some degree of imagination those convictions and values which brought into being that specific understanding of human existence. In this respect religion stands on no different ground in the academic world than any other field where value considerations come to the fore. But it cannot appeal to any principle extraneous to the nature of the academic community itself to justify its incorporation into the state university curriculum. For this reason, if for no other, those who defend the position of religion as a legitimate field of scholarship and teaching must turn their backs on proposals for denominational representatives chosen on the basis of sociological considerations. If religion is to be taken in all seriousness as an academic area worthy of students' attention and professors' efforts, it must show its maturity by insisting that it be treated like any other subject within the framework of the university.

To those who see the integrity of their religious faiths endangered if the three major religious traditions in America are not represented in the teaching of religion, it must be firmly said that if well-educated people of differing religious persuasions cannot recognize competence in religion scholarship and instruction wherever it appears, then it is foolish to expect that secular-minded critics of the teaching of religion in state universities can detect it. Religious bodies which deny the possibility of fair treatment of their unique tenets by other than their own representatives are free to establish their own institutions where these tenets may be inculcated. They are not free to use tax-supported institutions for the promulgation of their doctrines by appeal to a principle of a religious pluralism which takes account of the beliefs of only a portion of the American public and which, when practiced, subverts the principles upon which the universities themselves are founded. Religious sectarianism is a fact of church life, but it can be and is being transcended in the teaching of religion in many colleges and universities.

❧ IV ❧

RELATIONS OF UNDERGRADUATE DEPARTMENTS OF RELIGION TO THEOLOGICAL SEMINARIES AND GRADUATE SCHOOLS

INFLUENCES OF GRADUATE EDUCATION ON FACULTY AND CURRICULUM

Teaching and scholarship in religion normally are found at three institutional levels. In the undergraduate college they usually appear in one of the humanistic fields. In the theological seminary they appear in the form of theological studies and constitute a major portion of the training of prospective clergymen and others preparing for church vocations. In the graduate school various phases of the field are intensively studied, normally with an eye to teaching and further research.

Distinctions among the three levels at first glance seem to be definite and logical, but close examination of the actual work done at the seminary level soon shows that the distinctions are less clear than may be supposed. The theological seminary in one sense is a graduate institution offering courses to students who have completed four years of college or their equivalent.[1] Presumably its courses build upon the foundations laid at the undergraduate level and are therefore of a graduate quality. However, after the normal three-year seminary course the graduate is awarded a bachelor's degree in divinity on the assumption that he is taking the first degree in a different sequence of study than that established at the undergraduate level. Furthermore, not all of his work has been of a graduate type. He often has taken introductory courses in religion, theology, or Bible as well as in new fields relevant to his vocational training. Thus the seminary serves as a graduate, undergraduate, and professional school at one and the same time, focusing mainly on the

[1] Reference in this chapter is primarily to Protestant seminaries.

life of the church. Its primary aim has not been humanistic in the broad sense, but professional or vocational for the service of the church.[2]

Should the graduate of the theological seminary seek an advanced degree in religion, he finds before him two options. The more common one is that of a graduate division in religion or theology in a university of which the seminary faculty is a constituent body. In the graduate division he finds many of the same seminary faculty members he knew in his B.D. days and occasionally members of other departments or of the undergraduate department of religion if there is one. The other option, a more recently developed program, is a graduate school or division in religion of a university, staffed by a faculty which is not drawn from the ranks of a seminary. As yet, relatively few teachers of religion have taken this direction, and programs of this type are still relatively scarce.[3] The purpose of graduate training is the preparation of professors and scholars in religion, whose primary commitment may be to the field of religion as a humanistic area and not necessarily as a function of a religious institution.

With the exception of the last-named type of graduate study, it may readily be seen that the theological seminary stands in a dominating and crucial position in respect to the development of the field of religion and the preparation of instructors in it. The first graduate work of the student ordinarily takes place there, and his continued graduate studies take place largely

[2] Some of the larger interdenominational seminaries provide so wide a range of courses that, with the possible exception of laboratory work in the natural sciences, a liberal arts education is available! The expansion of courses in these institutions has been so great that they have virtually become universities.

[3] Among the best-known programs of the university type are those at Brown, Columbia, the State University of Iowa, Pennsylvania, and Princeton.

under the tutelage of a seminary faculty. Without entering into the details of seminary education itself, it is desirable to recognize that the interplay between the seminary on the one hand and the undergraduate and graduate fields of religion on the other has created problems for the understanding of religion as a humanistic field. The impress of the seminary program has been felt in the preparation of instructors and in the programs of study offered at the undergraduate and graduate levels, thereby defining to a certain extent the field itself.

The influence of the seminary under present conditions is first of all felt at the point of the preparation of religion professors. Certain questions have been raised by critics concerning the dominant position of the seminary in this area. Does the fact that graduate faculties are largely made up of seminary faculty members, whose principal efforts are normally directed toward ecclesiastical interests, adversely affect the quality and the direction of graduate preparation? Is the work offered comparable in rigor and depth to that found in graduate studies in other humanistic fields? [4] In spite of the generally high scholarly achievements of these faculties, is there a tendency to direct graduate work too narrowly toward the churches' life rather than toward the academic community? Another line of questioning deals with the problem of comparative isolation from secular currents which a seminary-influenced graduate education

[4] Uneasiness on this score is also found among Catholic observers. Gustave Weigel, S.J., has said that "the seminary is not the locus of high scholarly endeavor," and that "it is not in general the function of priestly and religious training to produce scholars." Dr. J. T. Ellis quotes a statement made by Bishop Spalding some years ago which Ellis feels may still be true: "The ecclesiastical seminary is not a school of intellectual culture, either here in America or elsewhere, and to imagine that it can become the instrument of intellectual culture is to cherish a delusion." [*American Catholicism and the Intellectual Ideal,* ed. F. L. Christ and G. E. Sherry (Appleton, 1960), pp. 220, 222, 269.]

affords. Are the major grounds of opposition to theological reflection and religious convictions, common in the university culture of today, met during graduate training? Does the prospective religion instructor find among his classmates and faculty the concrete personal embodiments of skepticism or indifference? Does he feel the shock of intellectual conflict which he is likely to meet on any "live" campus? Are the main currents of opposing value positions running through the seminary-induced atmosphere, or does this atmosphere, consciously or unconsciously, shield the graduate student from the full impact of the major problems our culture faces? Does he meet the downright ignorance about religion elsewhere often found even among otherwise highly educated academicians? Are the contributions and viewpoints of fields adjacent to or even sharply divided from religion met, evaluated, and in some cases, appropriated?

General answers to these and similar questions are not to be lightly given. Institutions vary widely in "tone" and "temper," and it would be most misleading to suggest that wherever seminary faculties control graduate work, an inevitable decline of quality and narrowness of perspective occur. However, questions about "isolation" may be answered with some authority on the basis of the Niebuhr study of theological education. [H. R. Niebuhr, J. M. Gustafson, and D. D. Williams, *The Advancement of Theological Education* (Harper, 1957), pp. 64-65, 72, 136.] It was concluded in this report that theological schools did tend to be isolated from the broader cultural and secular forces of our society, and recommendations were made for overcoming this condition. Contacts with articulate spokesmen from outside the seminary who held views both congenial and uncongenial to certain theological perspectives were discovered to be minimal for both faculty and students. Therefore it was suggested that advances should be made in opening these schools to a more full-bodied encounter with contemporary culture in order to produce a more realistically minded and relevant clergy. It may be noted, however, that graduate students in most of the major theological centers are not usually so isolated from the total university milieu as are the B.D. students in seminaries independent of universities. There are usually opportunities in and out of the seminary classroom at the university for catching the temper of an institution in which the winds of controversy incessantly blow. Nor should it be thought that among graduate religion students in a given institution the quiet of a single harmonious viewpoint prevails. Graduate students themselves bring to their studies a variety of backgrounds and interests which reflect more of the world about them than sometimes the outsider supposes. Yet, having conceded this much to the intellectual vitality of these centers, we still face the question of how vigorously graduate preparation for teaching can enter into significant dialogue with other cultural forces so long as the seminary atmosphere remains decisive.

Furthermore, doubt has been expressed of whether education in this context provides the best type of preparation for the graduate's encounter with the university world. In the seminary, the field of religion and its disciplines are accepted naturally as of prime importance, and they are normally studied, without question, as relevant to the professional aims for which the theological or graduate school exists. It is pointless to ask what the study of the Bible, church history, theology, or ethics has to do with becoming a clergyman or a professor of religion. If the student does not recognize the relevance of his studies to his future profession, the fault does not lie with the field or the discipline. Either the professor has failed to relate his work to the professional aim or the student has simply failed to grasp the connection. The materials and methodologies stand firm;

only the manner of presentation and reception is called into question. This scene abruptly changes for the religion professor as he begins to teach in the undergraduate college. Relevance can no longer be taken for granted. The terms, thought patterns, and issues which have been the common stock of theological education seldom carry the same importance they once had. No longer can the religion professor presuppose the community of religious faith which formerly undergirded, if even loosely, the intellectual commerce of the seminary. Questions by students and colleagues center not only upon the contents and methods of religion courses but upon the relevance which the whole field has to the education of men and women who will be entering medicine, law, engineering, public schoolteaching, homemaking, and the like. Accordingly the religion professor finds he must reshape his materials and methods of approach. He is now in a situation where the relevance of his work may be challenged, where assumptions about the religious institutions and their aims are put into question and where he is an educator rather than the representative of a church or religious tradition. He must constantly be confronted with the task of showing the truth of his subject in this arena and its contribution to the broadening and deepening of the intellectual and evaluative powers of persons who may or may not ever be participants in religious institutions. He will meet the crosscurrents of sophisticated secularism, narrow pietism, ignorance, prejudice, disciplined thinking, and new insights now concretely embodied in those who disagree with him. He has surrendered whatever measure of comfort and intellectual security the seminary has provided for an atmosphere which may be relatively free but which is often little inclined to take for granted the significance of his contribution to the dialogue among competing viewpoints. He may develop a defensive attitude toward his role in the university or he may embrace this new situation as one of exciting possibilities. As time passes he may also become convinced that those seminary or graduate professors who sometimes express interest in teaching part-time in undergraduate institutions are simply out of touch with the problems to be faced there. In whatever manner he evaluates his position, the one factor which remains constant is that of relevance, and the question which will repeatedly stand to the fore will be that of the degree to which a seminary-influenced education has prepared him for handling this issue. On this question opinion is divided, but there is increasing uneasiness about the graduate education which is largely carried on at a considerable remove from the mainstreams of American higher education.

Questions concerning the quality and direction of graduate training yield no set of ready-made answers. The danger of ecclesiastical domination of graduate preparation, for example, can be exaggerated, but it is nevertheless present. One serious implication of the seminary's influence upon graduate preparation may be found at the point of admissions policies. Since the seminary exists to serve the churches, it is natural that often criteria of a religious type should be used in the acceptance of students. But since the seminary also normally provides the first steps in graduate education for those going into teaching, such criteria may act as a deterrent to those whose interest in the field may be largely intellectual or whose religious positions have not been formulated in terms acceptable to the seminary authorities. Yet until a comparatively recent date few other means for procuring a graduate education in religion existed except those provided through the seminary route. It remains a serious question whether religious criteria applied as a condition of entrance into graduate work or by the institution at which the graduate is to teach are compatible with either the needs of the field itself or academic freedom.

It would seem that a place exists in religion instruction and scholarship for both the religiously committed person and the uncommitted person. So long as each meets the requirements of intellectual excellence, no question should arise. As has been previously noted, presuppositions are unavoidable. If the peril of a bias excessively favorable to religious positions hovers over the workmanship of the religiously committed teacher and scholar, no less does the danger of a spurious objectivity or antireligious spirit threaten the integrity of the uncommitted teacher and scholar. And because of these parallel dangers religion instruction and scholarship need the services of each acting upon the other as a corrective. If the seminary continues to provide entry to the field and insists upon religious criteria as the condition of entry, the need for graduate schools of religion in which these criteria are not used becomes all the more apparent.

Some religion instructors, by virtue of personal conviction and the seminary auspices under which they have done their graduate work, will leave graduate school believing that theirs is a Christian ministry of teaching which must be exhibited in an ecclesiastical allegiance and a narrowly apologetic frame of mind. Others, holding similar convictions, will quietly go at the tasks of teaching and scholarship, believing that the best testimony to their personal religious convictions is the fidelity they show to the disciplines in which they are prepared and to the academic community of which they are now a part. Others may enter the profession with interests completely involved in the intellectual challenge of their work, lacking any sense of themselves as servants of a religious body.

Of course, intellectual interest and participation in church life can be justified on academic grounds. The study and interpretation of religion must take account of its institutional forms. Just as the study of government without reference to specific governmental forms is unthinkable, so the study of the vitalities of religious experience without reference to the historical and contemporaneous structures in which it is embodied would be unrealistic and vacuous. The advantage of a seminary-influenced graduate program is most apparent at this point, for it gives an opportunity for understanding the nature and function of the church which purely philosophical, theological, or biblical studies might avoid.

Attention to the nature of the church as a part of graduate preparation, however, is a different matter from the development of a personal attitude which interprets one's academic career in ecclesiastical terms. In spite of the structuring of some graduate programs about the church and its problems and possibilities in several of the most influential theological centers, it does not appear that a narrow denominational loyalty has been developed which would interfere with the prosecution of one's duties as a faculty member. There seems to be little ground for supposing that these graduate programs are supplying blind apologists for the churches, or that their graduates conceive their task as teachers to be that of supplying docile, uncritical laymen for the churches. It may be possible, however, that too much of contemporary American graduate training has been cast in terms of the importance of the Protestant churches, or in some cases, the ecumenical perspective.

Another more clearly demonstrable inadequacy which may be laid at the door of the seminary's influence does appear in graduate training. If men are to be prepared for teaching religion with some degree of breadth, the areas of world religions, Roman Catholicism, Eastern orthodoxy, and Jewish thought and practice should play a larger part in that preparation. Because of the predominantly Protestant cast afforded to graduate training by seminary faculties and their programs,

197

because it is difficult to find capable instructors in these areas, because financial limitations have often prevented the establishment and growth of departments, these fields have seldom received the attention they deserve as part of graduate training.

Although some attention is paid to world religions in the seminary program, the Niebuhr report concludes "unquestionably it is badly neglected." [*Ibid.*, p. 100; cf. pp. 24-25.] Studies in Eastern orthodoxy, Judaism, and Roman Catholicism fare even worse. It may be understandable that B.D. curriculums should omit these studies, but if their faculties profess to be preparing men for positions in the academic world, the omission becomes one of reprehensible proportions. Not only does the control of the supply of professors of religion lie largely with the seminary, but so also does the control over the possible fields of concentration. Again it appears that a partial remedy for this situation may lie in the increased development of graduate schools and divisions independent of the seminaries where scholars in these now largely neglected fields may be developed.

The problem of limitation of scope in present-day graduate training should not be used to becloud the issue of the quality of such education. The issue is a treacherous one in which rash evaluations can only lead to inaccuracy and ill will. Obviously, standards vary among institutions and even among departments within institutions. Certain institutions, manned primarily by seminary faculties, have attained and maintained prestige positions. Others struggle for recognition, while independent graduate programs have yet to make their influence widely felt. Future research should be done on this question to determine more precisely the advantages and disadvantages of graduate preparation under seminary and independent auspices as well as to develop estimates of the degree of preparation for religion teaching and scholarship needed compared with that in other fields. This ambitious project falls outside the scope of the present essay, which must be content with several general observations.

The majority of religion professors have carried on programs of preparation extending over more than three years beyond the collegiate degree—a period of five or six years is not unusual. This period of graduate work does not compare unfavorably with that in other fields, but clearly mere length of time expended on graduate studies is not proof positive of either high or low quality in the training itself. The previously noted, general upswing in the quality of teaching, however, seems to argue that this graduate preparation has proved to be satisfactory, although improvements certainly could be made along the lines suggested above.[5] Pending further empirical studies of this problem, it may not be too rash to conclude that graduate training for teaching has generally been at least as intensive and rigorous in the major graduate theological centers as it has been in comparable humanistic fields. It should also be recognized, however, that there are relatively few of these centers compared with a larger number which aspire to produce professors of religion, but do so with indifferent results. This situation has evoked concern about the unevenness of doctoral standards and has been referred for study to the Council on

[5] Dr. Robert Michaelson, on the basis of a sample survey among religion teachers who have graduated within the last ten or fifteen years, reports that most of this number have been satisfied with their training, much of which has been done under the auspices of seminary faculties. He notes, however, that some have felt that their graduate work was merely a "bigger dose" of materials which they had at the B.D. level, that too often there has been a "party line" in graduate training and that little opportunity was given for contact with such lines of thought as logical empiricism, the relation of religion and science, depth psychology, sociology, and other fields which impinge upon the field of religion. ["The Training of Teachers of Religion for College and University," *Religion in Life,* XXVIII, 1 (1958-59).]

Graduate Studies in Religion. [Niebuhr, Gustafson, and Williams, *op. cit.*, p. 202.]

The seminary makes its influence felt not only in the preparation of the religion teacher, but also by the impact it has had upon the curriculum, which defines the field at the undergraduate level. By virtue of his training in certain disciplines, the religion professor takes for granted that these disciplines, with appropriate modifications, should be offered to undergraduate students. If he does so, he may soon find himself caught in a cross fire of criticism. Critics speaking from a liberal arts perspective charge that he has only reproduced a selection of seminary courses fit, at best, for the preparation of pretheological students. If the charge be valid, he has then endangered his right to be considered a contributor to liberal education. On the other hand, if he gives himself and his department over to pretheological education, he is bewildered to discover that his efforts are so far deprecated by authorities speaking for seminaries that they consider his department to be less desirable than others as a major for pretheological students. His well-intentioned efforts to treat the field of religion in the form in which he has been taught seem to have been misguided.

If he moves to meet the challenge of those of the "liberal arts" type by turning his teaching into the channels of general service and terminal courses, he soon finds he has locked himself into the dead end of a constant round of elementary courses, which erodes his incentive for carrying out scholarly work of his own. He is no longer repeating seminary courses, as the criticism runs, but neither is he advancing his own intellectual powers or those of his students. Buffeted by criticisms from both sides of the academic arena, and not without a sense of having been betrayed by the seminaries, he stands confronted with two incompatible goals, neither of which, it appears, he can achieve to the satisfaction of his critics.[6]

Two basic issues may be distinguished in this connection. The first is that of the degree to which seminary or graduate training properly determines or influences the curriculum and method of approach to the field of religion when it is conceived as a humanistic study. The second is that of the relation between pretheological studies and the seminaries, a problem which will be discussed in the next chapter.

When the seminary acts as a graduate school its work in fact does define the field of religion by the disciplines it develops. To be sure, a variety of courses appear in the seminary curriculum which are inappropriate at the undergraduate level, but the major segments of the field have been firmly established. Biblical, historical, theological, and philosophical areas within which specific courses occur remain the principal stock in trade of the field at every level of higher education. These divisions naturally serve as controlling factors in the undergraduate domain even when religion is conceived as a humanistic field. No proprietary authority over religion curriculums has been vested in the seminary or graduate school so far as humanistic aims are concerned, but the religion professor cannot evade the general structuring of the field which scholars in these schools have developed. Tension can occur only when seminaries connected with colleges or uni-

---

[6] The freedom with which seminary faculties pronounce upon the nature of undergraduate instruction and the character of undergraduate institutions, especially those of a Christian type, without reference in some cases to those who teach in these institutions is nothing less than remarkable. For example, the commission which drew up a statement on "The Theological Foundations of the Christian College" was comprised of ten members, only one of whom had taught at the college level. [*Christian Scholar,* XLI (Special Issue, August 1958), 273 ff.]

versities attempt to dictate the manner of approach or the content of courses at the college level—a possibility which fortunately is as rare as it would be disastrous to the freedom of the college. So long as religion remains a humanistic study, it must forego professional intent while at the same time being governed by the general structure of the field which has been largely established by graduate faculties. To this degree then the seminary properly makes its influence felt upon the undergraduate teaching of religion.

When the charge is made that undergraduate departments repeat seminary curriculums, it must then be understood in the first place that the structuring of the field itself calls for offerings within these disciplines. Unless the field has been falsely interpreted at the graduate centers, no legitimate reason may be offered in opposition to the giving of similar courses at the undergraduate level. For example, a course in the analysis of the gospel of John may be as rewarding and appropriate to the liberal education of an undergraduate as is a critical course in the writings of Blake, Lawrence, or Rilke. But it must equally be insisted that a wide margin of freedom exists for the religion department to develop courses and methods of its own independent of seminary or professional influences and in line with its humanistic content. Undoubtedly religion professors have too often lacked the academic imagination and vigor to break with the lockstep of traditional offerings. They have often failed to use their opportunities for incorporating sociological, psychological, or philosophical viewpoints into their courses. They have not always responded convincingly to the impact of world cultures upon the treatment of theological issues. Less often than might be expected have they made use of a comparative method in treating Christianity or Judaism in relation to other religions, and too often have they failed to dare to enter into dialogue with viewpoints in other departments which are uncongenial to them. Where this lack of creative effort exists and the traditional disciplines alone are offered, the semblance of truth is given to the charge of repetition as made by both the seminary and humanistically minded colleagues. Yet no mere collation of similarly titled courses in undergraduate and seminary catalogs establishes the charge of repetition. Differences of approach, in detail of treatment, and not least of all, in the context where such courses are offered, make decided differences between these courses as offered at the two levels. Nor should it be overlooked that when "repetition" takes place, the "repetition" is not necessarily effected by the undergraduate course.[7] If courses in religion offered in the college are of the same type and degree of intellectual intensity as those found in the seminary, the fault of overlapping may be properly assessed to the seminary rather than to the college. Certainly if seminaries fail to advance to programs of a genuinely graduate caliber, this fact cannot be used to discourage undergraduate departments of religion from carrying on work at as high a level as is maintained in other departments of the liberal arts program.

The conclusion must then be that the seminary or graduate school does greatly influence the conformation of the field of religion as found in the humanities and that it does so less by any explicit effort than by its training of teachers and the development of the disciplines within the field. The hold of the seminary upon graduate education involves certain dangers

---

[7] Whereas in the eighteenth and early nineteenth centuries, theological subjects and ancillary studies were often accepted in the collegiate program as a matter of course, today the seminary sometimes chides departments of religion for offering courses in these subjects which it asserts belong solely to its domain. There is something of historical irony in this. [Cf. Roland Bainton, *Yale and the Ministry* (Harper, 1957); also Robert F. Goheen, "The Seminary and the University," *Princeton Seminary Bulletin,* LIV, 1 (July 1960).]

to the broadest possible treatment of religion, and it may be that in the future more attention should be given to the establishment and strengthening of graduate divisions of religion in the university apart from the professional interests of the seminary. In spite of the dangers or shortcomings, however, ample credit must be given to the seminaries whose graduate work and scholarship have been the principal source of the supply of professors of religion. The training provided by these institutions has been generally of a high intellectual order and has not been excessively marked by a sectarian or biased spirit.

ᵊᔑ 11 ᔐᵊ

PRETHEOLOGICAL TRAINING AND UNDERGRADUATE RELIGION INSTRUCTION

Instruction in religion at the undergraduate level may be understood as part of the humanities, but its relation to pretheological studies has proved to be a thorny issue. The undergraduate professor has discovered that seminary authorities seldom express themselves upon the values of the study of religion as part of the humanistic area, but that they are most explicit on the advantages of a liberal education as preparation for further theological work. The official body of the divinity schools, the American Association of Theological Schools (AATS), has issued recommendations on the types of courses considered to be desirable for future seminarians. These statements, which have appeared from time to time, have produced mixed reactions among college religion instructors, many of whom feel that these pronouncements tend to de-emphasize the study of religion in the eyes of pretheological and general students as well as in the sight of faculty colleagues and adminstrators. In consequence a discussion of some warmth has been carried on between proponents of the AATS position and those who believe it to be injurious to the cause of religion throughout higher education.[1]

[1] Dean Ernest C. Colwell, in a sharply worded criticism of the AATS position, refers to theological faculties as "looking down their noses" at college professors of religion, as regarding themselves as "superior," and as manifesting "arrogance" toward these professors. He notes the "lively resentment" felt by some undergraduate professors toward theological faculties. Additional indications of the vigor and heat which have characterized the debate may be found in the following: C. A. Holbrook,

205

As early as 1940 the AATS published recommendations for preseminary students which emphasized the importance of a broad liberal arts education and the avoidance of "preprofessional studies." It was suggested that Bible or religion account for four to six hours out of three-quarters of the total college program of the college student. In 1948 a new statement appeared which, although it did not substantially change the recommendations on religion, did omit the phrase *preprofessional studies*. The latest published set of recommendations came out in 1956 and represented a shift of opinion. Instead of speaking of specific courses or hours, it referred to the kinds of understanding and techniques which a seminary student should have achieved as a result of his undergraduate experience. Fields of study believed to lead to the development of these understandings and techniques were outlined. In religion, the statement reads, "a thorough knowledge of the content of the Bible is indispensable, together with an introduction to the major religious traditions and theological problems in the context of the principal aspects of human culture." This formidable achievement is correlated with the recommendation of at least three semesters in the field. Of the possible areas of concentration or major work, "English, philosophy and history are regarded as the most desirable." The AATS reminded readers of the statement that its recommendations were minimal and

"College Religion Courses and the Seminaries," *Iliff Review*, VI, 1 (1949); J. Paul Williams, "But Don't Major in Religion," *Christian Century*, LXXI (June 16, 1954); *Journal of Bible and Religion* articles as follows: J. A. Easley, "Statement on Pre-Theological Studies," XXV (July 1957); Correspondence from Charles L. Taylor and J. Arthur Baird; Ernest C. Colwell, "Closing the Gap Between College and Seminary"; Earl Cranston, "Historical Backgrounds in College and Seminary," XXVI (January 1958); J. Arthur Baird, "Pre-Theological Training: An Empirical Study," XXVII, 4 (1959); and Paul Ramsey, "Theological Studies in College and Seminary," *Theology Today*, XVII, 4 (1961).

intended as suggestions for the guidance of both students and seminaries. The primary emphasis of the statement was placed upon a "liberal arts" program, a "broad and comprehensive college education."

Of course, in evaluating this statement, the right which this representative body has to lay out guide lines for preseminary preparation for clergy is not at issue. Considering the variety of backgrounds and preparations with which students are accepted into seminaries, it is understandable that moves should be made toward minimal standardization of preparation. In fact, there are grounds for believing that seminaries have been too lax in entrance requirements compared with other professional and graduate schools. Apparently, the predominantly professional concern of the seminary has weakened the emphasis on intellectual criteria for admission. The pressures by ecclesiastical agencies to accept students of inferior preparation, the high evaluation placed upon the entering students' personal qualifications, especially the depth of his commitment to the Christian faith, as well as the insistent demand of the churches for more clergymen, have often placed the seminaries under an embarrassing stress. The Niebuhr study frankly states that theological schools seldom "make a detailed assessment of the students' college record" or "require further college work in areas where he is deficient." Although admittedly practical problems impede progress toward higher entrance requirements, the report concludes that more rigor should be exercized. [H. R. Niebuhr, J. M. Gustafson, and D. D. Williams, *The Advancement of Theological Education* (Harper, 1957), pp. 91-92.] With this conclusion probably most college religion professors would heartily agree.

But for the same reason, among others, some religion professors object to the assumptions and implications which the statement involves. Although the recommendation on religion is stated in minimal terms, thus seeming to encourage the student to take more work in the field, it is felt that the statement serves to discourage rather than encourage this result. Over the years a climate of opinion has been generated by the AATS and those persuaded of the validity of its position which implies that at best only minimal course work should be carried out in the field because serious, high-level theological studies begin only in the seminary. Since concentrated work in religion has never been assumed by the AATS as an integral element in the undergraduate's seminary preparation, it is natural to read the present statement, in spite of its minimal formulation, as no significant advance toward the elevation of preparatory standards in religion.[2] This impression is strengthened by the conspicuous omission of religion from the list of the "most desirable" fields in which to major.

Critics of the AATS position find several of its assumptions exceedingly disturbing. It appears, for example, that undergraduate work in religion is advanced neither as a primary option by which "a broad and comprehensive college education" may be procured nor as a basis for future theological studies. If the study of religion in some depth was regarded as serving either or both of these purposes, presumably the statement would have placed religion among the most desirable fields for concentration. On the contrary, the statement places religion as an adjunct to a liberal arts program which more fittingly focuses on some other field such as English, philosophy,

[2] Paul Ramsey makes the point that although the statement is couched in minimal terms, it does not emphasize the need which the student has for building a firmer base in religion studies by extending the time needed for acquiring the minimal understanding the AATS finds desirable. The minimal formulation means only that "many other elements in one's college courses" may be taken "while still working in what the Association regards as the first essentials." ["Theological Studies in College and Seminary," *op cit.,* p. 476 n.]

or history. But can it be seriously argued that religion courses are inherently less liberalizing, less productive of knowledge of man's nature, history, or aspiration, less stimulating to the mind, than courses in classics, advanced mathematics, statistics, economic theory, or psychological studies? By what ingenious twist of logic can the serious professor of religion be brought to believe that there is some relatively objective way of determining that courses in nineteenth century French poetry, symbolic logic, Renaissance art, or English history from the Glorious Revolution to the present are inherently liberalizing, whereas courses in world religions, the prophets of Israel, the history of Christian thought, or contemporary trends in theology are by the same indefinite standard mere adornments or even deterrents to a liberalizing educational experience? Experience strongly suggests that no criteria exist for determining the question, yet the AATS statement seems to build on the supposition that they do.

Objections properly can be raised if the assumption behind the recommendation is one which presupposes that college religion courses are as such essentially constrictive, whereas the taking of almost any other combination of courses is inevitably broadening in its effect on the student. Charles L. Taylor, speaking as the executive officer of the AATS, reveals the Achilles' heel of the argument against college education in religion when he writes: "Let me put the real problem in the form of a question. Is the danger greater that future ministers shall suffer an irreparable hiatus in their education because they fail to take courses in religion at the college level or that these men shall *narrow* the field of their studies prematurely and suffer all their life long for lack of thorough exposure to those other studies also requisite for the best education?" [Italics mine. Charles L. Taylor's Correspondence, *Journal of Bible and Religion* (January 1958), pp. 50-51.] This is sheer question begging, of course, since the sting of the question resides in the word *narrow*. Taylor's question presupposes, but does not establish, as it obviously cannot, that religion courses constitute a narrowing of a student's education. The alternative possibility that religion contributes to both breadth and integration of college students' education seems to lie totally outside the range of his attention. Of course, the study of religion should not be conducted on narrow lines, but, as a report of the National Association of Biblical Instructors puts it, "any discipline that fills a genuine and important role in liberal education ought hardly produce an opposite effect by virtue of being studied intensively." [*Journal of Bible and Religion* (April 1958), p. 140.]

Clearly, no objection can properly be raised to the desirability of providing a liberal arts background for future seminary students, but as Ramsey has pointed out, this breadth is to be secured "along with, not instead of, the student's acquiring a foundation of three or four years of study in the subject he intends to pursue in graduate work." [Ramsey, "Theological Studies in College and Seminary," *op. cit.,* p. 469.] Dean Colwell puts the issue in a different light by arguing that the seminary's justifiable desire for a broad, liberal education is vitiated by its naïve confidence in the thoroughness with which majors are prosecuted. He states: "The theological faculty's confidence in the depth contribution of the college major rests on an ignorance of what is actually taught in these majors today in college." ["Closing the Gap Between College and Seminary," *op. cit.,* pp. 107-08.] Others have detected in the AATS recommendations a certain presumption in attempting to tell the colleges themselves what constitutes a liberal arts education and how it should be constructed. Presumably colleges have not been devoid of ideas and plans on this subject in respect to the future professional plans of their students in many fields. However the question of a liberal education be posed, at least it must be insisted that the study of religion, whether as a major or as part of a liberal education at the undergraduate level, is not by definition a narrowing experience in spite of unsupported assumptions to the contrary.

Of course, this issue of the liberalizing contribution which religion makes to the preseminary student is not one to be decided by the use of arguments and counterarguments based primarily on subjective impressions on both sides. A study is needed which would determine generally whether students majoring or taking substantial amounts of work in religion have thereby been prevented from securing that breadth of learning believed to be requisite for seminary studies. Careful examination should be made, for example, of the spread of course work outside the field of religion taken by religion majors, as compared with similar academic spread for majors in other fields. Preliminary, small-scale investigations by the author show that religion majors have had as much or more opportunity for "exposure" to other disciplines than have majors in other fields. A survey being conducted at the College of Wooster has confirmed this provisional impression. "Of the various majors represented in the group studied it appears that only those who majored in religion felt that their major provided a sufficiently broad background in college." There is a strong consensus among the young ministers who were studied "that the notion that a non-religion major automatically means breadth of background is more fictional than tenable." ["Pre-Seminary Preparation and Study in Religion," *Journal of Bible and Religion* (April 1959), p. 142 n.] The sense of breadth reported is probably due to a combination of factors. In some cases the religion major may not call for more than the minimum number of hours allowed by the particular college, thus allowing the student more ample opportunities for electives in other fields. The course materials themselves are of a type which enlarge the students' understanding of both religion and its relationship to other fields, whereas in certain majors, the more advanced courses concentrate upon technicalities which point more directly to professional use in those fields, but which have little connection with the theological studies the student will be taking up in seminary. The common use of "bridge" or "cognate" courses with other departments as part of the religion major has also contributed to the enrichment of perspective which a religion major can provide. In any case, more precise study must be given to the actual effects which various majors have upon the acquisition of a genuinely "liberal" education.

Sometimes it has been argued in defense of the AATS posture that courses in religion are of so poor a quality that the seminaries rightfully discount them on grounds of their contribution both to a liberal education and to preprofessional training. One can readily recognize the validity of this line of reasoning if facts support it. In spite of great improvements made in the quality of religion instruction, probably too many inferior courses are being taught. The distinction between the teaching of religion as a "religious" subject and the teaching of it as an intellectual discipline has not fully won its way. The weight of pietistic, dogmatic, or ecclesiastical influences is still felt. Overburdened small departments, often not so by design of their members, stagger on, attempting to "cover" the field. And there are always poorly prepared professors, sometimes pulled from successful pastoral careers by overenthusiastic, ill-informed administrators. Then there are those who, discouraged by prevailing academic policies or administrative attitudes, have given up all pretense of the use of scholarly disciplines which once they had, and who have settled for a comfortable mediocrity. All this unfortunately must be frankly conceded. At the same time, it should be noticed that the problem of the quality of religion courses is only one aspect of the larger issue of the quality of all courses submitted for admission to theological schools. Students, general or pretheological, should no more be expected to take inferior courses in biology, psychology, or philosophy than in religion. But neither should seminaries accept, almost casually as the Niebuhr report points out they do, courses in fields such as these while acting with suspicion or negligence toward the entering student's work in religion. Furthermore, disparaging estimates of the quality of undergraduate religion courses are seldom put in proper relation to poor seminary education. After all, as Dean Colwell has put it, "in our good colleges the faculty in religion has the same education as the faculty in theology, has studied in the same universities, received the same degrees, and in more than one instance, is superior in individual quality." Nor need the religion faculty "fear the most exact comparison with other departments in the colleges." ["Closing the Gap Between College and Seminary," *op. cit.*][3] Thus when comparisons of quality of work are made between seminaries and colleges, let the balance be held equally between those at the same stage of development. Poor college work is no more to be compared to work in our best seminaries than are the poorest seminaries with their small staffs and their inadequate libraries and facilities to be compared with our best departments of religion in colleges and universities. The appli-

---

[3] As long ago as 1936 a study of religion courses in American colleges and universities reported that "teachers of religion have a scholastic training equal to that of the teachers in the other college departments. And their scholastic status is improving. . . . Teachers of religion are no longer merely pulpit orators and successful ministers; they are scholars in their own fields." [Gould Wickey and R. A. Eckhart, "A National Survey of Courses in Bible and Religion in American Universities and Colleges," 1936, p. 17; reprint from *Christian Education* (October 1936).] The trend detected in this survey has certainly not been reversed in more recent years, but the seminaries seem to have lagged in their appreciation of its implications for preseminary studies.

cation of a double standard of quality is certainly not calculated to beget confidence.

The problem of the religion major itself has been discussed from the standpoint of its contribution to the vocational training of the future clergyman or teacher of religion. In this connection the omission of religion from the "most desirable" fields of concentration raises additional doubts about the principles which apparently govern the minds of those responsible for the statement. The basic assumption in this case is that concentration in religion is regarded as undesirable because only in seminary can serious theological study be undertaken. The normal three-year seminary course presumably will provide sufficient theological preparation.

The cogency of these ideas is vulnerable, and their effect may be highly misleading. So far as facts are discernible in this murky area they seem to support positions which are the exact opposite of this assumption. Considerable experience has shown that undergraduate study in religion not only can but has provided innumerable entering seminary students with the rudiments of biblical, historical, theological, and philosophical studies as bases upon which more advanced work has been done. The acquiring of knowledge of terms, problems, theological perspectives, biblical content, etc. is not an esoteric or difficult achievement beyond the capacities of undergraduates. Yet students who are expected to be sufficiently mature to have grasped the essentials of art, history, foreign languages, psychology, philosophy, or English strangely enough are supposed to appear at the seminary's gate lacking any but the most superficial acquaintance with the field of religion! While other students in the college have been attacking in some depth the fields which lead to their life's work, future theological students are apparently to be encouraged to adorn their nonreligion majors with bits and scraps from the field of religion wherever it is offered.

While his advancement in intellectual comprehension, skill in oral and written expression, and knowledge of other fields is presumably going on, the future theological student is encouraged to stand still in his intellectual development in religion, unprepared not only for advanced studies, but equally unprepared for the unsettling intellectual give and take of the university campus, in the classroom and out. Furthermore, it would be a disservice if he were directed away from the intensive studies in religion when by them he would have the opportunity of understanding religion not in its professional context, but as part of the total educative process. The college study of religion affords the student, perhaps for the last time in his educational career, the chance to participate in the interplay of religion as an academic subject with secular subjects and viewpoints. The bifurcation of the "sacred" and "secular" has too often removed the study of religion to the graduate or professional school and thereby strengthened the popular opinion that these two "branches" have no point of intersection. The seminary alone is incapable of removing this idea of dichotomy from the academic or popular mentality, but it can encourage its future students to explore as fully as possible ways to eliminate the idea of separation. In the college the student may be helped to see that the area in which he will do his professional work is no sheltered, cloistered affair, but a definite domain of inquiry in constant dialogue with the intellectual viewpoints of a culture which all too readily permits religion the dignity of a place among graduate and professional studies, but by the same device consigns it to irrelevance in the academic world at large. Without the systematic study of religion, the undergraduate is prevented from entering into this dialogue with the same degree of intellectual sophistication which his fellow students possess in their fields. Into that encounter, so vital to his own development, certainly he should not be asked to enter without the knowledge and techniques available in our best undergraduate departments of religion.

The central justification of the work which the future clergyman will undertake lies in the broad area of theology. In this area he will make his contribution, and from it he will draw his inspiration and insight. He prepares for a life vocation in which knowledge of and about God—his operation in history, in the personal lives of men, and in social structures—is the foundation. As a clergyman, he need not compete with experts in literature, economics, physics, or psychology; he justifies himself in his chosen vocation by having something worth saying and doing because the nature of God and man are what his reasoned belief has found them to be.

If this is the rationale for the minister's work, and no serious alternative appears possible, then the pretheological student should begin his preparation for theology in the college. It seems a dereliction of religious and academic responsibility to counsel such students to wait until seminary to begin a sustained and systematic attack upon the theological field broadly conceived, on the highly misleading assumption that three or four years of study allow him to begin to settle the issues raised there.

The case might be otherwise if seminaries did actually give full time to theological subjects, but seldom is this the case. Instead, the theological student finds his curriculum a mixture of theological studies, practical courses in pastoralia, and "new" ancillary courses which Ramsey calls the "God and . . ." type. Psychology, politics, literature, drama, sociology, group dynamics, biography, juvenile delinquency, storytelling, hymnology, art, etc. are now to be brought into relation with what too often is a nonexistent theological core of study. Outside the classroom the student's life is weighted down with "fieldwork," partly on professional and educational grounds and usually for financial reasons. Consequently, if the recommendation on religion offered by the AATS were taken seriously by a pretheological student, he might well find that there would be no period in his career, in college or seminary, for full-time prosecution of theological studies. Precisely because this danger is not purely hypothetical, the professor of religion may be excused for discounting remarks in the AATS statement which suggest that it be treated as merely "informational," "suggestive," and "not binding," since, as an authoritative statement by a reputable academic body, it in fact does encourage a de-emphasis upon preseminary preparation in religion. Its assumptions concerning the limited validity of intensive undergraduate study in religion and the opportunities for concentrated graduate theological study appear to be wildly divorced from the facts and the needs of theological education at both levels.

Confidence in the realism of the framers of the AATS is not markedly heightened when it is implied that "a thorough knowledge of the content of the Bible, together with an introduction to the major religious traditions and theological problems in the context of the principal aspects of human culture" may be achieved in three semesters. Although the qualifying phrase *at least* is placed before *three semesters,* false hopes are nevertheless engendered in the unwary undergraduate by the correlation of three semesters with the possibility of acquiring this enormous quantity of intellectual freight. Realistically viewed, double the proposed number of credit hours would probably be required to approach the pitch of thoroughness which the statement contemplates. And considering the breadth and diversity of the disciplines within the field, as well as their relation to the "context" of human culture, the number of hours would rise to the level of a full major. No respectable department of religion would or could pretend to undertake responsibility for developing in students the level of understanding which the recommendation suggests is possible in "at least three semesters."

Furthermore, although the student may have had considerable course work in religion, seminaries often fail to take cogni-
zance of the student's understanding of the field upon his entry
into divinity school. As Ramsey complains: "The fact is that he
is exposed to additional general courses in Bible, and courses
introductory to the major religious traditions and to theological
problems in their cultural context all over again. . . . The
statement that he may already have made a beginning serves
often only as an ideological formulation having no relation to
the realities of seminary education." ["Theological Study in
College and Seminary," *op. cit.,* p. 476.] Exceptions to this
observation occur, as we shall see, but its validity originates in
the not uncommon experience of those who have been bored
and vexed by the repetition of undergraduate courses in seminaries.

When it has been suggested that concentration in religion be
made a prerequisite to seminary education, or that it at least be
placed among the "most desirable" fields for a major, the customary answer has been that many candidates come to the seminary from technical schools or state universities where the study
of religion is not offered. Thus a statement made by the
National Association of Biblical Instructors (NABI) points
out that "the American college students who are enabled to
select courses identified as 'religion' comprise a minority,"
though the empirical grounds for this judgment might be further studied. [*Journal of Bible and Religion* (April 1959), p.
141.] This observation is sometimes regarded as a sufficient
basis for closing off further debate on the subject. After all, the
"call" to the ministry comes where it will, and man-made
restrictions should not hamper its summons lest a potential supply of future clergy be cut off at its source. Here again we find
the vocational and graduate purposes of the seminaries in ten-

sion with each other and reflecting that tension into undergraduate departments of religion.

Seminaries generally seem often to have lacked the will to commit themselves to any firm standards of achievement in religion or in other fields beyond that of a college degree. If preoccupation with the diversity of sources from which students come, rather than a due regard for their own integrity as educational institutions, is permitted to dictate academic policy, the theological schools will be seriously weakened in their efforts to become genuine graduate institutions. Surely deficiencies in academic preparation cannot be used as a guide to an admissions program without a noticeable dilution of both the graduate and professional functions of these institutions.

Certain clear alternatives to much of present practice and planning already exist. The standard of admission to theological education should be a major or high degree of concentration in the field of religion. Those without this preparation should be treated as exceptions who must make up deficiencies, either by taking courses in adjacent undergraduate departments of religion, intensive reading courses followed by qualifying examinations, or, as seems most likely, the taking of seminary noncredit, introductory courses designed for this purpose rather than as components of graduate education. Similar practices could be carried out in respect to deficiencies in English, philosophy, history, psychology, and sociology. Adoption of policies of this kind may prove to be cumbersome or even discouraging to prospective students, but the need for a more effective way of dealing with deficiencies has long been overdue. Furthermore such policies might put an end to the common practice of treating entering students as a "class" which must move as a single unit through theological education rather than as individuals with varying degrees of preparation. There need be no cutting off of candidates from technical and state schools on this basis. They, compared with those from liberal arts colleges with serious background work in religion, must expect to extend their period of seminary training. By the same logic, the better-trained student could shorten his seminary course or further enrich his training by taking advanced studies if wider use were made of advanced placement tests and more careful consideration were given to his preseminary studies in religion.

The benefits of an undergraduate religion major to graduate religion study become even more obvious in respect to the preparation of those who hope to become professors of religion, a group whose needs are not taken into account by the AATS recommendations. Accordingly, recommendations which may serve the purposes of preministerial training are not necessarily to be taken with the same seriousness when applied to those who aspire to an academic career. Because the college student interested in becoming a professor of religion needs the amplest possible training in the field, the reasons for his concentration in the field at the undergraduate level are more persuasive than for the embryonic minister. Presumably, the aspiring religion professor has "taken fire" intellectually because some course or professor has revealed to him the advantages and rewards of a life of scholarship and teaching in some segment of theological studies. He should accordingly be spurred on to work intensively in religion in college, while also achieving mastery of languages and other fields, and to anticipate with enthusiasm his entry into graduate work at the seminary or graduate school. If he should be persuaded by the AATS statement, however, to decline major work in religion, or if he finds in seminary that his studies are scarcely more advanced than those of his college years, his impetus will be seriously checked. Like the student preparing for the ministry, he may find that others have prepared themselves for graduate work and gone on into advanced studies while he has marked time.

Unquestionably the position of the AATS has had a wide influence. College students who have become acquainted with it have laid out their courses in its light. Pastors, seminary officials, and some college professors have been guided by it in counseling students. This influence understandably has been directed to the aim of securing to the seminaries the best-trained student body, a goal which cannot be challenged. The preceding critical discussion of the AATS position is therefore based not upon opposition to its ultimate purpose, but rather upon a recognition that a sharp difference of opinion exists as to how this aim is to be achieved insofar as undergraduate religion instruction is properly a part of the student's preparation.

The problem which remains is that of the effect which the AATS proposals may have upon the welfare of undergraduate departments themselves. Some professors of religion have felt that these recommendations have weakened their positions and that of their departments in the eyes of the academic community at large. The proposals seem to have taken for granted that departments will continue to flourish, that course offerings will continue to improve, that pretheological students will take some work in the field, that the general student will be attracted to the study of religion, that administrations will provide budgets for these departments, that faculty colleagues will respect the study of religion as a contribution to humane learning, and that professors of religion will maintain high morale in teaching and scholarship—all in the face of statements by an authoritative professional body which in fact, though not by intent, de-emphasize undergraduate study of religion. Since the concentrated study of religion is not even mentioned in these statements as one of the possible avenues to a liberal education and is shunted aside as a relatively secondary part of the preparation for graduate theological studies, what grounds remain for supposing that the field itself will be accorded a significant place in higher education? What rationale can then be offered for its existence except that of a "service" department of the college? Acquiescence to this status leads only to small, inferior departments bound to an interminable round of introductory and terminal courses. The encouragement which faculty members normally receive from teaching advanced courses is denied, and the motivation for research in one's specialization is dampened.

Under these conditions religion would be regarded as an exception among the basic fields of learning, as a field having a kind of adornment value which in the eyes of the university community did not warrant the offering of specialized courses or the employment of a scholarly faculty. It may be argued that these dire consequences are purely imaginary, and that there are religion departments which offer no major yet engage the services of a scholarly faculty. But it must be pointed out that these arrangements are themselves indications of a surrender to a way of thinking which denies to religion a fullfledged place in the university. Unfortunately there already exists a readiness on the part of some who speak for the place of religion in the university to settle for any niche within the academic structure. And it is not uncommon for college authorities to welcome religion departments which will limit themselves to a small faculty and a few courses. But neither is it uncommon for those working in such departments to find themselves working under handicaps not usually found in other departments of the college.

The issue is not solely that of whether major work in religion should be offered both for pretheological students and for students in general. Decision on this point must be made on the local scene and fortunately is not one upon which the position of the AATS need bear unduly, since many students who take a major in religion do so with no thought of continuing these studies in a seminary or graduate school. They accept the religion major as one of the alternatives by which to receive a liberal arts education. Offering a major is justified on this ground alone.[4] What further is at stake is whether strong academic work in religion can be encouraged as a part of humanistic education when an influential body representing and in large measure controlling graduate theological education publicly sets forth positions which move in the direction of depressing the importance of undergraduate religion studies rather than encouraging it. Fears on this score have not been idle. More than once the college professor has found his efforts to develop his field overshadowed and hampered by administrative opinions in part drawn from the AATS position which has proved a handy instrument for denying to religion its authentic place among other strong departments within the humanities. When this happens, unquestionably the influence of the seminary upon the place of religion in the college or university has proved to be unfortunate. It is highly unlikely under these circumstances that religion can make its best contribution to liberal education, to say nothing of its potential services to pretheological training.

Although the relation of seminaries and graduate schools to undergraduate departments has been marked by tensions, there

---

[4] The impression that the religion major has been developed solely for the benefit of pretheological students should be sharply qualified by the fact that a considerable number of students who have taken religion majors enter other fields of graduate study and vocations not directly related to their college major. I know of students who have entered nursing, public school teaching, social work, medicine, international relations, law, journalism, the teaching of literature, philosophy, history, anthropology, and sociology.

223

are also brighter aspects of the situation. At present a study to investigate the nature of pretheological studies is being carried on jointly by the NABI and the AATS with the assistance of a grant from the Lilly Foundation. This study marks a turn toward a more mature and realistic evaluation of the relation between the college and the graduate institutions. Although its primary interest will focus upon the needs of the church, its findings may also assist in clarifying the position of religion among the humanities.

Other concrete evidences of a lessening of tensions are to be found. There has been an increasing sense on the part of college instructors of their professional responsibilities toward the larger academic community and the seminaries. They have realized their own failures as teachers and scholars and have recognized that they have sometimes adopted an excessively defensive attitude in respect to the seminaries. Another heartening evidence of an improved situation is the fact that certain seminaries and graduate schools now give credit for work in religion done at the undergraduate level.

Colgate-Rochester Divinity School places students with adequate preparation in advanced courses in Bible. Drew Theological Seminary permits exemption from its introductory biblical courses on the basis of undergraduate work. An interesting testimonial to the quality of undergraduate preparation in religion is found in the fact that the class entering in 1960 had 50.5 per cent exempted from both Old and New Testament introductory courses. In addition, 2.5 per cent were exempted from the Old Testament course and 9.5 per cent from the New Testament course. Only 37.5 per cent were required to take both introductory courses. ["Theological Study in College and Seminary," *op. cit.*, p. 481.] Boston University's Divinity School encourages students with strong records in Bible and philosophy of religion to seek enrollment in advanced courses. Union Theological Seminary has used qualifying examinations in both Bible and philosophy of religion. Vanderbilt's School of Theology makes allowance for proficiency in religion as a prerequisite for the M.A. and Ph.D. degrees. Yale accepts students for graduate work who have not completed the B.D. degree but who show high-quality credentials.

Among the graduate schools not affiliated with seminaries, a similar practice has developed. Admission to the new program in graduate study in religious thought at the University of Pennsylvania does not require a religion major, "though the student with insufficient preparation will need to extend his period of graduate study proportionately." The brochure on graduate work in religion at Princeton University states: "Ideally the college senior who contemplates entering our program should have majored in a department of religion with courses equivalent to those offered in the undergraduate department at Princeton. . . . A student who has not concentrated in religion as an undergraduate and who wishes to enter directly after the completion of his college degree will normally be required to spend his first year as a 'qualifying student.' " Dean Ernest C. Colwell states: "We who teach at the seminaries should, so we believe at the Southern California School of Theology, encourage students either to take courses in religion throughout college, or to major in religion in college." [*Journal of Bible and Religion*, XXVI, 2, 108.] Students are excused from elementary courses at this institution on the basis of an interview in which the undergraduate work is evaluated. It is hoped that more seminaries and graduate schools will follow methods similar to these. With advanced placement having become a commonplace of American education even in graduate schools, it would seem that seminaries and graduate schools of religion can no longer fail to take advantage of the preparation provided by college departments of religion.

Another sign which promises to be of advantage to religion as a humanistic field is the relatively recent development of graduate divisions dedicated to the preparation of scholars and teachers of religion. In these graduate divisions, attention is focused on the field of religion itself and is not diverted into the channels of professional training of clergymen, as is usually the case where the first steps in graduate work are taken in the seminary. The establishment of these divisions is based on the conviction that it is not enough to locate seminaries near universities as the centers of our intellectual life, valuable as this may be. [Charles L. Taylor, "Seminaries and Universities in Partnership," *Princeton Seminary Bulletin,* LIV, 1 (1960), 14.] Graduate education in religion must be in the university itself. Nor is it sufficient to think that private universities alone should develop graduate programs in religion. Fully as important for the development of the field as a genuine humanistic domain is the establishment of these programs in state universities where they would complement the undergraduate religion studies and assist in placing them in the proper perspectives as humanistic studies freed of ecclesiastical entanglement.[5] Beginnings in these directions are small compared with the much larger number of graduate programs which fall under the supervision of the seminaries, but the signs are encouraging.

Of course there are problems in establishing these programs: overcoming the impression that theological and religion studies properly belong to the province of church-related schools; dispelling the reluctance of those who fear indoctrination; securing high-caliber students and capable staff so that specialized courses may be given at the level on which the better seminaries

[5] See the supporting comments of Robert Michaelson, *Journal of Higher Education,* XXX, 4, 220; and Hubert C. Noble, *Religious Education,* LIV, 2, 140.

now offer them; and, not least of all, the provision of financial support. Considering the recognized shortage of competent seminary faculty, the problem of staffing may be as important as any other; however, competition for faculty may present somewhat less difficulty than first appears. In spite of the prestige which is associated with seminary professorships, salaries offered in these institutions sometimes do not compare favorably even with those of undergraduate institutions. It is possible that salaries of graduate divisions, when they are firmly established within university budgets, may prove more attractive than salaries offered by seminaries, which depend for the most part on relatively small endowments and denominational contributions.[6] Even seminaries associated with universities are not in a markedly advantageous position in comparison with other graduate divisions of the university or, in some cases, with undergraduate departments of religion.[7]

This fact may well give pause to any extravagant ideas that graduate divisions will soon take over the education of professors and scholars in religion, but the advantages of these programs seem undeniable. They will establish religion in the midst of the university structure. They offer opportunity for the employment of a faculty along nonsectarian lines, a feature

[6] A comparative study of salaries in seminaries independent of universities, seminaries associated with universities, and undergraduate departments of religion would be highly instructive.

[7] One aspect of this situation is evident in the Yale Divinity School. President A. W. Griswold has reported the following comparative figures. Between the years 1900 and 1955, monies budgeted for the Medical School rose from $24,000 to $3,179,000; for the Law School, from $32,000 to $747,000; for the Divinity School, which lost its initial financial advantage, from $52,000 to $589,000. [*In the University Tradition* (Yale, 1957), p. 138.] I know of two major seminaries at which salaries for full professors fall below those offered in the religion departments of some colleges.

which some seminaries lack. They enable the prospective candidate to enter directly and speedily into graduate studies.[8] They are able to provide an atmosphere for study and intellectual confrontation similar to that which may be found on the campuses where their graduates will eventually teach. And the university setting may prove to be more exciting and attractive to faculty members than that of the seminary. Whether all these possibilities are converted into realities remains to be seen. A slow shift in the direction of graduate divisions is occurring and it may be anticipated that this shift will be of benefit to the development of the field of religion among the humanities.

[8] Professor Waldo Beach underscores the problem of the length of time spent in graduate work by the religion Ph.D. "If one assumes a three-year minimum for the B.D. and three more for the Ph.D., the college senior who is interested in teaching religion faces the prospect of a minimum of six further years of preparation—a prospect which, however exhilarating scholastically, is economically and psychologically depressing, especially when his fellow graduate students . . . are enabled to move directly into a graduate program from the B.A. . . ." Dr. Beach concedes, however, that at Duke competition for places in the graduate program favors the mature seminary student over the undergraduate senior with a major in religion although both may have high academic records. In this case at least, the college senior is virtually forced into a seminary course of study or to seek admission at one of the graduate religion divisions of another university. [Waldo Beach, "Graduate Study in Religion at Duke University," *Journal of Bible and Religion,* XXXI, 1 (January 1963), 39.]

❧ V ❧

SCHOLARSHIP IN RELIGION

❧ 12 ❧

TYPES AND EVIDENCES OF SCHOLARSHIP

The common impression prevails that the undergraduate professor of religion contributes little to the realm of scholarship.
Certainly there are features of his situation and his reaction to
them which would seem to support this impression. He is
widely regarded as a teacher, a role too easily substituted for that
of a scholar. When additional duties, such as those of college
chaplain or advisor to religious groups, are tacked on to his instructional responsibilities the possibilities for scholarship are
indeed remote. He may find himself in a small department,
lacking secretarial assistance, operating with inadequate library
facilities, and seldom given the stimulation of working with
graduate students. In these not uncommon circumstances he
comes to feel that he is out of touch with what he regards as the
mainstreams of thought in his discipline. In a nostalgic mood he
looks back longingly and enviously to the seminary or graduate
school where he is convinced the truly exciting scholarly work
is being done. He realizes, with some justification, that he is not
advantageously placed for securing grants which would enable
him to re-establish contacts with the world of scholarship he
once knew. He finds, or believes he finds, that as a college professor of religion it is more difficult to get a book published
than for his seminary counterpart, who may even be the judge
of his manuscript for a publishing house. He may sense that the
administrators who have authority over his professional advancement have not the slightest glimmer of understanding of what
constitutes a scholarly production in religion. In this mixture
of fact and fancy, there is much to discourage the college pro-

231

fessor from getting on with scholarship; he may be tempted to renounce his responsibility for scholarship, while comforting himself with the thought that his is a teaching function.

There are, however, other factors which may shape his ideas in a more active scholarly direction. He may recognize that being a teacher is never enough, since the wells of insight and information soon run dry without active participation in some phase of scholarship. He notes that some of his colleagues are busy with scholarship in their respective disciplines. As he looks about, he recognizes that active scholarship in religion is carried on by men who are identified neither with departments of religion nor with seminaries.[1] He also discovers that a sizeable number of scholars who now teach and publish in seminaries or graduate schools have been drawn from undergraduate departments of religion where they first won their spurs as scholars. And there are others who hold respected positions in religion scholarship whose scholarly productivity has not been confined to those periods of their lives when they were identified with seminaries or graduate schools.[2]

[1] In support of this statement, the following list may be accepted as typical but not exhaustive: Roy Wesley Battenhouse, Peter A. Bertocci, Edwin A. Burtt, Maurice S. Friedmann, Horace L. Friess, Roland M. Frye, A. C. Garnett, R. C. Good, T. M. Greene, John H. Hallowell, E. H. Harbison, Hans Jonas, Douglas M. Knight, William Haller, S. R. Hopper, Walter Kaufmann, Rollo May, Richard Schlatter, H. W. Schneider, W. T. Stace, T. S. K. Scott-Craig, Marcus G. Singer, S. E. Stumpf, John Wild, Harry A. Wolfson, Milton Yinger.
[2] In support of these statements the following list of names, from a much longer one, is offered: W. F. Albright, Bernhard W. Anderson, Philip H. Ashby, E. E. Aubrey, Dwight M. Beck, Fred Berthold, R. R. Bonthius, Robert W. Bretall, Edmond La B. Cherbonnier, William A. Christian, W. G. Cole, Virginia Corwin, Horton Davies, Fred J. Denbeaux, Paul J. R. Desjardins, Malcolm L. Diamond, John Dillenberger, R. A. Eckhart, J. D. Eusden, Erwin R. Goodenough, Hans Frei, Paul M. Harrison, M. H. Hartshorne, Roger Hazelton, C. A. Holbrook, John A. Hutchison, A. Leland Jamison, Gordon D. Kaufman, C. W. Kegley,

His nostalgia for the seminary environment may abate in the face of these encouraging prospects for scholarship. As he sees the need and possibility for a scholarship which arises within the college or university context proper, he may also come to a new appreciation for the intellectual breadth available there. Perhaps he has overestimated the time and opportunities available for scholarship in the theological school, for he, after all, experienced the seminary as a student, not as a faculty member whose life was quite as much subject to distractions as now he feels his own is.

He may further observe that the stream of intellectual leadership he attributed to the seminary or graduate school does not only run in one direction, downward to the colleges. Conspicuous leadership in biblical, historical, and theological scholarship has ordinarily been found in the better seminary faculties, but certain issues which later were to find expressions or responses in the seminaries were first met and formulated at the college level. Among the most obvious of these have been the impact of philosophical analysis on philosophy of religion and theological issues; the exploration of the relations between religion and literature, art, music, and drama; as well as the problems arising out of the relations among the social sciences, religious convictions, and norms of truth. The onset of interest in existentialism took place in literature, philosophy, and religion departments at least contemporaneously with its influence in the seminaries, and the present discussions on the ethics of atomic warfare have been as diligently prosecuted in the university setting as in sem-

Thomas S. Kepler, Cornelius Loew, E. L. Long, Jr., Vernon S. McCasland, A. C. McGill, J. A. Martin, Robert Michaelson, Alexander Miller, Kenneth Morgan, A. W. Munck, A. S. Nash, R. R. Niebuhr, P. E. Pfuetze, C. E. Purinton, Paul Ramsey, R. B. Y. Scott, Roger L. Shinn, Huston Smith, Edmund D. Soper, William A. Spurrier, G. F. Thomas, J. C. Trever, Joachim Wach, Claude Welch, Rolland E. Wolfe, Frederic H. Young.

inaries. Accordingly, the college professor of religion need not feel that he has cast his lines in barren places where scholarship is totally stultified. He may and should reconstruct his notion of his role as a scholar, and take new heart in the venture of scholarship.

Admittedly, scholarship for the average college religion professor is the result of a hard-fought battle for time and facilities. His published works may less often attract the favorable attention of scholars who set the trends or of college administrators who preside over his academic fortunes. Nevertheless, opportunities exist for carrying out scholarly work, and there is some evidence to suggest that the undergraduate professor has not been altogether idle in taking advantage of them.

How then is the situation in religion scholarship to be described? Assessment of religion scholarship must take into account several ways of approaching this subject. In the narrower and more familiar sense the term *scholarship* refers to substantial works published in learned journals, monographs, and books. The enormous quantity of this material as well as its variety of subject matter warns the interpreter of the dangers of a too simple analysis of its nature and value. But in a broader sense scholarship includes formal oral presentations of materials which may never come to print. Therefore a fair estimation of scholarship cannot be based solely upon published results. Then there is that form of scholarship which never reaches either the formal oral or written stages but which presumably makes its influence felt in the classroom; the results of this type of scholarship, however, are impossible either to discover or to evaluate with any certainty. In addition, to understand more fully the conditions of scholarship in religion it is imperative to take account of those indications of scholarly activity which themselves do not constitue scholarship but which encourage and express it It is necessary to make note of the existence of professional so-

234

cieties and learned journals and to estimate the amount of scholarly contribution made to them.

The existence of professional societies is usually regarded as evidence of scholarly activity. In the field of religion there are several which may be mentioned as typical. Two of the largest of these groups are the Society for Biblical Literature (SBL) and the National Association of Biblical Instructors. The first and older of these has flourished since 1881 and now has about 2,158 members. It is composed mainly of those active in the study of biblical languages and thought and draws its membership primarily from seminary and graduate faculties, although a fair proportion of its constituency also comes from the ranks of undergraduate professors. No distinctions for membership are drawn on the basis of religious affiliation. The society holds regular annual meetings at the national as well as the regional levels. Its journal usually contains technical articles on various phases of biblical studies. The National Association of Biblical Instructors, now slightly over fifty years old, has about 1,416 members, some of whom also hold membership in the SBL. The majority of NABI members is drawn from undergraduate religion and philosophy departments and a number come from seminary and graduate schools. It is the only nationwide society which deals with all disciplines within the field of religion. Its regional divisions hold regular meetings, as does the national body. Its *Journal of Bible and Religion* includes a wide range of articles dealing both with pedagogical problems and with technical matters.

Other, smaller professional groups support scholarly activities in various aspects of the field of religion. Typical of these are the American Church History Society, the American Textual Criticism Society, the National Association of Professors of Hebrew, the American Society for Oriental Research, the American Theological Society, and the American Society for Christian Social Ethics. Scholarly competence and interest in the particular segment of the field which the society serves, not religious affiliation, determine qualification of membership.

Certain groups exist whose purposes include encouragement of religion scholarship. Among these are the Christian Faculty Fellowship, the Society for Religion in Higher Education, the Catholic Commission on Intellectual and Cultural Affairs, the Jewish Academy of Arts and Sciences, and the American Academy for Jewish Research. Among the foundations which in various ways have assisted scholarship are the Alexander Kohut Memorial, Danforth, Lilly, Rockefeller, Seatlantic, Ford, and the Frank L. Weil Institute.

The most recent signs of increased scholarly vitality among professional societies may be seen in the establishment of the Society for the History of Religions—the initial impetus for which came from the American Council of Learned Societies—and the establishment of the Society for the Scientific Study of Religion. Each of these new groups has begun publication of its own journal.

It has been observed that not all which counts as scholarship achieves printed form, and some evidences of scholarly activity may be drawn from a brief analysis of the oral presentations made to the programs of learned societies. To be sure, similar contributions are made to groups of a restricted membership, such as those made before the Week of Work of the Society for Religion in Higher Education or before the meetings of the American Theological Society, but these are little known outside the groups themselves. The annual programs of the SBL and of the NABI yield more definite results. Contributions to the annual national programs of these two societies indicate that scholarly activity is undertaken by faculty members at all levels of the academic world and that contributions are also made by persons outside the colleges, universities, and seminaries. A survey of the programs of the SBL for the past seven years provides the following information. Out of 351 presentations to these programs, undergraduate and graduate religion professors (i.e., nonseminary faculty) contributed 121 presentations, the large majority of these by undergraduate faculty members. Of the remaining 230 program items, about 35 were made by persons not identified with college, university, or seminary. The remaining 195 contributions were by seminary faculty members.

The annual programs of the NABI include some contributions which cannot be regarded as scholarship, even on the loosest possible construction of that term. Among the contributions, however, there are many substantial items. A sampling of the programs of this association, as made available in its journal, reveals that for five annual programs there were about 62 presentations.[3] Of these presentations, 38 were made by members of undergraduate or graduate religion faculties, the undergraduate faculty predominating; 12 were by seminary faculty and 11 by those falling into neither classification.

This account does not take into consideration the quality of the contributions themselves, nor has any attempt been made to analyze the regional meetings of these societies. Study of the programs of other societies would probably show differing proportions of contributions in the three categories used above. It would be expected, for instance, that higher proportions of contributions from seminary and graduate faculties would be found in the programs of the American Society for Oriental Research or the Church History Society than from undergraduate faculties. It should especially be noted that scholarly contributions in

[3] Each of the members of a panel program was considered as a contributor for the purposes of this survey. A more detailed study of program participation, with more rigid distinctions drawn between scholarly and nonscholarly offerings, could be carried out.

these groups often come from persons who are engaged in studies in such fields as archaeology, ancient history, classics, and languages of the East.

The existence of journals in the field of religion may also be regarded as a sign of scholarly activity. Two types of journals may be distinguished: those given over mainly to scholarly articles in some area within the field, and those which, although not regarded as scholarly journals, do publish with some regularity articles of a scholarly character. Examples of these two types may be found below.[4] There are also journals whose purposes are not identified with religious matters, but which frequently publish scholarly articles bearing on religion. The number and variety of these journals is extensive. Representative titles are given below.[5]

A spot check of several journals of the last-named type indicates that undergraduate professors of religion and seminary faculty seldom contribute to them. Much of the scholarship which can be rightly identified as religion scholarship in these journals is the product of undergraduate and graduate professors working outside the field of religion proper. For example,

---

[4] Scholarly journals: *American Academy for Jewish Research Proceedings, American Jewish Archives, American Ecclesiastical Review, Benedictine Review, Catholic Biblical Quarterly, Church History, Harvard Theological Review, Historia Judaica, History of Religions, Jewish Quarterly Review, Journal of Biblical Literature and Exegesis, Journal of Bible and Religion, Journal of Jewish Studies, Journal of Religion, Journal of the Scientific Study of Religion, Review of Religion, Theological Studies,* and *Worship.* Religious journals which publish scholarly articles: *Christian Scholar, Interpretation, Jubilee, Religion in Life,* and *Theology Today.*

[5] *American Journal of Archaeology, Antioch Review, Catholic Historical Review, Jewish Social Studies, Journal of the American Oriental Society, Journal of Cuneiform Studies, Journal of the History of Ideas, Journal of Near Eastern Studies, Journal of Philosophy, New England Quarterly, Personalist, Philosophy, East and West, Philosophical Review, Speculum,* and *Thought.*

from 1951 to 1960, the *Journal of the History of Ideas* contained only one article by a Roman Catholic seminary professor and another which might possibly have come from a Protestant clergyman. During the same period many articles bearing on religious subjects were published from the pens of men working in philosophy, history, or literature. A survey of the major articles bearing on religion in the *Journal of Philosophy* and the *Philosophical Review* shows the same pattern; the scholarship is contributed almost entirely by professors of philosophy, as might be expected.

A random sampling of the sources of scholarly publications in some of the journals ordinarily considered to be the principal outlets for religion scholarship in America yields similarly interesting results.[6] *Church History* for the years 1954-55 and 1957-60 contained 118 major articles: 2 were contributed by college professors of religion, 34 by seminary professors, 1 by a graduate professor, and 64 by faculty members in other disciplines; 13 were contributed by "others." The *Harvard Theological Review* for the years 1952-53 and 1956-57 contained 56 major articles: 3 were contributed by college professors of religion, 10 by seminary professors, 6 by graduate professors, 18 by faculty members in other disciplines, and 19 by "others." The *Journal of Biblical Literature* for the years 1956 and 1958-60 contained 97 major articles: 15 were contributed by college professors of religion, 47 by seminary professors, 5 by graduate professors, 1 by a faculty member in another discipline, and 28

---

[6] No attempt has been made to survey all the journals of this type, nor have rejection rates been considered. Distinctions made between undergraduate, seminary, and graduate professors of religion are not rigid. Whenever it has been possible to identify the author by his status, I have done so, but there are probably some authors in the graduate category who have been placed in the seminary category. Foreign scholars, graduate students, clergymen, and unidentified contributors were placed in the miscellaneous category "others."

by "others." This journal is given over to biblical studies, and it appears that professors in fields other than religion seldom publish in its pages. The *Journal of Religion* for the years 1952-57 contained 101 major articles: 15 were contributed by college professors of religion, 37 by seminary professors, 4 by graduate professors, 33 by faculty members in other disciplines, and 15 by "others." In recent years in twenty issues of The *Review of Religion,* each containing about three major articles, only one seminary faculty member and one college professor of religion contributed one article apiece. The first copies of *History of Religion* contain a number of articles by foreign authors, a fact which may indicate a desire on the part of the editors to make the journal a truly international one, as its subtitle suggests, or which may imply that American scholarship in the history of religions has lagged behind that abroad. The *Journal for the Scientific Study of Religion* in its first issue contains articles by members of seminary, graduate, and undergraduate faculties of religion with a substantial number by members of sociology and psychology departments.

The impressions which this brief and by no means exhaustive survey leaves are these. College professors of religion and seminary faculty members are not publishing scholarly articles at the same rate as do those from other fields who are interested in the field of religion. One might be tempted to decide that religion scholarship is being carried on primarily by those outside the field. With the exception of the area of biblical studies, college religion faculty members are not contributing as much to scholarship as might be expected. However, when compared with the output of seminary faculties, their showing is respectable; compared with that of scholars outside the field, the showing is far from impressive. In biblical studies their record is not bad. Only in biblical studies do seminary faculty seem to be publishing scholarship at the rate one might expect. It should be noticed, however, that some scholarly productivity by American professors of religion at all levels, but especially at the seminary level, is published abroad. The *Hibbert Journal,* the *Journal of Semitic Studies, New Testament Studies, Novum Testamentum,* and other foreign journals often contain major contributions from scholars on this side of the Atlantic. And in some cases the scholarly output of seminary faculties finds its way into the journals published by the seminaries themselves.

A survey of these journals and those under Roman Catholic and Jewish sponsorship reveals another dimension of the problem of scholarship as reflected in learned journals. A few contributors from the ranks of Roman Catholic and Jewish scholarship are found in the survey above. These contributions are usually in biblical, linguistic, and historical areas. Jewish scholars apparently are somewhat more ready to publish in non-Jewish journals than are Roman Catholic scholars to publish in non-Roman Catholic journals. In the main, however, Protestant scholars or those not identified with any religious body do not publish in journals identified with Roman Catholic or Jewish scholarship, and Roman Catholic and Jewish scholars do not publish widely in journals which, although they are not identified as Protestant, do carry a preponderance of Protestant scholarship. In the case of Catholic scholars it appears that foreign journals are favored as publication outlets, probably because much graduate education of Catholic professors still takes place at theological centers abroad. This state of affairs suggests strongly that much remains to be done in bringing into more fruitful confrontation the scholarly output of scholars from these several religious groups. Obviously, there are particular subjects germane to each of these groups which are ill suited to national journals aimed at wide-gauge scholarship, but the need remains for a more effective engagement of scholarship stemming from these diverse religious strands. The relative paucity of journals which by design or accident encourage the cross-fertilization of scholarship from these sources may in part account for the tendency for scholarship to be encapsulated in journals whose vigor, interest, and circulation is confined to certain religious bodies, rather than to the professional academic world as a whole.

In turning to the analysis of religion scholarship represented in books and monographs, the sheer quantity of output calls for the adoption of some pattern by which this material may be brought into manageable compass. A convenient but by no means exact method by which this may be done is to distinguish three types of scholarship: technical, perspectival, and pivotal writings. Although these categories will be found to overlap at certain points, they do introduce a measure of rough structure into an otherwise highly complex territory. They do not provide criteria of the quality of the scholarship examined, but rather suggest the categories of workmanship being considered.[7] Each is a valuable component of religion scholarship taken as a whole.

Technical scholarship is ordinarily restricted to intensive study of some one problem or area of fairly narrow range. It typically aims to add information to the present store of knowledge and often is less weighted, though not lacking, in the direction of interpretive principles. It is customarily identified by the thoroughness of detail with which it operates and by the external signs of scholarly apparatus such as extensive use of footnotes and references. Perspectival scholarship is ordinarily built upon the foundations provided by technical scholarship, but its emphasis is placed upon the exposition of broad principles by means of which some segment of the field may be interpreted. In some respects it is less concerned with providing new

[7] Examination of scholarship by disciplines within the field of religion may be found in another volume of "The Princeton Studies." See *Religion,* ed. Paul Ramsey (Prentice-Hall, 1964).

information than in effecting a creative reorientation of information already attained. It seeks understanding rather than knowledge as such. It attempts to set available knowledge in new perspectives and to restate and reinterpret crucial problems. Pivotal scholarship achieves its status by a combination of circumstances. It may be of either a technical or perspectival type; it may win immediate recognition upon publication as a decisively influential work; it may languish upon bookshelves for years before scholars by accident or research recognize its value and timeliness; it may even lack the refinements of scholarly research or be of inferior quality judged by the requirements of technical scholarship. But it must have the power to turn the whole range of discussion in a specific area in a different direction from that hitherto followed or it must synthesize a development of thought into a comprehensive unity which was previously lacking. It must be "fertile" in the sense that whether or not its insights are widely accepted as valid, it furnishes over a period of time fresh starting points for discussion and scholarship. It is the kind of workmanship which in one way or another forces the scholarly world to take it seriously as a continuing source of productive insights and as the object of repeated criticism. The selection of examples of pivotal scholarship in certain respects is the easiest of tasks, since they are the books which are most often referred to in scholarly treatises, but it is also a matter of considerable delicacy, since works which at one stage of scholarly development may appear of crucial importance sometimes sink into obscurity with the passage of time. In all three types of scholarship, and even that which is scorned as pedestrian, the basal minimal qualifications are serious, honest, and careful treatment of subject matter.

This threefold pattern may now help to delineate the features of religion scholarship over the past three decades. The titles of the books mentioned will sufficiently classify their subject fields.

As a part of the evidence of scholarly activity, although not itself counted as scholarship, certain foundational work has been carried out which places in scholars' hands the tools of research. For example, the microfilming of the entire Vatican Library and the proposed microfilming of the Ambrogiano Library at Milan by the universities of St. Louis and Notre Dame respectively should be noted. In these rich and relatively untapped deposits, now being made more widely available, scholars dealing with linguistic, theological, historical, and philosophical matters will be greatly aided. In a similar fashion the identification and translation of the Dead Sea Scrolls, as exemplified by Millar Burrows' *The Dead Sea Scrolls of St. Mark's Monastery* may be counted as foundational work for further scholarship. Among major works of translation which are the results of scholarly achievement and which provide the basis for further studies, the following can be mentioned: the Revised Standard Version of the Bible; "The Library of Christian Classics," a translation of the church fathers and reformers, carried out by Protestant seminary faculty members in this country and in Britain; "The Fathers of the Church: A New Translation" by Roman Catholic scholars; *Luther's Works,* edited by Jaroslov Pelikan; the translations of the works of Sören Kierkegaard by Walter Lowrie and F. D. Swenson; the "Yale Judaica Series," mainly executed by American scholars; and the new translation of Aquinas's *Summa contra gentiles.*

Technical scholarship of a different type embraces a wide assortment of books which make accessible new information drawn from research in original sources or which place such information in new systematic structures. Books of this type are not confined in their aim to the purposes of other scholars, but also appeal to a wider cultured public. The line previously drawn between technical studies and perspectival studies is a difficult one to maintain at this point, but with certain exceptions it is possible to indicate by example, if not by definition, the nature of these technical works of scholarship.

Among works in this category *The Interpreter's Bible,* a commentary of exegesis and homiletical exposition running to twelve volumes, exemplifies the problem of classification. Much of the content of these volumes rates as scholarly work of a technical and informational type, although its technical apparatus is seldom set forth in detail. Since the commentary is intended to serve the purposes of clergymen and a public which may be interested in biblical studies, its general character, while remaining within the broad area of scholarship, does not suggest the high degree of technical scholarship usually associated with the biblical field. Other recent or forthcoming examples of technical scholarship of a similar type are *The Interpreter's Dictionary of the Bible* and the new *Catholic Encyclopedia.*

The problems associated with the classification of commentaries, dictionaries, and encyclopedias among scholarly works of a technical or semitechnical nature are reduced when particular books or series of books are considered. The following examples of American scholarship in religion more faithfully represent the technical category: K. S. Latourette's *The History of the Expansion of Christianity* in seven volumes; W. F. Albright's *From the Stone Age to Christianity;* the Yale edition of the complete works of Jonathan Edwards, of which two volumes of a multivolume project have appeared; Edward Duff, S. J., *The Social Thought of the World Council of Churches;* M. S. Enslin, *Christian Beginnings;* Horton Davies, *Worship and Theology in England,* two volumes of which have been published; "The Morris Loeb Series" in Jewish studies, four volumes of which have appeared to date; William Haller, *The Rise of Puritanism;* Erwin R. Goodenough, *Jewish Symbols in the Graeco-Roman Period,* as well as his studies in Philo; Henry Davis, *Moral and Pastoral Theology* in four volumes; Walter J. Ong, S. J., *Ra-*

mus; Method and the Decay of Dialogue; Millar Burrows, two volumes on the Dead Sea Scrolls; Harry A. Wolfson, *The Philosophy of the Church Fathers;* D. C. Macintosh, *The Problem of Religious Knowledge;* R. H. Pfeiffer, *Introduction to the Old Testament;* Joachim Wach, *Sociology of Religion;* Milton Yinger, *Religion, Society and the Individual;* and Jack Finegan, *The Archeology of World Religions* and *Light from the Ancient Past.*

Certain books mentioned above, such as those of Davies, Haller, Ong, Latourette and the critical introductions by Paul Ramsey and J. E. Smith in the Edwards volumes are distinctly interpretive as well as representative of technical research. The same observations may be made of such works as W. W. Sweet's several volumes on American church history and his efforts to relate Christianity to the growth of American culture; M. S. Bates, *Religious Liberty;* and the four-volume study entitled *Religion in American Life,* edited by J. W. Smith and A. Leland Jamison, assisted by Nelson R. Burr. The last-named publication contains a critical bibliography on the subject which would normally place it definitely within the category of technical scholarship, but the essays which comprise the first two volumes are explicitly perspectival in character.

In assigning a certain work to the category of perspectival scholarship one cannot overlook its relation to technical scholarship. Technical scholarship may refer primarily to publications which are explicitly based upon research in documents, artifacts, and monuments, but its influence is felt in writings which are clearly interpetive in character. The arts of critical analysis, appraisal, and creation of explanatory theories are seldom developed apart from thorough acquaintance with the results and practice of technical scholarship. Even as no scholar works without reference to some interpretive pattern, so also does no scholar operate without reliance upon the resources of technical studies. The distinction between perspectival and technical scholarship is then largely determined by the degree of stress which is placed on one or the other of these two complementary forms. The examples of scholarship offered below are considered to be perspectival because they appear to emphasize the use of interpretive principles rather than to exhibit the familiar characteristics of technical studies. They also suggest the range of subject matters, the diversity of skills, and the variety of religious and academic backgrounds to be found among religion scholars.

The list of works representative of perspectival scholarship includes: Roland Bainton, *Here I Stand,* a study of Luther; Nels Ferré, *Christianity and Society* and his theological works; J. C. Bennett, *Christians and the State;* Paul Ramsey, *War and the Christian Conscience;* Perry Miller, *The New England Mind* and *Orthodoxy in Massachusetts;* A. N. Wilder, *Eschatology and Ethics in the Teaching of Jesus;* H. R. Niebuhr, *The Kingdom of God in America* and *Christ and Culture;* Paul Tillich, *Systematic Theology* in three volumes, two of which have been published; Reinhold Niebuhr, *The Nature and Destiny of Man* and many of his other books; George H. Tavard, *Holy Writ or Holy Church;* Will Herberg, *Protestant, Catholic, and Jew;* Abraham Heschel, *God in Search of Man;* Claude Welch, *In This Name.*

Works of a pivotal type are not easily identified, partly because one seldom knows what book now being discussed among scholars is likely to become a focal point of further studies, and partly because books now considered to be central may lose their present position of esteem. Books may be popular even among scholars and yet prove to be merely passing enthusiasms. An even more embarrassing difficulty lies in the fact that on whatever grounds one identifies a work as pivotal, relatively few such works are the products of American scholarship. In many of the disciplines found within the field of religion the decisive impetus has been given by foreign rather than American scholars. In this area American scholarship has been largely the offshoot of British and Continental influences. Given this widely recognized fact, are we to say that no pivotal scholarship has originated on this side of the Atlantic? Within this country there have been certain developments which, although they may not have won recognition abroad, have proved to be crucially important in the growth of domestic scholarship. The fields of philosophy of religion, Christian ethics, American religious culture, and, in some respects, that of Bible have produced scholarly works of a high caliber. The late Twenties and Thirties saw the development of an empirical philosophy of religion which owed its origins to the work of H. N. Wieman at the University of Chicago and D. C. Macintosh at Yale.[8] Wieman adopted a process conception of deity and defended vigorously in his earlier books (*Religious Experience and the Scientific Method, The Wrestle of Religion with Truth,* and *The Issues of Life*) the scientific method as a way of securing knowledge of God. Building upon insights drawn from Whitehead's metaphysics and Dewey's methodology, he forged a distinctive philosophy of religion which in many respects might be regarded as a uniquely American contribution to the philosophy of religion. By the novelty with which his views challenged traditional ways of thinking, his work virtually forced scholars in theology and philosophy of religion to take a stand on his position. Whatever were the shortcomings of Wieman's scholarship in the fields of historical and epistemological studies, he set

[8] Macintosh's *Theology as an Empirical Science* expressed a less radical form of empiricism than that of Wieman. Although unquestionably his writings were buttressed with a heavier weight of philosophical and historical scholarship than Wieman's, their more traditional caste seems to have denied them the same eminence as that enjoyed by Wieman's works.

248

new ideas coursing through American religion scholarship, and the sharpness with which liberals and conservatives attacked his position showed his work to be of a pivotal type.

By the mid-Forties the empirical tendency had spent much of its force, a consequence greatly hastened by the appearance of theological conceptions from the Continent. The writings of Barth and Brunner became dominant influences at many theological centers, and the names of Kierkegaard, Buber, Berdyaev, and Bultmann were as familiar to Protestant scholars as were the names of Gilson, Garrigou-LaGrange, and Maritain to Roman Catholics. The impact of such thinkers as these upon American scholarship has been great, but at the same time the creative influences of the Niebuhrs also grew. They had been among the principal interpreters of Continental viewpoints, but they had not been mere transmitters of these perspectives. Their own writings sharply reoriented American scholarship in theology, philosophy of religion, and Christian ethics to Continental insights without surrendering the liberal, social, and biblical heritage of American religious thought.

It then can be said that in American scholarship the Niebuhrs have contributed pivotal works. H. R. Niebuhr's *The Meaning of Revelation* and *Christ and Culture* may be mentioned, as well as Reinhold Niebuhr's Gifford Lectures on *The Nature and Destiny of Man*. The latter's writings on the relation of Christian faith to political and economic problems have also been generally regarded as of high significance. With the coming of Paul Tillich to these shores another crucial influence has been released in philosophical and theological studies, and his position, although much criticized, as are all pivotal works, has been firmly established by his *Systematic Theology*.

Examples of pivotal studies similar in impact to those mentioned above can be culled from other fields. The works of Perry Miller, William Haller, and M. M. Knappen on American and English Puritanism stand out for having set new directions in that field. It is noteworthy that none of these authors is a member of a theological or undergraduate religion faculty. In church history, K. S. Latourette's *History of the Expansion of Christianity* may claim a position of decisive importance, as also may W. W. Sweet's earlier studies in American church history. The areas of biblical and Near Eastern archaeology and thought remain deeply indebted to the brilliant studies of W. F. Albright. In New Testament scholarship the writings of the so-called Chicago School of the Thirties, including E. J. Goodspeed, S. J. Case, H. R. Willoughby, and others, played a dominating role. The contributions of S. W. Baron, Julian Morgenstern, and Julian J. Obermann, among others, remain as landmarks of Jewish scholarship.

A more extensive survey of major works in all categories would probably further confirm the impression that American scholarship in religion has been vigorously prosecuted, although its record in respect to pivotal studies is less impressive than might be expected. In considering all forms of scholarly activity, evidence of participation by undergraduate religion faculty members is not lacking. By their contributions to the programs of professional societies and journals and their publication of several interpretive books, they have shown signs of scholarly responsibility. When the number of these faculty members is taken into consideration, however, it would seem that much more remains to be done to break the image of the undergraduate religion professor as one lacking in scholarly interests and achievements. The bulk of major technical, perspectival, and pivotal scholarship remains in the hands of scholars in theological institutions, in graduate departments of religion, or in other fields. But perhaps the most surprising fact about religion scholarship is that so much of it is carried on by scholars who are not attached to departments of religion, theological schools, or graduate departments of religion. Except for the field of biblical studies, professors of literature, philosophy, history, sociology, and archaeology seem to bear a disproportionate share of the burden of scholarship.

←§ 13 §→

EVALUATION OF THE SITUATION IN
RELIGION SCHOLARSHIP

Opinions of the health of American scholarship in religion over the past three decades are various. In 1943 Professor Erwin R. Goodenough, commenting upon one discipline in the field, announced: "In this country and abroad New Testament scholarship has hit the nadir. Not at any time for a century and a half has so little of importance been written." [*Journal of Biblical Literature*, LXII (1943), xi.] Since the time of this depressing pronouncement conditions have materially changed. The discovery of the Dead Sea Scrolls and the Gnostic library in Egypt set off fresh activity in New and Old Testament studies and Judaica. The problems of hermeneutics and demythologizing, largely introduced by Bultmann, seized scholarly attention.

The spirit of Goodenough's remark about New Testament scholarship, however, has been echoed by writers commenting upon the state of scholarship. In 1936 M. J. Ahern, S. J., had boasted that "the output of works in religion of American Catholic authorship is several hundred yearly," but three years later a far different estimate was given. "Our record of productive scholarship in all but a few fields is still a pitiful one," wrote Martin R. P. McGuire. [*American Catholicism and the Intellectual Ideal,* ed. F. L. Christ and G. E. Sherry (Appleton, 1961), pp. 108, 120.] Professor J. Tracy Ellis and others also expressed the judgment that Catholic scholarship in all areas, including that of religion, has been in the doldrums. ["American Catholics and the Intellectual Life," *Thought* (Fall 1955).] J. Paul Williams, writing as a college professor of religion, decried the lack of basic research in religion and called for a more energetic attack upon the problem. ["The Present Status of Research in Religion," *Journal of Bible and Religion,* XV, 1 (1947), 3 ff.] On the one hand, it then would appear that scholarship in religion has been woefully lagging; on the other hand, enormous quantities of materials have been coming from the presses, a fair amount of which certainly must be regarded as scholarly in nature. Furthermore apologetic attitudes about American scholarship persist even while ever increasing numbers of articles, monographs, and books flood the market.

This anomalous situation suggests that differing standards are being applied in the judgment of what constitutes scholarship. The more pessimistic estimates probably originate in the conviction that pivotal scholarship alone can properly be regarded as true scholarship. Technical or perspectival publications which do not attain this level accordingly are ruled out or relegated to secondary positions. Writings which dwell upon minutiae in a pedantic manner may not even be accorded the dignity of the title *scholarship.* More favorable evaluations of the situation adopt a less rigorous standard as to what constitutes scholarship, accepting even pedantic works as part of the scholarly output. However, agreement is reached when pivotal scholarship is in question. There seems little doubt that American scholarship has been notably weak in this area and that Continental and British scholars have outsped their American colleagues.

The indebtedness of American scholarship to foreign learning cannot be denied. Advances in biblical studies, church history, and theology have often been made by British and Continental scholars. The names of Harnack, Troeltsch, Barth, Brunner, Eichrodt, Weiss, Schweitzer, Lietzmann, Dibelius, Schmidt, Bultmann, Cullmann, Nygren, Pedersen, Heim, Noth, Aulen, and van der Leeuw are familiar to American scholars.

Scarcely less impressive has been the influence of such English and Scottish figures as Dodd, Taylor, Black, the Baillies, Tennant, Temple, Dickie, MacKinnon, and Farrer. Similar admissions of dependence upon foreign scholarship have been made by Roman Catholic scholars in this country. "The fact is that although American Catholics have the largest and most expensive educational system of any national Catholic group in the world, a genuine Catholic intellectual life is still dependent upon translations of European works and books of British origin. "When the American Catholic reaches the point in his intellectual development at which it is necessary to change his intellectual diet from milk to meat, he by necessity becomes an importer. . . . It is hardly necessary to stress these facts, because they are generally recognized by large numbers concerned with the viewpoint of Catholic intellectual life." [Thomas F. O'Dea, in *American Catholicism and the Intellectual Ideal,* p. 245.]

Certainly it would be wrong to explain this dependence as due to the slothfulness of American scholars. Their sizeable output of publications should be sufficient to scotch the notion that they have been idly waiting for the latest word from abroad. Rather, the influence of foreign scholarship upon this country may be explained in part by the accident of past historical associations. From the beginning American culture in all its aspects has been deeply indebted to the achievements of Europe and Britain. The roots of our spiritual and intellectual heritage lie there and, although a distinctive civilization has been developed on this continent, those roots have continued to nourish our arts and religious life. It is all but unavoidable in these circumstances that religious thought in this country should listen with respect to what scholars in foreign lands say.

But there is more than past historical associations at work here. The deference paid to foreign scholarship in religion in the last analysis is due to the excellence of that scholarship. It commends itself to American scholars by virtue of its thoroughness and creativity. It need not be supposed that foreign scholars possess mental faculties inherently superior to those of scholars on this side of the Atlantic, but they do have an intellectual tradition in respect to matters religious which America does not as yet possess. Theological scholars abroad, for the most part, are members of autonomous faculties within universities. They have inherited and developed a recognized tradition of academic excellence which is oriented to basic research and pioneering efforts on religious issues. Their work has not been evaluated on the grounds of its immediate relevance to the religious life of their culture and churches. It has stood on its own feet as scholarship, while at the same time it has had profound effects upon the modes of religious activities and parish responsibilities carried on in the churches. These scholars in the main do not offer instruction in the practical fields of pastoralia, but leave to other church agencies the task of preparing men for ecclesiastical duties. The traditional disciplines of the field of religion are given high significance, each of which with its subdivisions offers the greatest possible opportunity for specialization. From this specialization have come the major works which by their profundity and originality are to be counted as milestones of scholarship. Since they normally teach graduate students who themselves possess the necessary linguistic skills for theological studies, these scholars can deal with their materials in the classroom at a level of sophistication beyond that found in many American seminaries. Thus it appears that the conditions under which foreign scholars work encourage scholarship in religion as a lifetime vocation. The tradition of scholarship in religion is firmly established as an integral part of the university situation.

One need not be swept along on a tide of uncritical adulation of foreign scholarship, nor need American scholars envy in all respects the conditions under which their colleagues abroad work. From the American point of view there are serious deficiencies as well as benefits in it. The scope of foreign scholarship has seemed unnecessarily limited. It has been noticed that European scholars are seldom familiar with the work of either British or American scholars, perhaps because some of them cannot read English. There are also signs of a religious and cultural provincialism which in the case of both British and European scholars assumes as a matter of course that the theological issues met within their respective cultures are of universal and crucial significance elsewhere in the world. In the field of church history, for example, Dr. Franklin H. Littell points out that the German scholar Dr. Karl Heussi some time ago produced a manual on church history which proved widely influential. It passed through a dozen editions in fifty years, yet concluded with only three pages on Christianity outside of Germany! By way of contrast, Littell mentions Professor Ernst Berg of Marburg who, after studying Latourette's *History of the Expansion of Christianity,* was moved to comment favorably upon the breadth of its scope and to note the comparative provincialism of much European historiography. [Littell, *From Church to Pluralism: A Protestant Interpretation of Religion in American History* (Doubleday, 1962), p. xvii.] The relative freedom with which the foreign scholar is enabled to carry on his work may also have restrictive consequences. He may enjoy a certain autonomy within the university, but he also seems set apart from the ebb and flow of critical secular opinion originating outside the circle of theological scholarship. He may therefore be less aware of the cultural conditioning which undetected enters deeply into his scholarship. One may wonder, for example, whether the massive and learned theology of Karl Barth would have developed as it has if it had stood fully in the cross fire from secular philosophers, historians, and non-European biblical scholars. American scholars may envy their colleagues abroad their opportunities for specialization, but this advantage must also be weighed against the resultant narrowness of some of their work and its failure to relate theological considerations to other humanistic and social science studies.[1] The strictness with which the traditional disciplines of Old and New Testament, church history, and theology have governed the field of scholarship have also served to de-emphasize or omit from consideration certain areas which may properly be counted as appropriate to religion scholarship. For this reason fewer leads have come from foreign scholars in such fields as the following: psychology and sociology of religion; Christian ethics as related to the empirical data set forth by the social sciences; the philosophy of religion, which in Britain, the Scandinavian countries, and the United States has assumed new importance but which has left Continental scholarship relatively untouched; and American church history, which deals with the unique and vital developments in this country and need no longer be treated as a minor addendum to European church history. [Littell, *op. cit.*, pp. xvii-xviii.]

In spite of these serious limitations, American scholars sometimes tend to be ill at ease when comparisons are made between them and foreign scholars. Some feel that the supreme accolade for their work can only come from abroad and others accept as a fact their secondary status as scholars. Still others are irritated at what they believe to be the highhanded manner in which European scholars especially refuse to take seriously works produced in America. Probably the areas of greatest sensitivity are those of theology proper and church history, where it sometimes seems to be taken for granted that little of merit has been forthcoming from American scholars. In biblical scholarship, on the

[1] Exceptions to this opinion may be found in Karl Heim's studies in the relation of theology to modern science and in Bultmann's use of Heidegger's ontology.

257

other hand, a genuinely international flavor exists. American scholars such as H. G. May, S. L. Terrien, James Muilenburg, B. M. Metzger, Carl H. Kraeling, R. B. Y. Scott, W. F. Albright, G. Ernest Wright, and J. M. Robinson are respected as contributors and editors for foreign journals and as authors of scholarly books. For example, the series of excellent monographs entitled "Biblical Theology" has as its American editors F. V. Filson and G. Ernest Wright; the forthcoming "Old Testament Library" has as its American editors John Bright and G. Ernest Wright, and *Vetus testamentum* has Millar Burrows and H. G. May on its editorial board. The scene is different in theology where few American theologians are known abroad with the possible exception of Reinhold Niebuhr, who curiously enough declines the title of theologian!

In turning to evaluate more fully the situation in American scholarship, one is irresistibly drawn to conclude that the acknowledged lack of pivotal scholarship is due to certain shortcomings in the academic and cultural situation in which American scholars operate. A country which boasts 3,500 full-time teachers of religion in universities, colleges, and junior colleges, to say nothing of those in seminaries, should be able to produce a quality of scholarship second to none. [*Teacher Supply and Demand in Universities, Colleges, and Junior Colleges, 1959-60, and 1960-61*, table 30 (Research Division, NEA, 1961), p. 55.] Yet the record is not impressive. We do not produce in proportion to our numbers or to the religious vitality of American culture.

Undoubtedly many factors could be brought forward to explain the fact that American scholarship has been tardy in producing major creative leads in religion, but the one which most clearly stands out is the absence of a consistently maintained intellectual tradition in American religious life. The scholarly tradition with which an influential segment of the clergy and laity of the seventeenth and early eighteenth centuries was familiar was seriously retarded by the excessive pietistic ardor in the evangelical movements of the mid-eighteenth and nineteenth centuries. A popular religion of the "heart" which took precedence over a religion of "head and heart" joined with a native pragmatism to depreciate the value of the intellectual life in matters religious. Today, in many quarters, the word *religion* has come to be associated with a nebulous, uncritical, emotional quality which is primarily valued for its pacification of the human mind and spirit or for its morally inspirational qualities. In the face of a culture which has been willing to settle for a religious outlook which makes so little place for the life of the mind, it is not surprising to find that any pretensions to scholarship have been given an extremely modest place. The notion that one might enter a life of scholarship in religion as a self-justifying vocation, carried on apart from considerations of immediate relevance to the churches or to the religious life of American society, has come to be regarded as visionary. The spirit of pragmatism has so dominated the American conception of religion itself that something very like an anti-intellectualistic attitude is to be found not only in the churches and culture generally, but even in some seminaries where one would expect the scholarly tradition to be most vigorously maintained. The Niebuhr study of theological education bluntly asserts: "Faculty members who attempt to turn the tide of anti-intellectualism must fight every inch of the way." [H. R. Niebuhr, J. M. Gustafson, and D. D. Williams, *The Advancement of Theological Education* (Harper, 1957), p. 197.] Yet if scholarly standards are to be achieved, if creative scholarship is ever to be produced in the quantities demanded by the present situation, this battle against anti-intellectualism and pervasive pragmatism must be incessantly waged. As Professor Robert L. Calhoun has pointed out: "If judged by the standard of the freest, maturest, most distinguished inquiries man has performed, much religious thinking has been vitiated by too constant subordination to ulterior practical demands . . . religious preoccupation which forever urges the thinker to find what shall be edifying, consoling, or somehow spiritually useful rather than just to find what is the case, is more than likely to shorten his perspectives, narrow his purview, and deflect his line of vision." [Perry Miller, R. L. Calhoun, N. M. Pusey, and Reinhold Niebuhr, *Religion and Freedom of Thought* (Doubleday, 1954), p. 43.] It is doubtful that American scholarship will realize its potential until this advice is taken to heart.

The cultural and religious changes of the nineteenth century moved the center of religion scholarship into the seminary, where it has since lived a precarious existence in the face of competing claims upon the time and energies of faculty members. As has been previously noted, the seminary has become a hybrid institution where undergraduate, graduate, and professional concerns mingle. The pressures for practical courses, originating in a desire to produce clergymen who would have at their fingertips the tools of church administration, counseling, preaching, community organization, and religious education techniques, have threatened the classical substance of theological education. The burgeoning of so-called practical courses has consequently not only taken up increasingly large segments of the seminary student's time, but for the professor it has also restricted, if not the time available in the curriculum for substantive scholarly work, at least the sense of importance due this dimension of theological education. In addition, seminary faculties soon find they are expected to enter into a wide range of extra-academic duties connected with the fortunes of the institution or the churches. These claims upon their time and energies include popular lectures at ministers' retreats—usually to be couched in nontechnical language the better to be rapidly converted into homiletical materials by the listeners—contributions to denominational journals and adult education programs, service on denominational boards, leadership for Religious Emphasis Weeks at colleges, recruitment of students, administrative duties, and the publication of lightweight books and manuals for the benefit of those who run better than they read. Some of these services are carried out to supplement inadequate salaries, and some are expected by denominational agencies, which in spite of their notoriously meager support of their educational institutions, often assume that these schools exist primarily to serve their interests.[2] In some cases, denominations that control seminaries further adversely affect the conditions for scholarship by limiting the faculty constituency to members of their own religious body, thereby losing the stimulating influence of personnel drawn from other religious groups and, in some cases, other academic disciplines. When the disadvantages for scholarship under which many undergraduate religion faculties labor are compounded by those of the seminary, there remains little ground for surprise that a steady academic tradition in scholarship has been difficult to establish and maintain. Rather, it is remarkable that so much capable scholarship has been produced by religion faculties on all levels of higher education.

Another point at which the lack of a scholarly tradition affects the development of scholarship is the reluctance of the churches, both Roman Catholic and Protestant, to encourage their young people to undertake the hard road to academic

[2] Charles L. Taylor quotes from a recent study made of denominational support of seminaries: "Eleven of the largest denominations are contributing to the budgets of their seminaries an average of less than one-half percent of the total amount these churches are giving for all purposes." ["Do Churches Support Seminaries?" *Christian Century,* LXXIX, 17 (April 25, 1962), 548. See *Support of Theological Education in the United States, by Selected Protestant Denominations* (AATS, Dayton, Ohio, 1962).]

excellence in religion studies. Efforts are constantly made to induce youth to enter church-related vocations or the ranks of the clergy, but similar attempts to set before them the advantages of a life of scholarship and teaching are comparatively rare. Yet the need is great. The mastery of languages, the techniques of research, and critical habits of thought are not quickly achieved; they must be developed over sizeable periods of time, but they also demand an atmosphere in which the intellectual virtues are as highly prized as a part of man's essential nature as are the ethical and spiritual values. Generally the churches have not contributed to the development of this cultural context. They seldom recognize or admire their intellectuals, scholars, or teachers in religion, and sometimes seem rather to regard them with suspicion as "rare birds" who, it is feared, may upset cherished religious ideas or who talk "over the heads" of both clergy and laity. What passes for scholarship in some churches is the distilled traces of scholarship found in popular paperbacks which appear on the literature racks in the entries of churches. Since the church expects to be talked down to and written down to, there are always authors who might otherwise produce scholarly works, who are ready to meet these expectations. This type of journalistic writing has not been without value to churchmen, but it has also abetted the erroneous impression that whatever there is of importance can be presented in digest form. Consequently, appreciation of the realm of scholarship and its demands has largely remained an alien territory even for the intelligent layman. Misapprehensions about what constitutes scholarship thus continue to flourish, and little in the way of encouragement is given to those young people who might otherwise find their way into the ranks of scholarship. Certainly the churches are concerned to develop their own leadership, but it seems equally important that they awaken to their responsibilities to foster an intellectual leadership which will take its place beside that found in other fields.

The lack of a scholarly tradition has borne severely upon American Roman Catholicism. Professor J. Tracy Ellis marks "an absence of a love of scholarship for its own sake among American Catholics," [3] even among those engaged in higher education. He suggests that the necessity for preparing men for the pastoral care of large immigrant populations in the nineteenth century prevented the growth of such a tradition. Edward J. Power has commented upon the heavy load of non-academic duties which fall to professors in Catholic institutions and concludes that "present conditions are such that it is only with some difficulty and perseverance that a teacher at a Catholic college can become an expert or a scholar." Father Gustave Weigel, S. J., finds that Catholic writing has too often been diverted from scholarly attainments by what he calls "an obsession with the apologetic defense of Catholic positions," the result presumably of what Professor Ellis has identified as a "self-imposed ghetto mentality." Oscar Perlmutter complains in a similar vein that "outstanding works, even in fields of direct Catholic interest, are written by non-Catholics." In a study conducted by Burnett C. Bauer, Catholic scholarship published in all fields made a poor showing. Bauer found that at most only one-fifth of all Catholic teachers in all fields and in all types of institutions of higher learning had published. This figure compared unfavorably with the publication rates at 35 colleges related to the Methodist Episcopal Church, where 35 per cent published. "Of these schools seventeen were institutions on the approved list of the Association of American Universities, and

---

[3] *American Catholicism and the Intellectual Ideal,* p. 274. The following statements by Power, Weigel, Ellis, Perlmutter, and Bauer are from the same work, pp. 194, 222, 276, 234, and 131-32, respectively.

41% of their total faculties have published. The remaining eighteen colleges . . . had 30% of their faculties who had published." Bauer concluded that his comparisons left "little room for complacency in the minds of those Catholics who are concerned about the influence Catholic scholars are exerting upon modern scholarship." In the light of these comments it need scarcely be argued that a profound uneasiness exists about Catholic scholarship generally, although probably religion scholarship comes off somewhat better than other fields when comparisons are made. In any case, some of the same features which hinder the progress of scholarship in religion generally in America can be detected: the emphasis on "practical" studies, the profusion of extra-academic responsibilities, and, above all, the failure to appreciate and develop an intellectual tradition in the field.

In spite of, or perhaps because of, its status as a minority group in American culture, Judaism has preserved its treasured tradition of learning and scholarship. Numerous learned journals, monographs, and books, as well as societies for the promotion of scholarship attest its continued concern with intellectual excellence. In the field of religion scholarship, however, Dr. Samuel Sandmel estimates that 90 per cent of Jewish scholarship emanates from five or six Jewish colleges and seminaries. It appears, as in the case of Protestant scholarship, that Jewish scholarship is closely linked with theological education and probably undergoes some of the same difficulties discernible in Catholicism and Protestantism. On the other hand, the contributions of Jewish scholars in other fields and in non-Jewish institutions to religion scholarship cannot be overlooked.

The identification of scholarship with the seminaries and with theological education generally has had certain other consequences which also bear upon the state of scholarship in this country. The precise effect of these is extremely difficult to assess, but there can be little doubt that in various and often subtle ways they have shaped the context of scholarship. First among these consequences—or, for want of a better word, factors—is the lack of freedom for what might be called pure research. This lack of freedom appears to be due to a combination of circumstances: the pressure for producing clergy armed with those practical devices which make for success in the ministry; the pressure of extra-academic duties upon faculty members; and in some seminaries the pressure to conformity coming variously from denominations, alumni, students, administrators, and the historic traditions of the school itself. [Niebuhr, Gustafson, and Williams, *op. cit.*, p. 195.] Clearly, pure research demands release from these conditions for its execution. A second factor which has had an inhibiting effect upon the breadth of scholarship is the relative isolation of seminaries from the university itself. Not only the seminaries which are set apart from university centers but those connected with them sometimes suffer from this detachment. It is possible that the quality of scholarship found in the seminaries does not lag behind that found elsewhere in the university, but it does run the danger of being cut off from those currents of thought which course through the university at large. It is these currents which do so much to form the intellectual atmosphere with which both the teaching and scholarship in religion must cope. A scholarship which finds its principal habitation in the seminary might be expected to be of superior quality in respect to the details of theological studies while at the same time it failed to engage fully with those insights and perspectives which might serve as the stimulus for fresh, creative starting points for scholarly efforts. It is notable, for example, that the most influential scholarship now being done is in those seminaries connected with university centers rather than in those removed from a university setting, but even in the former the tendency to isolation remains.

A third feature of the contemporary scene is closely connected with that of isolation. It is the relatively small number of first-class theological schools at which graduate work is done and from which creative scholarship may be expected. The paucity of these schools may affect scholarly activity in several ways. With all the difficulties which face faculty members in these graduate centers they nevertheless have better opportunities for carrying on scholarship than their less advantageously placed colleagues in other seminaries or in colleges. But the failure to establish a larger number of these centers means that relatively few scholars bear the brunt of scholarly productivity. This fact in turn means that in spite of their small numbers these scholars bring to bear a disproportionate impress upon the formulation of the principal currents of thought, the types and standards of scholarship, and the crucial problems of the field. Although unintended, their collective influence—not only through their writings, but also through their teaching— has produced conformities of thought which have narrowed the spectrum of religion scholarship. The dominating influence of these scholars has made it difficult for younger or less well-known scholars to break out on trails of their own or, if they do so, to be recognized for their contributions. Their work is often judged by its resemblance to or divergence from the accepted norms provided by what are at present considered to be the eminent scholars. Thus the scholarship which emanates from other academic centers has in recent years revolved about the issues set in a few theological centers or at worst has become a kind of unadventurous parroting or footnoting of the viewpoints found there. This is not to say that the scholarship which comes from these major centers is devoid of substance or that it fails to meet the highest requirements of scholarly attainment. It is to say that a constrictive force is at work in the field of religion scholarship which has discouraged the discovery of fresh starting points on the part of both those who do and do not have the opportunity of working at these centers. If one were to select one field in which this effect has been most often felt, it would probably be theology itself.

The fourth and last factor to be mentioned here is the method of preparation of scholars, which is largely carried out by graduate seminary faculties. In this instance, however, the difficulty lies less with the seminary orientation of graduate education as such than with the preparation afforded by the American system of higher education. In many cases graduate students have not provided themselves with the tools of scholarly research. Often they do not handle with ease the languages, ancient and modern, which are essential to scholarship. They therefore are unable to work in original sources from the beginning of their graduate work and are dependent upon translations of contemporary foreign authors and upon interpretations offered to them by their professors. Nor is it uncommon after the completion of their graduate education for them to leave behind whatever competence they have achieved in foreign languages. Their scholarship, in consequence, tends to deal with materials readily available in English. The total effect of this circumstance is a further reduction of the span of the scholarship produced and the forfeiting of opportunities for confrontation with the invigorating influence of authors outside one's immediate cultural and religious orbit. The provincialism noted in respect to foreign scholarship thus has also come to be a feature of American religion scholarship.

The recital of these negative factors which affect American scholarship in religion should not blind us to the definite positive features of that scholarship. In many fields left relatively untouched by foreign scholars American scholars have made impressive contributions. This is particularly true of the psychology and sociology of religion and of disciplines bridging theology and other humanistic fields. Even when American scholars have drawn heavily upon transatlantic sources, they have distinguished themselves by advancing beyond them. In Christian ethics the relation between Christian ethical insights and political and economic realities has been creatively worked out by John Bennett and Reinhold Niebuhr. H. R. Niebuhr's *Christ and Culture* marked an advance over the typology of Ernst Troeltsch, Paul Ramsey has made major contributions to the contemporary discussion on atomic warfare. In the studies of Puritanism, English and American, the names of Haller, Knappen, and Miller stand out. The problem of church and state has been extensively studied by A. P. Stokes, Leo Pfeffer, and J. Courtney Murray. Religion in higher education has developed as an identifiable field of study under the leadership of C. P. Shedd. Latourette's historical studies have received worldwide attention. Conservative Protestant scholarship, as seen in Carl C. H. Henry's *Christian Personal Ethics* and the theological constructions of E. J. Carnell, has undergone a remarkable revival by casting off the mantle of obscurantism which in the past identified it with an illiterate fundamentalism. Observations of a similar nature apply to Jewish and Catholic scholarship.

Creative pivotal scholarship cannot be made to order by edict. No mere rearrangement of the conditions under which American scholars work will automatically produce monumental scholarly works. At last the creative powers of the individual will prove determinative. But it is also obvious that steps can be taken which will provide a more encouraging environment for scholarship. It is possible that in certain respects American scholars have overrated the quality of foreign scholarship and underrated their own. Perhaps they have labored too long under a sense of inferiority. Perhaps they simply do not relish the prospect of producing large systematic treatises common in Continental scholarship. They may have failed to take advantage of the present opportunities which they have for carrying on a vigorous scholarly tradition. But neither is there the least doubt that they deserve a wider and more sustained support from cultural, religious, academic, and financial resources. The present situation may not be one which calls for abject apology, but neither should it be accepted with complacency.

◄§ 14 §►

THE ADVANCEMENT OF RELIGION
SCHOLARSHIP

The pathway of constructive proposals for the advancement of scholarship in religion is littered with shopworn suggestions. Even a summary of the categories into which these proposals fall yields a series of truisms which make up their shortcomings in originality by their obvious validity. Presumably no one would seriously challenge the assertion that responsibility for scholarly productivity rests finally with the scholar himself. Neither would it be denied that the total cultural climate decisively affects the chances of the scholar's success. And how in speaking of the future of religion scholarship can one avoid consideration of specific campus conditions within which scholarship is to be prosecuted? The issues of freedom, opportunities for research and stimulating relations among scholars, long repetitiously discussed in academia, once more claim attention. And only the remarkably unperceptive would imagine that problems such as these could be treated without confrontation at last with the fateful question of financial support for religion scholarship.

The case for financial support of scholarship in religion cannot be given pride of place in the consideration of these issues. A broader, more intangible problem must be raised first, although hopes for its resolution admittedly are not high. It has been suggested that American culture has harbored a certain apathy, if not antagonism, toward scholarly efforts in the humanities. The pragmatic coloration found in our society, with which even scientific research has had to contend, seems to have adversely affected humanistic scholarship, and in no area has this been more conspicuous than that of religion. The tendency to conceive religion itself primarily in practical, inspirational, and morally elevating terms has successfully damped enthusiasm and respect for the intellectual dimensions of that field. For some people it is all but impossible to understand that religion calls for sustained and purposeful investigation. The removal or the reduction of the influence of these conceptions is imperative for the advancement of humane learning. This task weighs not only upon scholars themselves but upon the leadership of religious institutions as well. Their influence and encouragement could have a beneficial effect in shaping some segments of the popular mind toward a more appreciative understanding of the scholar's tasks. Looked at from the standpoint of the scholarly world, however, the major responsibility for shifts in the cultural milieu remains with the academic community. The efforts of scholars may not be crowned with large-scale, favorable responses, and increased outputs of pedantic and technical scholarship will certainly not capture the public mind. On the other hand, a broadly conceived scholarship presented in attractive oral and written forms can help to create a more receptive attitude to an intellectual tradition in religion. The scholar need not be hemmed in by his technical vocabulary or by an assumed vulgarity of style, but in many cases he should be able to produce some portions of his specialized studies in a form which clarifies their meaning and which evokes the interest of a wider audience than that constituted of his peers. [See H. M. Jones, *One Great Society* (Harcourt, 1959), pp. 184-86.]

There are signs that something of this order already has taken place. Books on the Dead Sea Scrolls, some of the writings of Reinhold Niebuhr, Paul Tillich, and Martin Buber, in spite of their difficulty and even their stylistic inadequacies, have captured the attention of significant numbers of laymen.

271

More than once professors of religion have been struck by the eagerness with which lay audiences have laid hold upon relatively sophisticated religious conceptions. If these evidences of scholarship as presented to the public do not indicate a widespread turn to an intellectual understanding of religion, they nevertheless do imply that a sizeable intellectual curiosity exists. And the development of this curiosity may lead further to a genuine appreciation of the work which scholars in religion do.

Even when most optimistically regarded, the books and lectures of scholars may have only a limited effect in creating an atmosphere favorable to a scholarly tradition in American religious life. However, the scholar finds within the academic institution a more directly applicable fulcrum for affecting cultural conditions. By his own adherence to high standards of scholarship, by bringing his students face to face with major works of scholarship and by offering them opportunities for trying their hands at scholarly creation, the scholar may not only help to raise up new generations of scholars, but also to stimulate in those who are not to follow that direction an appreciative understanding of the value of scholarship. In fact, a considerable contribution to the advancement of scholarship would be made if colleges could increasingly pour into our common intellectual life persons who would insist upon a richer diet of thought in religious matters and who would spurn the shoddiness and superficiality of much that passes for religious thought. The undergraduate professor of religion has a special responsibility and opportunity in this respect, since he deals with those who in increasing numbers make up the American public and set the tone of its cultural aspirations.

It need hardly be said that encouragement should be offered to students who give promise of future achievement as scholars and professors in the field. This in itself is no small job. The continuing battles against anti-intellectualism within and outside college walls, the misunderstanding and indifference which surrounds religious thought, the limited enrollments of students in religion, to say nothing of the strongly competitive positions of vocations which appear to be more lucrative and immediately practical in the world's work, are formidable obstacles to the securing of first-class personnel. Yet in spite of these pressures, the effort must be made to seek out and develop candidates for the field if the future vigor of scholarship is to be insured. The intrinsic interest which attaches to studies in religion, the contributions which can be made to the clarification of human ends and problems, and the wide diversity of gifts and disciplines which can be exercised at a high pitch of excellence in the field can still capture the interest of alert students.

Problems more directly affecting the promotion of scholarship are to be found within the academic community itself.[1] First among these is the absolute prerequisite of freedom for the scholar. The idea of freedom may be construed in several ways, the most obvious of which is academic freedom. For the most part religion scholarship does not suffer hardship on this score. Seldom in the university or seminary are restrictions placed upon research, publication, or conclusions, although from time to time censorship has plagued Roman Catholic authors, and there are opinions which, if expressed within some Protestant seminaries, church-related or secular colleges, would meet severe disapproval.[2] Academic freedom therefore can

---

[1] The ensuing discussion has reference only to professors of religion, rather than to scholars in other fields who contribute scholarship to religion.

[2] "When the religious comes to express his thoughts in writing there looms upon the horizon the added hurdle of censorship. Sometimes censors deal rather severely with the first few articles of the burgeoning scholar." [A. A. North, S.J., in *American Catholicism and the Intellectual Ideal,* ed. F. L. Christ and G. E. Sherry (Appleton, 1961), p. 203; see also p. 205 for a similar comment by Sister Annette Walters, C.S.J.]

never be taken for granted, but in the wider intellectual world it appears that religious authority has neither the inclination nor the power to exercise control over scholarship. The enormous range of ideas on religion to be found in scholarly writings and the wide diversity of intellectual and religious backgrounds of authors argue that few inhibiting factors have limited productivity.

Freedom to think and publish is not the only requisite for scholarship. There must be freedom of time in which such work can be done. In this respect both seminary and university religion faculties are seriously hampered. The Niebuhr study emphasized the need for relief from administrative and counseling duties for seminary faculties, and undergraduate professors find themselves in even more desperate straits in respect to freedom for research, thought, and writing.

The addition of extracurricular duties to the tasks of the undergraduate professor is as notorious as is his casual acceptance of the responsibilities. Furthermore, the reluctance of administrations in many cases to provide adequate staff for religion departments results in excessive teaching loads or in the faculty member's having to offer courses outside the areas of his principal competence. Thus, those areas in which he is especially trained and in which he might make scholarly contributions are often left fallow. Whatever other disadvantages the seminary professor suffers, at least he is normally able to operate in the disciplines of his specialization, an advantage less often enjoyed by the college professor. Yet the great reservoir of scholarly abilities lies in the colleges and universities. There the number of professors is largest and the general atmosphere is most congenial for a broad-scaled attack upon problems in the field. There is scarcely a professor of religion in American colleges who does not cherish hopes for carrying out a scholarly project of some kind, but few of these under the present conditions will ever come to fruition. The opportunities for sustained study, research, and thought which come his way are few and the time needed for gathering materials or maintaining contact with other scholars with specialized knowledge is at a premium.

The favorite dream of the seminary and college professor of religion is one in which at last the sluice gates of funds will be opened in his direction. He sees himself then getting on with his scholarly projects. This dream should not be allowed to fade into fantasy, nor should efforts be slackened to transform it into substance. But while awaiting that golden moment, faculty members can take more decisive steps in controlling their fate as scholars by a more careful management of their time. Although nonacademic duties cannot be shed in their entirety in some cases, the assumption of a less compliant attitude in the face of these demands and a more professional attitude toward one's role as a scholar can make some impress upon those who foist these diversions upon the faculty member. More importantly, faculty members should make a discriminating reassessment of their educational practices, some of which are anachronistic and wasteful of time. In the seminary and graduate school especially, extraordinary amounts of time are consumed in preparing and delivering lectures on material readily available in publications. College graduates, with some guidance, should be able to dig out this material. Yet unfortunately, years of tradition, if not professional egoism, have exercised an almost hypnotic influence upon faculty members who have come to feel that unless they express this material in a lecture, it will never get home to the student's mind. Lectures probably should be curtailed and retained for those areas in which the professor has something of consequence to say out of his own research and thought or in which materials are unavailable to the student. It must be admitted that larger groups of students can be reached by lectures than by seminars or discussion groups, and there must be a place for the impact of the professor to express itself. In some instances, the lecture system may even be a timesaving device. But beside these advantages must be placed the fact that sizeable amounts of time and energy are expended in practices which could well be eliminated. Similarly, the notion that a certain number of contact hours with students is a fixed and sacrosanct feature of successful instruction should be re-examined. It seems probable that at all levels of higher education time could be salvaged for scholarship if the peculiar fascination of this idea were broken. It is even possible that the use of teaching machines in some instances could prove beneficial for releasing time for scholarly purposes.

Although nothing can take the place of funds with which to "buy" faculty time for scholarship, faculty members must recognize their own responsibility in improving conditions. They cannot expect the treasure of time to be deposited in their laps by those outside the academic world unless they also take steps to overcome those rigidities of the educational system which hinder scholarship and for which they are, in some measure, responsible.

The importance of freedom for scholarship must also be understood in terms of opportunity for travel, which affords possibilities for meeting with scholars working elsewhere and for collecting materials outside one's immediate locale. Field studies are needed in world religions; examination of religious problems in other social contexts than those provided by American culture are needed in Christian ethics; currents of theological and philosophical thought abroad and in the larger domestic centers of theological education call for examination; and work with collections unavailable in smaller libraries is most desirable.

The development by American scholars of a sense of international scholarship remains relatively embryonic. This is especially true of scholars in undergraduate institutions where, even more than in the seminaries, opportunity for contact with foreign scholars has been minimal. The World Council of Churches provides an occasional opportunity for a limited number of Christian theologians to learn from each other, but this is a restricted avenue of international intercourse. Travel expenses are usually prohibitive, access to participation is limited, and the focus of the Council on the problems of world Christianity deters others whose interests do not lie in that direction. Few other international bodies exist which furnish stimulus for scholarship, with the exception of those in biblical studies. The college professor therefore often feels cut off from contacts which he realizes would stimulate and broaden his own scholarly efforts.

In this country, steps remain to be taken which would give institutional support for scholarship. The crucial position of the seminaries in respect to the training of scholars has been referred to in several connections. The values and limitations of such training have been discussed. Reference has also been made to the presence and need for centers for graduate education in religion which are not identified with the seminaries. It is necessary now to make clear that the establishment and support of these true graduate centers could provide an additional encouragement to scholarship in religion.

A review of the seminary's potential contribution to the production of both scholars and scholarship argues religion's need for new graduate institutions and divisions of universities. For the most part, the seminaries have been overcrowded with students and their faculties overworked with nonacademic duties. The orientation of the seminary program and curriculum is predominantly in the direction of preparation of clergy, and graduate work in some quarters is regarded as a mere append-age to a three-year course. In some seminaries an anti-intellec-tual atmosphere persists. [Cf. H. R. Niebuhr, J. M. Gustafson, and D. D. Williams, *The Advancement of Theological Educa-tion* (Harper, 1957), pp. 197, 212.] Ecclesiastical connections of the seminaries seldom provide either financial or psycholog-ical support for scholarly enterprises. Qualifications for entry into seminaries, even for those contemplating preparation for teaching and scholarship, often include religious criteria. The scope of subjects taught is limited by the purposes which the seminaries serve and the financial support available. Seminaries, even those connected with major universities, are often isolated from the mainstream of university education. Fellowships for graduate students are limited and, in some cases, library facili-ties are inadequate. Faculties are often chosen for their adher-ence to the religious bodies which sponsor the seminary. Oppor-tunities for faculty leaves of absence sometimes are not regularized. Departments are often small and therefore inade-quately represent their fields. Denominational interests con-tinue to influence the nature of the education provided.[3] Because the seminaries must be regarded as religious institu-tions of a sectarian nature, public tax funds are unavailable to them. Consequently, that segment of their work which is directed to nonsectarian scholarship and the preparation of scholars and professors of religion, as distinct from their train-ing for church services, remains without the financial support which under other circumstances they might receive. The sup-port of scholarly projects, research, and salaries and the as-sistance of graduate students must depend largely upon de-nominational resources, endowments, support from the private

[3] "There is still far too much unjustifiable denominationalism in theo-logical education." [Walter D. Wagoner, "Ecumenicity and Seminary Archaism," *Christian Century*, LXXIX, 17 (April 25, 1962), 516.]

university, and gifts from foundations, which to date have been relatively few and small.[4]

It has been made clear in previous contexts that seminary-influenced graduate education has not been without advantages in the preparation of religion professors and scholars. It has also been noted that a creditable amount of the scholarship produced in this country comes from these seminary faculties. But this is only to point to an achievement carried out by the persistence and ability of major schools operating in the face of the formidable obstacles mentioned above. Nor can it be supposed that the continuance of these conditions is either desirable or necessary if scholarship is to make the advances of which it is capable, given the inherent abilities of American scholars and the opportunities which should properly be theirs.

Some of the advantages to be derived from the establishment and support of graduate departments of religion within universities and the problems they may face have been mentioned at the end of Chapter 11. The possibilities for the broadening of graduate curriculums, the placing of first importance upon the development of younger scholars in an atmosphere where contact is made with a wide range of disciplines and viewpoints, and the challenge offered to faculties for carrying on their

[4] Denominational organizations contribute about 20 per cent of the cost of theological education, whereas tax monies provide about 50 per cent of the income for medical schools. [Niebuhr, Gustafson, and Williams, *op. cit.,* p. 224.] "Corporations and foundations shy away from contributions to denominational enterprises and even to those that are interdenominational." [Charles L. Taylor, "Do Churches Support Seminaries?" *Christian Century,* LXXIX, 17 (April 25, 1962).] A study of foundation grants shows that less than one third of the larger foundations contribute to causes in the category identified as *Religion.* Of the total grants made to Religion, 44 per cent went to theological schools, $3 million of the less than $4 million given to Religion was donated by a single foundation. [*The Foundation Directory,* Edition One, ed. Ann D. Walton and F. Emerson Andrews (Russell, 1960), pp. xliii and xliv.]

scholarly work in this context would seem to be extremely attractive. In this direction, Dr. Geddes MacGregor sees the study of religion taking its place in the university in a way which is impossible for the present seminary pattern to realize. He writes: "Our modern universities are so strong and so influential that, ideally, they can become the site for the realization of the vision of a truly free School of Religion in which men of all faiths may earnestly study the immensely valuable, theological traditions to which they are heir, and in full view of the humanistic and scientific work being conducted in so many different forms within these citadels of modern learning." ["Graduate Study in Religion and the University of Southern California," *Journal of Bible and Religion*, XXX, 2 (April 1962), 111.] The placement of religion squarely within the university setting should provide stimulus for the graduate student and the faculty member alike.

The Niebuhr report maintains that no need exists for more schools offering education at the graduate level. The primary need in the eyes of the report is for better work to be done in those now existing. [See Niebuhr, Gustafson, and Williams, *op. cit.*, p. 213.] Certainly the mere proliferation of graduate institutions of indifferent quality would serve no purpose. But it is another matter when it becomes clear that a genuine service for the training of personnel for scholarship is not only possible in university divisions of religion but is needed to offset the present dominance of the seminary-controlled pattern itself. Improvement of present practices is needed, but it is not a sufficiently radical step with which to meet the need for men trained in the heart of the university program or for the encouragement of a scholarship which can arise from within that context. It is probably too radical or unrealistic to suggest that existing seminaries be converted into professional training schools with definite sectarian allegiances to the denominations which support them and which depend upon them for their clergy, but this procedure might allow the universities to become centers for genuine graduate work and scholarship. In looking ahead, it should not be forgotten that no unbreakable logic binds graduate work or scholarship to the present pattern of seminary-influenced higher education and scholarship. Study and scholarship in religion is no more necessarily linked to church-related institutions than is political theory or economics to government or the business world. Nor, as our brief survey of the sources of contemporary religion scholarship has shown, must religion scholarship spring only from theological schools and religion professors. The amount of scholarly work which emanates from departments of Oriental studies, history, literature, and philosophy shows that it is possible, and perhaps even desirable, that scholarship be pursued across a broad front outside the seminary context.

Apart from arguments concerning the academic feasibility of placing graduate religion education squarely in the university, there remains the problem of financial support for scholarship when it takes place under the auspices of the seminaries. References to the financial difficulties of seminaries indicate not only that they are showing signs of failing to compete successfully with universities and some colleges in securing faculty, but that resources for leaves for faculty and the underwriting of scholarly projects are inadequate or unavailable. This is due to the failure of religious bodies to underwrite the costs of their theological institutions and to the inability of schools considered sectarian to draw upon public funds or to attract substantial endowments or grants from foundations. If religion scholarship were more widely disengaged from theological institutions and placed within the framework of humanistic studies in universities, public and private, it could become a recipient of funds now inaccessible to it. Just as historical, philosophical, linguistic, sociological, psychological, and archaeological studies which are divorced from religious purposes are counted fit recipients for these funds, so the field of religion, which has the counterparts of these disciplines, also could be a beneficiary of wider financial support. But there seems no way of this happening so long as the notion persists that religion scholarship is necessarily sectarian in nature or that its future inevitably is linked with the fortunes of theological schools. One way that religion professors and scholars can make clear that this judgment is of limited validity is to emphasize the role of religion as a humanistic subject at both the undergraduate and graduate levels. Once this role is firmly established, perhaps there will follow increased opportunities for the grants and support now made available to other humanistic scholars, limited as these are at present.

Another type of institutional move should also be seriously considered by those concerned for religion scholarship. The greatest possible benefit would accrue to the establishment of either an Institute for Religion Studies or a number of such institutes located at strategic places in the country. There already exist institutes of national and international repute in other fields such as the Institute of Advanced Studies at Princeton, the Institute for Behavioral Sciences at Palo Alto, and the Institute of Philosophical Research in San Francisco. The Frank L. Weil Institute for Studies in Religion and the Humanities, presently centered at Hebrew Union College in Cincinnati, is still in the formative stages, but promises to make a major contribution to bridging the gap between religion and other humanistic fields. The Institute for Research in the Humanities at the University of Wisconsin, now centered upon history, philosophy, language, and literature, is another example of what can be done on a broader scale.

The establishment of an institute would provide a place for those engaged in religion studies to carry on research, either in company with other scholars or independently. It could offer the opportunity for consultation among experts, library facilities, and above all an atmosphere in which the scholarly task could be undertaken in breadth and depth. It could conceivably open new directions for scholars whose present interests have been too narrowly channeled. It could help to move the field of religion from the position assigned to it at the circumference of the present academic scene and bring it into mutually fruitful confrontations with other disciplines. If conceived along lines of the greatest breadth in respect to diversity of religious convictions and fields of study adjacent to religion, if supervised by a competent staff and supported by monies which would permit the offering of fellowships sufficient to attract scholars of stature, such an institute could help to stimulate religion scholarship to a degree hitherto unknown in this country. Even if these conditions seem to throw the plan into the realm of utopian fantasy, it should be remembered that support has been found for projects far more ambitious when the need has been clearly seen. After all, the problem of support does not depend for its solution solely upon the quantity of money available in America, but on its wise allocation.

A less ambitious but no less desirable step would be the more extensive establishment of councils of humanities at colleges and universities where professors of various disciplines as well as religion could meet together and pursue their scholarly interests. Arrangements could be made to free faculty members temporarily from major parts or all of their teaching duties for this purpose. An even greater impact upon the cause of religion scholarship would be possible when visiting scholars of distinction could be brought to campuses to participate in colloquiums and to carry on their studies. Not only would the institutions themselves realize the benefits of intellectual enrichment which this program provides, but those who most need opportunities for the pursuit of scholarship, the under-graduate professors of religion, would secure the time and atmosphere for prolonged and concentrated work.

In addition to these proposals for institutional innovations, there remain the more prosaic needs which must be filled if scholarship is to be continued even at its present levels. Professional societies, including the American Council of Learned Societies, are ever operating in financially reduced circumstances; financial support for grants and the publication of scholarly works, especially those of a technical nature, call for support; learned journals which operate on close margins require subsidies; graduate fellowships in religion are relatively scarce; and support for regional and national meetings of scholars in religion is difficult to find. These more obvious needs persist and, as with the humanities generally, are not being met in a degree commensurate with their worth.

At last, then, all proposals for scholarship in religion bring one face to face with the hard question of the source of financial support. Too much is expected for too little expenditure of funds both by the churches and by the public at large. Clearly, talent and wisdom cannot be purchased, but opportunities for their exercise and development can be provided, and to that end more money is needed.

The federal government provides little for the humanities taken as a whole, and of that practically nothing finds its way into the areas of religion scholarship. Russell Kirk has recently estimated that out of federal funds set aside for research only 1 per cent was earmarked for the humanities. ["Growing Dangers in Campus Research," *New York Times Magazine* (September 17, 1962), p. 22.] The plight of the theological seminaries in attracting funds has been underlined in the studies made by the Niebuhr committee and others. The Rockefeller Foundation's program of grants to college graduates is directed to the development of clergy for Protestant churches rather than to development of those who might choose college teaching and a life of scholarship. The Seatlantic Fund has provided a measure of relief to seminary faculty members by grants which release a number of them from normal duties for scholarly purposes. The Danforth Foundation has given considerable aid in the form of fellowships to graduate students preparing for college teaching in all fields inclusive of religion, but as yet has not made major strides in assisting scholarship directly. The Lilly Foundation has initiated a postdoctoral fellowship program for professors of religion in colleges and those teaching in seminaries with associate membership in the American Association of Theological Schools. Professors in other fields who are interested in the field of religion are also eligible for these grants. The expressed purposes of these grants are "to facilitate scholarly pursuits and to advance vigorous teaching in the area of religion"; preference is given to teachers at the instructor and assistant professor levels and to those who, having taught a number of years, have lacked opportunities to develop research interests. The institution at which the applicant teaches is also expected to contribute to his budget. The Society for Religion in Higher Education, now in the process of merging some of its activities with the Danforth Foundation, has made contributions to scholarship both by fellowships to graduate students in religion and by support of a number of scholarly projects, but its resources to recent date have reached a greatly diminished condition. The American Council of Learned Societies has from time to time made grants to scholars in religion and has supported scholarly publications in the field, but its funds have also been at a premium. In 1959, H. M. Jones estimated its endowment as only $65,000 and its annual budget, supported by foundation gifts, at about $500,000. In 1957, for example, it had $100,000 available for fellowships, but could

285

offer grants of no more than $7,000 to individual scholars. Even with additional aid jointly donated by the Ford Foundation and the Carnegie Corporation, only a small number of the applicants of superior abilities could be cared for. [H. M. Jones, *One Great Society,* p. 236.] When such figures are compared with those available for the natural and social sciences, the rosiest dreams for the encouragement of humanistic scholarship in general and of religion scholarship in particular fade rapidly.

Greater efforts might be expended on bringing to the attention of churches their stake in the support of their institutions of higher learning from which some scholarship might be expected. Colleges and universities in their encouragement of scholarship generally may more fully recognize the place of religion faculty members. Programs of financial assistance for those undertaking research and publication could be further investigated as part of the fringe benefits accorded their faculties. As previously argued, the placing of religion fully within tax-supported colleges and universities should make available to religion faculties resources which in some cases are presently denied to them. Foundations and college authorities could also re-examine the stipulations under which grants are offered to see if legal tax exemptions are available by which the tax burden might be lightened for recipients of grants.[5]

When accounts are realistically cast up, however, only two major sources of financial assistance remain, the private foundations and government resources. The latter can be called upon with any hope of success only when it is clearly understood in all quarters that many of the aspects of religion scholarship rightfully belong among the humanities or, in some cases, the social sciences, where they are unbounded by sectarian interests.

[5] See Maurice C. Greenbaum, "The Scholar and Income Taxes," *Scholarly Books in America,* vol. III, nos. 2 and 3 (U. of Chicago, 1961).

This case has yet to make its way more convincingly and widely than it has been able to do in the face of misunderstandings and bickerings tenaciously engaged in by the religious bodies and secular forces of American society.

Hope then lies at last with the private foundations for the underwriting of religion scholarship. These must be approached by individuals, representatives of learned societies, universities, and colleges who deeply believe in the cause of such scholarship and who can offer not only specific and creative new proposals but also plans for the support of less dramatic but no less significant programs now being carried on under great difficulty. It may well be that a committee made up of representatives of the major professional bodies concerned with the study of religion should be formed to draw up these proposals and to assist the foundations in making a deep and more comprehensive survey of the dimensions, needs, and opportunities of religion scholarship, since the present hit-and-miss system of making appeals has not yet yielded responses proportionate to the magnitude of the problem.

Inevitably the question is raised of why aid should be given to this cause. To those engaged in the field the reasons appear obvious. Old problems in the various segments of the field call for fresh statements and solutions; new problems burst forth daily, insistently demanding attention; materials accumulate awaiting the scholar's touch to bring them to life in an ordered fashion and to set them relevantly before the people of his age. And there stands always the intrinsic interest which the field holds for scholars. But the minutiae of technical scholarship or the reaches of perspectival scholarship may strike no responsive chord in the minds of those outside the field. The problems which fascinate the scholar or his consuming interest in the values which the field holds for him may be persuasive reasons for his continuance in his tasks. He may regard them as sufficient answers to the question as to why his work deserves support. But they are not likely to win sympathetic attention from those he most earnestly wishes to convince of the significance of his task. His appeal must then be made on broader grounds than these.

The scholar knows that religion holds interest not only for the scholar or for the churchman but for the layman of whatever persuasion. Its fascination, when viewed historically and contemporaneously, remains a constant feature of man's intellectual and spiritual horizon. Men continue to live with it in its myriad guises of devotion to the supernatural, its sacralizing of the natural and commonplace, its variant secular forms of nationalism, Marxism, racialism, or sexualism. They read of it in the daily newspaper, they express opinions about it on the street corner, and occasionally they think deeply about it. Yet their ignorance of religious phenomena, traditions, beliefs, and institutions is colossal. Scarcely an area of human experience elicits more interest, yet is so befogged by misconceptions, inaccurate information, and narrowness of vision. In few fields of such universal interest and experience are men's judgments less influenced by sober understanding, factual information, and critical appreciation. Yet religion in all its confusing variety has won and lost empires, molded cultural aspirations, sent saints into desert places and cities, inspired the ethical sentiments of man for good and ill, both opened and blocked the way to learning, social justice, and the practice of the arts.

In the face of these conditions can it be seriously maintained that there is no need for men trained in the exercise of their finest intellectual and spiritual talents? Can it be said that the comprehension of this pervasive phenomenon in depth and breadth deserves no attention? Is the attempt to impart critical understanding and appreciation of humanity's values, past and present, to be made an insignificant side issue in the human panorama? Should not any society which values its existence have placed before it discriminating and imaginative portrayals of those visions by which men today and in the past have guided their steps? To be sure, these visions by which men live and the realities to which they have given their ultimate loyalties are not gleaned simply from the study of texts, artifacts, and monuments. Seldom does the scholar find that ennobling insights entertained in the study survive unchanged when transferred into the common life of mankind. His daily tasks may at times eclipse his search for comprehensive interpretations of the human situation, but without his persistent, discriminating gleanings, the devotion of men may as easily follow the spurious and delusory as the valid and authentic.

A scholar need not feel charged with the responsibility of saving civilization, although more than one has moved his age into new and fruitful channels of human effort. He may not read his mandate as one which summons him to transform the modes of man's existence, although his thoughts may at last persuasively enter the common consciousness of men. His duty, more modestly put, is to lay before his generation his knowledge and assessment of the past, its appalling failures and disfigurements of the human and divine images no less than its highest aspirations and spiritual achievements. It is his business to know the difference between the shoddy and the sublime in man's religious devotion and to share his judgments with others. He gives to the present a sense of the past as individual memories die and are irretrievably lost. His studies may offer an understanding of that mystery of existence against which the restless seekings and defiant doubts of man unceasingly pound. He does not flinch from wrestling with the idols for the sake of the gods, nor from being present at the death of the gods when deeper insights into the mystery of existence demand their extinction. He brings the world's religious literature to men who speak in tongues foreign to that in which the literature was first formed and guides them in their understanding of it. He knows the uses of dialectial skills, but declines to employ them as a means of blanching the vividly complex texture of religious experiences to suit the strictures of abstract speculation. He examines and evaluates contemporary readings of the purposes of human life and debates his case with those of contradictory opinions. And if nothing more, he adds to the sum of human knowledge as he penetrates into little-known and unexplored areas of human experience where men believe they have been encountered by the divine and have expressed this encounter in traditions, acts of worship, architecture, and social systems.

No scholar pretends to live in all the dimensions of the total task of scholarship. No scholar worthy of the name imagines himself to be a disinterested spectator of the religious scene or a mere sideline commentator upon the human venture. He too moves inescapably among the relativities of time, circumstance, and personal convictions. His work is never final or all-comprehending in its scope. He knows that scholarship in religion is not to be identified with the religious life as such. But neither is his task merely an optional adornment or an expendable luxury of the human enterprise. He is directly and pertinently related to a most important area of human life—an area where the ultimate convictions by which men live and die are wrestled through, where faith moves men to action or reduces them to passivity, where the interpretations and justifications of human existence are ever at stake, where the battle against barbarism, fanaticism, and superstition must be incessantly waged. Without the scholar's contribution this region is turned into a morass of unprincipled prejudice and ignorance lacking intelligibility—a battlefield rather than a meeting place. Scholarship and teaching bring the profound religious convictions of mankind into comprehensible focus while safeguarding the uniqueness of the variant traditions in which men have reached toward the eternal or have been met by it in the depth of their being. As such they remain indispensable professions in humanity's endless struggle for knowledge and significance.

INDEX